NEW FORMATIONS

EDITORS:
David Glover
Scott McCracken

REVIEWS EDITOR
Timothy Bewes

EDITORIAL ASSISTANT
Helen Pendry

EDITORIAL BOARD:
Sara Ahmed
Timothy Bewes
Laura Chrisman
Jeremy Gilbert
David Glover
Priyamvada Gopal
Ben Highmore
Cora Kaplan
Neil Lazarus
Mandy Merck
Scott McCracken
Bill Schwarz
Brett St Louis
Jenny Bourne Taylor
Wendy Wheeler

ADVISORY BOARD:
Ien Ang
Angelika Bammer
Tony Bennett
Jody Berland
Homi Bhabha
Victor Burgin
Lesley Caldwell
Hazel Carby
Erica Carter
Iain Chambers
Joan Copjec
Lidia Curti
Tony Davies
James Donald
Simon Frith
Stuart Hall
Dick Hebdige
Colin Mercer
Alasdair Pettinger
Renata Salecl
Gayatri Chakravorty Spivak
Judith Squires
Valerie Walkerdine

PRODUCTION CO-ORD...
For enquiries/bookings contact Vanna Derosas, Lawrence & Wishart.

SUBSCRIPTIONS:
UK: Institutions £132.50, Individuals £40.
Rest of world: Institutions £132.50; Individuals £40.
Single copies: £14.99 plus £2 post and packing.
Back issues: £14.99 plus £2 post and packing for individuals;
£45 plus £2 post and packing for institutions.
Payments can be made by credit/debit card (no American Express).

CONTRIBUTIONS AND CORRESPONDENCE:
Send to either: The Editor, David Glover, School of English, Dept.
of English, University of Southampton, Highfield, Southampton
SO17 1BJ, dg6@soton.ac.uk; or The Editor, Scott McCracken,
School of English, Keele University, Keele ST5 5BG,
s.mccracken@engl.keele.ac.uk

BOOKS FOR REVIEW:
Send to: Ben Highmore, Reviews Editor, *new formations*,
School of Cultural Studies, University of the West of England, Bristol,
St Matthias Campus, Oldbury Court Road, Bristol BS16 2JP
Ben.Highmore@blueyonder.co.uk

new formations publishes themed issues, themed sections and discrete articles. Contributors are encouraged to contact the editors to discuss their ideas and to obtain a copy of our style sheet, which can also be obtained on our website at http://www.newformations.co.uk

Manuscripts should be sent in triplicate; experts in the relevant field will referee them anonymously. The manuscripts will not be returned unless a stamped, self-addressed envelope is enclosed. Contributors should note that the editorial board cannot take responsibility for any manuscript submitted to *new formations*.

The collection as a whole © Lawrence & Wishart 2005

Individual articles © the individual authors 2005

No article may be reproduced or transmitted in any form or by any means, electronic or mechanical, including photocopying, recording, or any information storage and retrieval system, without the permission in writing of the publisher, editor or author.

ISSN 0 950 237 8
ISBN 1 90500 7 34-5

Printed in Great Britain at the University Press, Cambridge.

new formations is published three times a year by
Lawrence & Wishart, 99a Wallis Road, London E9 5LN
Tel: 020-8533 2506 Fax: 020-8533 7369
Website: www.newformations.co.uk

Orders and Subscription payments to:
Lawrence and Wishart, PO Box 7701
Latchington, Chelmsford CH3 6WL
landw@btinternet.com

NOTES ON CONTRIBUTORS

Clive Barnett teaches human geography in the Faculty of Social Sciences at the Open University. He is author of *Culture and Democracy* (Edinburgh University Press 2003) and co-editor of *Spaces of Democracy* (Sage 2004).

Jody Berland is Associate Professor of Humanities, York University, Toronto, member of graduate faculties of Communication and Culture, Humanities, Sociology, Music, and Social and Political Thought. She has published widely on cultural studies, Canadian communication theory, music, media, culture and the environment and the cultural technologies of space. She is co-editor of *Theory Rules: Art as Theory, Theory and Art*, YYZ/University of Toronto Press (1996), and *Cultural Capital: A Reader on Modernist Legacies, State Institutions and the Value(s) of Art*, McGill-Queen's University Press (2000), and is editor of *Topia: A Canadian Journal of Cultural Studies* (www.yorku.ca/topia). Her book, *North of Empire*, is forthcoming with Duke University Press.

Janelle Blankenship is Assistant Professor/Faculty Fellow of German at New York University. She is the author of articles on early German film and film theory. In 2002 she edited a special issue of *Polygraph* entitled *Media and Spatiality in Deleuze and Guattari*.

Peter Brooker is Professor of Literary and Cultural Studies and Director of Research in the Department of Critical Theory and Cultural Studies at the University of Nottingham. He is author, amongst other works, of *New York Fictions* (1996), *Modernity and Metropolis: Writing, Film and Urban Formations* (2002), and *Bohemia in London: The Social Scene of Early Modernism* (2004). He is co-editor with Andrew Thacker of a forthcoming three volume *Critical and Cultural History of Modernist Magazines* and is a co-editor of *Key Words: A Journal of Cultural Materialism*.

Ian Buchanan is Professor of Critical and Cultural Theory at Cardiff University. He is the author *Deleuzism* (Edinburgh 2000), and *Michel de Certeau* (Sage 2000). He is the editor of *Deleuze Connections*, published by Edinburgh University Press.

Richard Cavell is author of *McLuhan in Space: A Cultural Geography* (2002); he teaches at the University of British Columbia.

David Cunningham is Lecturer in English Literature at the University of Westminster and an editor of the journal *Radical Philosophy*. He is currently writing a book on the concept of avant-garde, as well as co-editing, *Adorno and Literature*, a collection of essays forthcoming from Continuum.

Jess Edwards is Principal Lecturer in English at Manchester Metropolitan University. He is the author of *Writing, Geometry and Space in Seventeenth-Century England and America* (Routledge 2005).

Gerry Kearns lectures in Geography at the University of Cambridge, UK. He works on three topics: the history of urban public health, Irish identities and the relationship between Geography and Imperialism.

Laura Marcus is Professor of English at the University of Sussex. Her most recent publication, co-edited with Peter Nicholls, is *The Cambridge History of Twentieth-Century English Literature*. She is currently completing a study of literature, film and modernity.

Scott McCracken teaches in the English Department at Keele University. His most recent publication is *Benjamin's Arcades: an Unguided Tour*, co-authored with Peter Buse, Ken Hirschkop and Bertrand Taithe (Manchester University Press 2005). He is co-editor of *new formations*.

Miles Ogborn is Professor of Geography at Queen Mary, University of London. He is the author of *Spaces of Modernity: London's Geographies, 1680-1780* (New York 1998) and is currently completing a study of the uses of script and print in the world of the English East India Company in the seventeenth and eighteenth centuries.

Richard Phillips teaches Cultural Geography and Development Studies at Liverpool University. His publications include *Mapping Men and Empire: A Geography of Adventure* (Routledge 1997), the co-edited *De-centring Sexualities: Politics and Representations Beyond the Metropolis* (Routledge 2000), and *Sex, Politics and Empire: A Postcolonial Geography* (Manchester University Press 2006).

Peter Sjølyst-Jackson teaches rhetorical theory and cultural studies at St Clare's, Oxford. He has recently completed a DPhil on the literary works and fascist politics of Knut Hamsun at the University of Sussex.

Andrew Thacker is Senior Research Fellow in the School of English at De Montfort University, Leicester. Recent publications include, *Moving Through Modernity: Space and Geography in Modernism* (2003), and *Geographies of Modernism* (2005). He is currently completing a short book on the Imagist poets.

CONTENTS

NUMBER 57 WINTER 2005-6

The Spatial Imaginary

new formations

Special issue - Happiness
Edited by Sara Ahmed, Goldsmiths College

Call for papers

In the last few years there has been a proliferation of books on the science of happiness, which measures 'happiness indicators' within and between nation-states. A paradox has been identified: more wealth does not mean more happiness. One writer has recently suggested that the government should monitor our happiness as closely as it monitors the gross domestic product. Such an argument presumes there is something that is happiness, which can be measured. But what is being measured? How does happiness come to be seen as a property of cultures, persons or things? The special issue will offer a cultural approach to the question of happiness, and the modalities of its various affects and effects. Of course, happiness has long been at the centre of philosophy, posed as the moral question of what counts as the good life. Different traditions within philosophy have offered very different arguments about what is happiness, how it can be achieved, and who can achieve it, ranging from idealist models to the most starkly utilitarian. Rather than simply follow from this history, which begins with the question, 'what is happiness', we ask instead, 'what does happiness do?' what do we appeal to when we appeal to happiness as something that we have, once had and have lost, or have yet to find?

The special issue will join the increasing scholarship within cultural studies that takes emotions and affects seriously as things to think with. Much of this recent work attends to what we might call 'the politics of bad feeling' (shame, pain, grief, trauma, anger and resentment), although such emotions are often shown to be ambivalent, rather than simply negative. By taking happiness as its starting point, this issue will ask what happens if we begin not with the ambivalence of so-called bad feeling, but with the ambivalence of positive emotions such as happiness. We could ask, for instance, about the relation between happiness and the securing of the social ideals that 'make' others into failures, or read 'them' as the embodiment of failure. We could consider how happiness slides into other emotions such as anger and resentment. We might be angry towards others for their failure to embody our ideals, a failure which is often described in the language of deprivation (the other has deprived 'us' of the good life). Indeed, if happiness is intentional in the sense of being 'about something', or directed towards an object, then we might ask the question: What difference does it make 'what' happiness is directed towards? Does the desire for happiness ensure an investment in social ideals defined in terms of the public good? How does happiness get promised as a return for such investments? What is the relationship between happiness and new social movements that challenge the very scripts that are assumed to lead to 'happy endings'? What do we invest 'in' when we invest 'in' happiness as what is lacking in the present, or as what is hoped for in the future?

In considering the cultural politics of happiness, we invite contributions that open up different ways of thinking 'with' as well as 'about' this concept. Possible areas of enquiry include: consumption, poverty, the body, nation, capital, globalisation, sex, race, work, leisure, lifestyle, justice, ethics, protest, science, violence, welfare; as well as theoretical accounts of happiness as an emotion, affect, action, narrative, temporality, or practice. Papers should be 6000-8000 words. Further information for contributors is available on the journal website www.l-wbks.co.uk/journals/newformations/contents.html

The deadline for submissions is 3 april 2006. Please send your submissions as an email attachment to sara ahmed (s.ahmed@gold.ac.uk). All submissions will be peer reviewed.

Why not Subscribe?

New Formations is published three times a year. Make sure of your copy by subscribing.

SUBSCRIPTION RATES FOR 2006 (3 ISSUES)

Individual Subscriptions
UK & Rest of World   £40.00

Institutional Subscriptions
UK & Rest of World   £132.50

Back issues: *£14.99 plus £2 post and packing for individuals*
                   £45.00 plus £2 post and packing for institutions

Please send one year's subscription
starting with Issue Number ————————————————

I enclose payment of ————————————————————

Please send me ———— copies of back issue no. —————

I enclose total payment of   ————————————————

Name ——————————————————————————

Address ————————————————————————

———————————————————— Postcode —————————

Please return this form with cheque or money order (sterling only) payable to *Lawrence & Wishart* to: Lawrence and Wishart (Subs), PO Box 7701, Latchington, Chelmsford, CM3 6WL. Payments may also be made by credit/debit card (not American Express).

EDITORIAL

Richard Phillips and Scott McCracken

Fredric Jameson has called for a rethinking of 'cultural politics in terms of space and the struggle for space'.[1] This issue of *new formations* looks at where the spatial imagination is taking cultural criticism. Five of the articles (by Clive Barnett, Richard Cavell, Jess Edwards, Gerry Kearns, and Andrew Thacker) were originally given as papers at a conference session, 'Textual Spaces, Spatial Texts', at the Royal Geographical Society in London in 2004. That three other articles drawing their impetus from the same disciplinary intersection were submitted to the journal during the editorial process suggests that the session reflected broader debates in cultural studies. These currently operate around: textual space (a term deployed by Stephen Muecke); mapping strategies and territorial disputes (Graham Huggan); maps of meaning (Peter Jackson, after Raymond Williams); cognitive mapping (Frederic Jameson); geographies of writing (Nedra Reynolds); writing space (Jay Bolter); geographies of reading (James Secord); conceptual space (Paul Werth); and spaces of print and cartography (Robert Mayhew).[2]

The first of these three articles, Peter Brooker's 'Terrorism and Counter Terrorism and Counternarratives; Don DeLillo and the New York Imaginary', asks how New York has been re-imagined since 11 September 2001. Looking at narratives as different as DeLillo's work from *Mao II* to *Cosmopolis* and Art Spiegelman's graphic novel *In the Shadow of No Towers*, Brooker asks how New York's urban imaginary as a 'lived perceptual and interpretive framework, operating in a dialectical relation with the physical fabric and institutionalised systems of the urban or metropolitan complex' has changed in the aftermath of the destruction of the World Trade Center.

Ian Buchanan's article 'Practical Deleuzism and Postmodern Space' takes the discussion from redefinitions of a city we think we know to the lack of definition of what Marc Augé calls 'non-places - malls, airports, freeways, office parks, and so forth, which prioritise cost and function over look and feel'. In his discussion of postmodern space, Buchanan moves through three separate, but related stages: cinematic anticipations; the mall as realisation; and the application of the concept of 'deterritorialisation' to its transformations. Understanding postmodern space in relation to land value and ground rent suggests, he argues, an application of Deleuzian theory that is in keeping with the practical philosophy Deleuze demanded.

In the third article in this section, Jody Berland examines the significance of a spatial imaginary to Canadian national identity. In 'After the Fact: Spatial Narratives in the Canadian Imaginary' she argues that in Canada 'the emphasis on land and space has both expedited and resisted forces of colonial power'. Berland's central metaphor for the forging of a national

1. Frederick Jameson, *Postmodernism or the Cultural Logic of Late Capitalism*, London, Verso, 1991

2. Graham Huggan, *Territorial Disputes*, Toronto, University of Toronto Press, 1996; see also: Peter Jackson, *Maps of Meaning*, London, Routledge, 1989; S. Muecke, *Textual Spaces: Aboriginality and Cultural Studies*, Kensington, New South Wales University Press, 1992; Nedra Reynolds, *Geographies of Writing: Inhabiting Places and Encountering Difference*, Carbondale, Southern Illinois University Press, 2004; Paul Werth, *Text Worlds: Representing Conceptual Space in Discourse*, London, Longman, 1999; Jay David Bolter, *Writing Space: Computers, Hypertext and the Remediation of Print*, New Jersey, Lawrence Earlbaum, 2001; James Secord, *Victorian Sensation: the Extraordinary Publication, Reception and Secret Authorship of Vestiges of the Natural History of Creation*, Chicago, University of Chicago Press, 2000; Robert Mayhew, 'British Geography's Republic of Letters: Mapping and Imagined Community, c. 1600-1800' in *Journal of the History of Ideas*, 65, 2 (2004).

imaginary is the train-radio that broadcast as it crossed the continent, making a Canadian space through the air waves. But Canada's ambivalent position as both part of North America and politically and cultural distinct from its powerful neighbour means that its national space is far from secure. Here spatial politics is an ongoing battle for definition and redefinition.

The articles that emerged from 'Textual Spaces/Spatial Texts' are framed by Andrew Thacker's call for 'a critical literary geography' and Miles Ogborn's 'Afterword'. Thacker, working in an English Department, traces the influence of geographical ideas as they have seeped into literary studies. He proposes 'a *critical* literary geography', stressing its difference to the 'effortless mapping of represented landscapes in literary texts'. Such a literary geography would, he suggests, 'raise more complex questions about space and power, and how space and geography affect literary forms and styles'. Ogborn, who responded as discussant to the conference papers on the day, here gives a considered response from the perspective of cultural geography on the distinctions and differences highlighted by the dialogues the articles establish.

The other four essays in this section, also demonstrate the transgression of disciplinary boundaries such dialogues involve. Gerry Kearns, who works in a Department of Geography, offers a nuanced analysis of the spatial politics of James Joyce's fiction. Jess Edwards, from an English Department, engages with early modern mathematics to respond with an account of the 'dirtiness' of early modern maps, which were used 'not just to represent space but also to negotiate the identity, the legitimacy and the agency of individuals, groups and ventures'. Clive Barnett, another cultural geographer, in 'Disseminating Africa: Burdens of representation and the African Writers Series' offers a new perspective on Heinemann's African Writers Series as not primarily 'ideological', but instead engaged in the generation of new public forms of space. While in the final article in the section, Richard Cavell asks in 'Geographical Immediations: Locating *The English Patient*', what impact the increasing hegemony of electronic mediation has had on the relationship between space and text. Writing from within an English department, Cavell argues that '"text" remains useful for our understanding of a fundamentally mediatised space only to the extent that it can be understood as having superseded the regime of writing, as in Barthes' suggestion that texts are networks'.

Such dialogues are not, of course, without disagreement. Cross-disciplinary misunderstandings are the inevitable consequences of differences in perspective, language and values: of different critical literacies. As editors we have had vigorous debates about the issue, debates coloured by our different disciplinary perspectives which changed in character and emphasis according to the spaces in which they were situated at the time. The conference, for example, took place on geographical terrain, while the editorial process was conducted in the context of a journal which includes, culture, theory and politics, but not geography in its title.

Despite the tensions this threw up, we accept that such debates reflect the difficulties and realities of interdisciplinary exchange. Situated inevitably amidst the realities of disciplinary power and influence, in the end, our dialogues were both critical and productive, resulting, we feel, in a better issue than if they had not taken place. Nonetheless, the dialogues go on. As Ogborn concludes, there are still significant differences. Speaking productively across boundaries is something that has to be worked at.

Terrorism and Counternarratives:
Don DeLillo and the New York Imaginary

Peter Brooker

There are terrible spirits, ghosts, in the air of America
D.H. Lawrence[1]

1. *Studies in Classic American Literature* [1924], London, Heinemann, 1965, p71.

USA! USA! USA! USA!

(Audience at the Republican Convention,
New York City, August 2004)

We are now over four years beyond the awesome events of September 11 2001, short-handed the world over as 9/11. At once 'beyond words' but the subject of endless words and around 40 million hits on the internet, 9/11 has proved paradoxically unrepresentable and endlessly represented. I want to explore this paradox and some of these modes of representation below, including photography, comics, and Art Spielgelman's graphic novel, *In the Shadow of No Towers*. Above all, however, I'm interested in the role of fiction and fantasy, and how, in a world of direct reportage and political commentary, these indirect, fabular or allegorical modes have taken the measure of such a fantastical reality. To put this more broadly, I am interested in the work of the imagination and its apprehension of the real, where this real is the spectacular nightmare of 9/11 and the embedded mythology of New York City. This leads me to consider the concept, firstly, of the 'urban imaginary' and, secondly, the example of the New York novelist Don DeLillo.

DeLillo responded soon after the initial impact of 9/11 in a prose essay titled 'In the Ruins of the Future'. There he offers some direct guidance to the writer amidst thoughts on how the terrorist narrative struck at the cherished symbolic identity of New York City and the contemporary meaning of America. His own fiction, however, works in a different, more analogical, tangential and, I believe, more deeply analytical way. I want to explore DeLillo's recent fiction, then, in the context of the shock to New York's urban imaginary, and indeed to a national imaginary, as an example of how the nostalgia and defensive, sometimes belligerent, patriotism provoked by 9/11 might be rethought. My question is whether fiction, precisely at its most oblique, can, in a set of terms introduced by DeLillo, present an alternative 'counternarrative' not only to the terrorist narrative but to the homogenising narrative which sought, in response to this crisis, to (over)identify New York City with the United States and the World. What is also at stake therefore are perceptions of the relation between the local, focused upon this scene in Manhattan, and the global.

THE URBAN IMAGINARY

The concept of the 'urban imaginary' offers to combine the physical, material reality of a city and its imagined or mythic contours. As defined by Edward W. Soja, the urban imaginary refers 'to our mental or cognitive mappings of urban reality and the interpretive grids through which we think about, experience, evaluate, and decide to act in the places, spaces, and communities in which we live'.[2]

The urban imaginary is a lived perceptual and interpretive framework, then, operating in a dialectical relation with the physical fabric and institutionalised systems of the urban or metropolitan complex. But often, in addition, it has been associated with the strategies of artistic or symbolic discourse, understood as a realm of critique and liberated alterity. Michel de Certeau, for example, talks directly of the 'magical powers' of language and myth and of the challenge a 'poetic geography' sets an underlying rationalised geography of 'literal, forbidden or permitted meaning'.[3] Material, literal reality becomes a restrictive zone and the 'poetic' a realm of magic and liberation.

What emerged in discussions of the 'postmodern' city in the 1980s and 1990s was a common sense that this relation and the supposed efficacy of the symbolic or imaginary, or the cultural, was in crisis, not simply in its capacity to intervene and rebut the diffuse mechanisms of contemporary control under globalisation, but in our ability to comprehend or give an inner geography to this system's operations. Hence Fredric Jameson's call, lost in the deep space of the Bonaventure hotel, for a newly configured 'cognitive mapping' and Soja's own propositions on 'restructuring the urban imaginary' so as to outface 'simcity', as he terms the 'postmetropolis' of hyperreality, theme parks and unrelieved media simulation. In a more conservative vein, writing in response to the perceived anomie of the postmodern city, Kevin Robins argued that we must 'attempt to re-imagine urbanity [by] ... recovering a lost sense of territorial identity, urban community and public space'. This amounts, he says, to 'a kind of return to (mythical) origins'.[4]

9/11, I believe, accentuated this crisis in 'cognitive mapping' and thus in an active and critical relation to the material and rationalised postmodern, global city. It prompted too, I think, the nostalgic or melancholy recourse to a 'lost ... territorial identity' or to some other place, an 'after life', beyond this loss. Thinking about 9/11 and its representations, I suggest will give us a deeper sense of this crisis and of the composition of a New York urban imaginary. We need to add two things immediately to these ideas, however: firstly a recognition of the particular articulation of the material and immaterial in this particular global city; what Rem Koolhaas termed the 'rigid chaos' of Manhattan's combined horizontal grid and vertical skyscraper architecture and the tensions this has dramatised between regulation and fantasy or rationalisation and excess.[5] I think also in general and manifestly

2. Edward W. Soja, *Postmetropolis: Critical Studies of Cities and Regions*, Oxford, Blackwell, 2000, p324.

3. Michel de Certeau, *The Practice of Everyday Life*, Berkeley, University of California Press, 1984, p105.

4. Kevin Robins, 'Prisoners of the City. Whatever Could a Postmodern City Be?', in *Space and Place: Theories of Identity and Location*, E. Carter, J.Donald and J. Squires (eds), London, Lawrence and Wishart, 1993, p304.

5. Rem Koolhaas, *Delirious New York*, Rotterdam, 010 Publishers, [1978] 1994, p20.

in relation to 9/11, that we need to recognise, in common with recent researchers, the emotional or affective dimension of urban geography. The urban nightmare of 9/11 was greeted with emotions of panic, shock and dread, together with a confusion of the real and unreal that made it a 'sublime' event of, so it seemed, literally unutterable horror. The urban imaginary, that is to say, comprises both the strategies of 'cognitive mapping', which strive for an integrated understanding of the globalised strata in *this* local place, and something like a seismograph of affect, which will register the emotional contours operating below or outside a formed response. The author Siri Hustvedt, in a short report on 9/11 in the collection *110 Stories* talks of children's devastated reactions. One child cannot be separated from her mother; one swears there were skeletons walking the street; one refused to let his feet touch the ground. These stories alert us, she writes, to 'the translations of horror when it enters the mind and body'.[6] Both discourses, of the mind and body - the symbolic and semiotic, the cognitive and affective - need to be part of our thinking on the urban imaginary.

6. Siri Hustvedt, 'The World Trade Center', in Ulrich Baer (ed), *110 Stories*: *New York Writes After September 11*, New York, New York University Press, 2002, p159.

THE TERRORIST AND THE NOVELIST

In Don DeLillo's novel *Mao II* (1991) the character Bill Gray, a novelist in retreat from his work and the world, sees the writer's public influence and authority as being overtaken by the totalising world narrative and fundamentalist conviction of the terrorist and gunman. His counterpart in Beirut, an Arab terrorist leader and dedicated Maoist, Abu Rashid, sees his son as continuing the cause; 'All men one man', he says.[7] Against this, Bill Gray sets the novelist, whose task is to transform 'the inner life of the culture' (41), and the novel, which shows us 'one thing unlike another, one voice unlike another' (159). This 'other fiction' pushes 'toward the social order, trying to unfold into it. A writer creates character to reveal consciousness to increase the flow of meaning', he says. 'This is how we reply to power and how we beat back our fear' (200). Though Bill Gray ventures beyond the boundaries of the US to meet the terrorist sect in Beirut, he fails to complete the journey. A photographer who does reach Abu Rashid, whips off the hood worn by his son to reveal a face of hatred; the look of the future to which neither the camera nor the novel, nor this novel's characters in New York City, in the end have an answer, for they dream in equivalent monolithic simplicities of a world of 'total control'. Tompkins Square is 'just like Beirut, it looks like Beirut', says one. Opposing civilisations in fact mirror and feed off each other, spliced by television and Coca Cola. The Andy Warhol print 'Mao II' has already cloned and recycled the Maoist image Abu Rashid means in his own terms to replicate. In such a world the culture of the novel or the novel of culture appears defeated.

7. Don DeLillo, *Mao II*, London, Jonathan Cape, 1991, p233.

Mao II was published shortly after the Rushdie affair and the Iran hostage crisis and reminds us that these themes have a history before 9/11. But this historical sense itself becomes part too of the present crisis in the urban imaginary, prompting feelings of nostalgia and yearning for another time in the before or after of this place, or an attempt at once to repair time and the physical city so as to bridge the psychic chasm represented by the fallen towers. What a dislocated New York imaginary had to contend with was, in one refrain, this 'silent, howling void', the psychic and physical absence where what had been in New York's past was no more, but where this nothing still cast a heavy pall - best expressed in the title of Art Spiegelman's graphic novel *In the Shadow of No Towers*.[8] Already, as this tells us, the apparent blank finality of loss and nothingness was less than final. What followed was an attempt to stabilise a battered imaginary haunted by its other, the shadow or spectre of absence, in a doubling motif of presence and absence aggravated by the image of the twin towers themselves.

8. Art Spiegelman, *In the Shadow of No Towers*, London and New York, Penguin/ Viking.

A MATTER OF TIME

To many, 9/11 seemed to bring a specifically contemporary history, the age of the skyscraper, or the age of irony, if not time and the world itself, to an end. 'The Sky Is Falling!' as Spiegelman titles his opening account. The event punctured and arrested time before sending it into the replay of what became a set of dominant emotions and images. A second response was to 'tell the story' - not only to repeat and repeat it again and so manage it in words, but to find the longer history which would contextualise events and emotions by conferring some fated sequence upon them. Such, I think, were the references to Hollywood disaster movies, such as *Towering Inferno* and *Independence Day*; to earlier novels, by Tom Clancy, for example, and fictionalised scenarios or images which seemed uncannily to anticipate this present disaster.[9] The cover image of DeLillo's *Underworld* was re-read in this way. Was it a bird or plane seen flying towards the World Trade Centre? Political commentaries, similarly, when they were not extrapolating 9/11 into a future crusade and war, sought in their own terms to situate this event in an explanatory history or critique.

9. Tom Clancy *Debt of Honor*, 1994 and *Executive Orders*, 1996. Other examples were *Seven Days in May* 1964, remade as *Enemy Within*, 1994, and the plot device of war games, including an attack on the WTC in the TV Show, *The Lone Gunman*, March 2001.

Don DeLillo's prose contribution, 'In the Ruins of the Future' was first published in December 2001.[10] 9/11, he argues here, interrupted the speeding onward course of information technologies and multinational corporations which had 'summoned us all to live permanently in the future, in the utopian glow of cyber-capital'. This was the narrative of America: 'technology is our fate, our truth. It is what we mean when we call ourselves the only superpower on the planet. We don't have to depend on God or the prophets or other astonishments. We are the astonishment'.

10. Don DeLillo, 'In the Ruins of the Future', *Harpers*, December 2001 and The *Guardian*, 22/12/ 2001, <http:// www.guardian.co.uk/ Archive/Article/ 0,4273,4324579,00.html>

But Al Qaeda was not astonished by the US example: 'Today again the world narrative belongs to terrorists', writes DeLillo. The effect of the assault, less an attack upon the global economy, he says, than upon America, was to send this identity crashing to ground zero and to drag the future back into the past. The Twin Towers, New York and America stand as one compound, now ruined, monument in this thinking: 'every wall, home, life and mind'

11. DeLillo's 'medieval' deserves some comment. John Gray in his study *Al Qaeda and What it Means to be Modern* (2003) argues that radical Islam is as modern as the free market liberalism it means to destroy. Terry Eagleton adds that it is more accurately described as 'modernist' since in its use of modern technologies and weapons and belief in a theocratic state it shares the conjunction of the archaic and the progressive characteristic of this movement (*Guardian*, 6/09/ 2003, p14).

12. See Noam Chomsky, *Power and Terror: Post- 9/11 Talks and Interviews*, New York, Seven Stories Press, 2003; Michael Moore, *Fahrenheit 9/11*, Optimum, 2004; Walter Mosley, *What Next: A Memoir Toward World Peace*, London, Serpent's Tail, 2003.

13. 'No New York writer can now set a novel in New York', says Hustvedt, 'without its referring in some way to 9/11' ('The Book Show' Channel 4, 27/12/ 2004). The most conspicuous recent examples of this 'post 9/11' 9/11 novel have been Jonathan Safran Foer's novel *Extremely Loud & Incredibly Close* (2005), Philip Beard's *Dear Zoe* (2005) and *Windows on the World* (2005) by the French author Frederic Beigbeder.

was invaded by dread, DeLillo writes. For the terrorist narrative was 'medieval', he says: reductive, narrow, suicidal, passionless; profoundly, in that bland phrase, 'anti-American'.[11]

To this terrorist narrative DeLillo poses a plethora of 'counternarratives' by which New York and America can reclaim the time and itself. These are the '100,000' stories of the day and its immediate aftermath: of children, families and friends, of shock and survival, but also of unity. Amassing the scraps and retold tales, the photographs of the missing, the memorabilia collected on the streets and fittingly at Union Square, including the false memories and internet rumours, New York can reply in the name of America to the 'massive spectacle' that was 'outside imagining'.

We might think DeLillo is contesting the discredited grand narratives of modernity with something like J-F. Lyotard's *petits recits*, but we'd be wrong. For the assembled testimony of human diversity, though set against a fundamentalist grand narrative, adds up to one unified story of Western modernity with, in the end, a disarmingly assimilative reach. DeLillo closes this account with the memory of a walk a month earlier on Canal Street. There, amidst 'the old jostle and stir unchanged for many decades' he saw a woman praying to Mecca, guided only by the compass of the Manhattan grid. The scene had confirmed the daily 'taken-for-granted greatness of New York', able to 'accommodate every language, ritual, belief and opinion', he says, and ends, 'Allahu akbar. God is great'.

Is this 'accommodation' a recognition or appropriation of difference? The second I think. The essay strives to assemble the broken parts of an older unified New York urban imaginary, to accommodate everything, while, from beginning to end, this is undermined by the figure of the 'other', branded as 'obsolete' and 'medieval' and outside the 'taken-for-granted greatness of New York'. The sense of 'Us and Them' DeLillo states early in the essay, in fact, 'has never been so striking, at either end'. The difficulty is that this extreme opposition will not hold either, for though the terrorist cannot be accommodated to the American 'miracle', 'parts of our world' in its present ruins, he concedes, 'has crumbled into theirs'. The vengeful, suicidal martyr who sweeps in from a pre-modern past, whose action was 'outside imagining' has already occupied the interior and planted the nightmare that haunts DeLillo's unifying counternarrative.

The immediate task of the writer in all this, says DeLillo, is to capture the moment, the 'primal terror' of the event - 'People falling from the towers hand in hand', and secondly 'to give memory, tenderness and meaning to all that howling space'. The first resembles the eye-witness accounts, the photographs and videos which documented the raw experience, 'the shock and horror as it is' in DeLillo's words, but this, he adds, is 'before politics before history and religion'. This distinction between a purely affective response to the raw event and its discursive aftermath, emerged as a common one. We might well want to question such a distinction but it evidently accords with the passionate sense of time having stopped dead: of the horror being outside time and beyond words, before the time of reflection, explanation and argument began again.

An entire discursive universe of narratives and counternarratives, openly marked by politics, history and religion, has of course since appeared, including works by dissenting American commentators such as Noam Chomsky, Michael Moore and Walter Mosley, as well as the bizarre conjunction of texts such as *The 9/11 Commission Report* and video statements from Osama Bin Laden broadcast by al-Jazeera.[12] There have been other kinds of fictional narratives too, however, which have acknowledged 9/11 in their background, or used it as a prompt, or deflected the disturbance of this event to a displaced realm in the past or to the analogical or allegorical realms of genre fiction or fable and fairy tale.[13] It is this more oblique story telling which intrigues me; and it is this, with DeLillo's essay and comparison of the victorious terrorist and defeated novelist in mind, that I want to consider. My chief interest, once more, is in the public role of fiction and the artistic imagination: the ways in which it sought in this case to replenish or redirect the urban or cultural imaginary; not by a direct encounter with the 'primal terror' of the event itself, but in registering the disturbances, as DeLillo puts it, in 'the grain of the most routine moment', or as 'translated', in Hustvedt's words 'into the mind and body'. I want to think, in addition, of this inner life of mind and body as part of the urban imaginary; and to ask what 'counternarratives', if this is what they were, emerged principally from DeLillo's own fiction.

THE REAL AND IMAGINED

I need first of all, however, to consider more directly the distinction between realism and fantasy which has so far hovered over these remarks, especially because of its resonance in relation to 9/11 and to New York City. In Manhattan's visual regime, the foundational grid plan and corresponding instrumental modernity have given rise to the apparently contrasting excess and fantastical bravura of its cultural superstructure. Apparently - for the rectangular and numerical at its base and the extraordinary and extravagant on high form a compound imaginary, the 'rigid chaos' of Rem Koolhaas's description. 'Real New York and imaginary New York aren't easily separated', Siri Hustvedt confirms.[14] What she has in mind is the way the attack on the material and symbolic fabric of the city made its mythology more poignant and more precious. An openly nostalgic love of the city rushed in, as it were, to fill the howling space of loss and mourning. Hustvedt tells, for example, how Paul Auster watching the closing scenes on TV of the film *42nd Street* 'felt tears come to his eyes, and ... gave way to a moment of hopeless sentimentality. "For the old New York," he told me', she says, '"not for 10 September, but for what used to be"'.

'The essence of Manhattanism was to live inside fantasy', Rem Koolhaas had concluded at an earlier time.[15] And Slavoj Zizek's reflections on 9/11

Earlier examples, not only by New York based writers, are William Gibson's *Pattern Recognition* (2003) and John Barth's collection of short stories *Nine Nights and One Night* (2004) which is framed by the challenge of 9/11 to the story-telling imagination. Pat Barker's *Double Vision* (2003) and Ian McEwan's *Saturday* (2005) pursue the aftermath to 9/11 in personal, professional and public life in England. 'At its core, a good horror novel', said the writer Brian Keene, 'deals with everyday issues and events twisted horribly awry' and this, confirmed Nick Mamata in the *Village Voice* (July 10 and 16/2002), 'was the state of the nation post 9-11': <http://www.villagevoice.com/news/0228,mamatas,36372,1.html> Examples from genre fiction have been *The Last Good Day* (2003) by Peter Blauner, in which a headless corpse found in the Hudson River two weeks after the terrorist attacks triggers tragedy and violence in the lives of a young professional couple, and *Small Town* (2003) by Lawrence Block, in which a man is driven to a killing spree in New York after the death of his family on 9/11. The story 'The Day the Laughter Died' by John R. Platt, written he has said in response to 9/11, tells of a plague which affected only clowns.

Neil Gaiman's rewriting of the tale of Hansel and Gretel in his novel *Coraline* is relevant here, so too is Hustvedt's own *What I loved* (2003) which explores loss, deceit, wickedness and art by way of ghoulish fairy tale. These are texts, I think, which tell a traumatised New York and America that it will find the terror inside itself, on its streets, in its families, and in its own houses.

14. Siri Hustvedt, 'New York. Big, bad and back to its ballsy best', *The Observer*, 10/3/2002, <http://observer.guardian.co.uk/waronterrorism/story/0,1373,665038,00.html>

15. Koolhaas, *Delirious New York*, op. cit., p10.

16. Slavoj Zizek *Welcome to the Desert of the Real*, London, Verso, 2002, pp14-19.

17. Hustvedt, op. cit., n.p.

18. alice rose george, gilles peress, michael shulan and charles traub (eds), *here is new york: a democracy of photographs*, Zurich, Berlin and New York, Scalo, 2002, <www.hereisnewyork.org>

19. Ulrich Baer (ed), op. cit., pp34-36, 49-50, 178-80.

confirm how any distinction between the real and imaginary was undermined, since what sliced through the symbol of fantastic America was not an intrusive 'reality' but a dreadful and spectacular image conjured in the domain of the 'Real' as theorised by Jacques Lacan: unutterable and beyond the reckoning of the symbolic, but lodged in the psyche - and in Hollywood's dream factory.[16] The attack was accordingly in some way expected, as many New Yorkers said. For this unspeakable scenario was already there, if not spoken, in one or another disaster movie. 'A hackneyed fiction', comments Hustvedt, 'remade ad nauseam by the studios was manipulated by the terrorists into grotesque reality'.[17] And immediately it was on TV, simultaneously a real and mediated happening. The fundamental co-ordinates of an already mythologised New York imaginary had, as it were, been co-opted, and this as much as the tragic human consequences sent the city into shock.

How does this relate to modes of representation? Above all, surely, 9/11 was represented in the many thousands of professional and amateur photographs taken of the event itself and its immediate aftermath. These belonged conventionally to the genre of reportage or documentary: the street level grid of realism, as it were, to the skyscraper of fable and fantasy. The collection of photographs, *here is new york*, for example, indexed the here and now of the event, the 'primal terror' of the planes bombing the WTC, the flames, the smoke, the astounded onlookers, the dust covered survivors, the heroic rescue workers, the skeletal remnant remaining at ground zero.[18] Prose writers responded too to this immediacy, tagging the sensation of panic and fear by time and day in diaristic fashion. The volume *110 Stories* contains several examples of this type: one from Paul Auster titled, 'Random Notes - September 11, 2001, 4.00pm', and others titled 'New York, 12 September 2001'; 'Shopping (3: 58 P.M. September 11)'; 'The Morning After That One'.[19] Even so, these stories are rarely if ever free of the space and time of reflection. Auster's piece, for example, is supplemented by later thoughts marvelling at the diversity and angelic patience of his fellow subway passengers. And more often the stories present oblique, adjacent and analogical narratives of, for example: being a Muslim woman alone in the city; a weight watcher's club which suspends its regime; a grandfather's death in another city in another country. And these are accompanied by dialogues, playlets and poems: one which rewrites an Old English poem, 'The Ruin'; one threaded with lines from Yeats and an allusion to Dante; while other pieces allude to Borges, Lorca, Whitman, Melville, and Hart Crane.

We might be inclined to attribute the immediacy and direct reference of documentary notation, on the one hand, and the variety of indirect, intertextual strategies, on the other, to the respective media and technologies of the photographic image and the written word. It would of course be a mistake, however, to assume the photographic record is free of art and editorial perspective. Time and again, the images collected in *here is new york* adopt an evident symbolism or aestheticising gaze, using light and setting, bodies, objects and buildings, the doubling effect of mirrors or windows or TV screens, or the counterpoint of text, street signage or graffiti to render what is at one and the same time an emotional and historic event.

What emerges in fact is less a blunt distinction between the real and imagined, than a visual discourse in which the more evidently fantastical and more apparently documentary collaborate in the making of an urban imaginary. We see this if we compare the photographic record with the two volume commemorative comic book issue produced by Dark Horse and DC comics.[20] As if to confirm that comics belong to the realm of fable and fantasy, Stan Lee in the second volume discovers a 'new' Aesop's fable. But the fantastical and everyday in fact combine here too. The cover of Volume Two shows the arch DC superhero, Superman, standing beneath and now subordinated to, a huge poster-window of the new-found heroes of firefighters, police and support services. 'Wow', he says. The stories themselves have predominantly children protagonists and invariably impart a code of values comprising love for family, friends, New York and nation, an end to prejudice and a belief in world peace. In one strip this goal is inspired by an alien intelligence, in another it is urged by a cast of world historical leaders, including Chief Joseph, Abraham Lincoln, Winston Churchill, Martin Luther King, Golda Meier, the Zulu Chief Shaka, and Mahatma Gandhi.

Effectively, the comics reaffirm an assimilative American national imaginary through the 'local' event of 9/11 in the 'global' city of New York. The anthology *here is new york* operates in a similar but in fact more direct way to affirm and 'globalise' American values, appealing explicitly in its prefatory statement to the Founding Fathers and the idea of democracy, enacted once more in the 'democracy of photographs' by 'anybody and everybody' which was the organising premise of the project.[21] In addition, the editors want to suggest that this event has world-wide ramifications. They understand their title '*here is new york*', they say, which is so evidently indexical, to mean that 'After 9/11, New York is everywhere' (9). *here is new york* is anonymous, democratic and realist in conception while the comics are explicitly authored, drawn and coloured, and co-produced by a major publisher of comic book fantasy. Both projects worked nevertheless to produce a replenished New York imaginary which renewed a combined sense of local belonging, patriotism and global centrality. The hallmark of this response to the shattering of the real and imaginary was to unify neighbourhoods, New Yorkers, America and the world under the banner of a notion of 'freedom'. At the same time neither the comics nor the anthology are vengeful or war-mongering, nor consciously propagandising.[22] Jointly they present a 'counternarrative' whose purpose was to combat despair and build solidarity around traditional American values. At the same time this was not, quite evidently, the dissenting counternarrative of a Michael Moore or Noam Chomsky or Walter Mosely. Nor, as we shall see, does the

20. *9-11 September 11th 2001, Vol 1, Artists Respond*, Milwaukee, Oregon, Dark Horse Comics, Chaos! Comics, Image Comics, 2002; *9-11. September 11th 2001, Vol 2, Writers and Artists Tell Stories to Remember*, Neil Gaiman (ed), New York, DC Comics, 2002.

21. george, et al (eds), *here is new york*, op. cit., p7.

22. The relevant comparison here is with the photographs of Joel Meyerowitz. Meyerowitz had exclusive access to ground zero and his resulting work *After September 11 Images from Ground Zero* was deployed by the Bush Administration in exhibitions outside the US for the explicit purpose of cultural diplomacy. In the words of the Under Secretary of Cultural Diplomacy and Public Affairs, Charlotte Beers, art and culture could play a part in countering, 'the myths, the biases, the outright lies' being circulated about the US throughout 'the Muslim world', quoted, in an admirable account, by Liam Kennedy, 'Remembering September 11: photography as cultural diplomacy', *International Affairs* 79, 2 (2003): 315-326.

identification of New York, America and the world which characterises these examples accord with the urban imaginary of DeLillo's fiction.

DELILLO'S COUNTERNARRATIVES

DeLillo has so far published three stories, two after and none directly about 9/11, but which I think orbit and work through some of its motifs: *The Body Artist* (2001), the short story titled 'Baader-Meinhof' or 'Looking at Meinhof' (2002) and the novel *Cosmopolis* (2003).[23] I want to consider the last two first and return to *The Body Artist*.

'Looking at Meinhof', to adopt this title, tells of a young woman who repeatedly visits the exhibition of paintings by Gerhard Richter titled 'October 18, 1977', which had been staged at the Museum of Modern Art first in 2000 and then as a part of a major retrospective in Spring, 2002. The first exhibition took place after the somewhat forgotten first attempted attack on the World Trade Center in February 1993, at the time noted as 'the gravest attack of international terrorism ... on American soil'.[24] Terrorism was a matter of concern and MoMA felt it necessary to issue a statement justifying their acquisition of the paintings and the exhibition.

The paintings themselves deliberately blur the clarity of 15 original photographs of the Baader-Meinhof group taken on the morning they were found dead in Stammheim prison, whether or not by their own hand. In viewing the paintings the unnamed woman in DeLillo's story looks intently at or for Ulrike Meinhof who had been found hanged earlier than the others in 1976. She names her and Gudrun Ennslen by their first names and supposes there must have been a reason for their terrorist campaign. Her inner thoughts are interrupted at the story's opening by a male visitor to the exhibition. He is killing time before an interview. They talk, leave, and go to a snack bar together and then to her apartment. She doesn't quite know how this happens and in the apartment where she lives alone becomes afraid of him. He assumes they will have sex and she is forced to hide in the bathroom. In time he leaves but the next day she goes to the exhibition and finds him already there.

Earlier, the woman scrutinises Richter's works and where the man sees nothing, 'no colour, no meaning', she finds beauty in the paintings and meaning in the terrorists' actions: what they did was 'wrong but it wasn't blind and empty', she says.[25] In one painting she detects a cross which makes her feel 'there was an element of forgiveness in the picture' and that though they were terrorists, the four men and women 'were not beyond forgiveness'. She then finds herself subjected to an episode of sexist 'terrorism' in her own apartment. This seems to be the point of the story's extension from the paintings and an episode of European terrorism to an average New York neighbourhood. The story 'increases the flow of meanings', shifting time and locale to show what a gendered New York urban imaginary might be like: cautious and curious, fragile and at risk.

23. Don DeLillo, *The Body Artist*, London, Picador, 2001; 'Baader-Meinhof', *The New Yorker*, April 2002; published as 'Looking at Meinhof', The *Guardian*, 17/08/2002, <http://books.guardian.co.uk/review/story/0,12084,775700,00.html>; *Cosmopolis*, London, Picador, 2003.

24. Statement by 'The Joint Terrorism Task Force', <http://www.adl.org/learn/jttf/wtcb_jttf.asp>

25. DeLillo, 'Looking at Meinhof', The *Guardian*, 17/08/2002.

Published *after* 9/11 the story shows that terrorism has a history outside the US and that it occurs in the unnoticed local spaces of the global city too. It brings, moreover, an ambiguity to this extension of meanings which passes from the 'nuances of obscurity' in the paintings to the woman's indecision, first wanting to tell the man nothing of herself and then telling him; wondering what she wanted, but knowing she does not want what he expects. He asks her to forgive him when he leaves and this echoes her thoughts on the Baader-Meinhof group. If they 'were not beyond forgiveness' what of him? And what does it mean when she discovers him at the gallery, looking at the painting where she had seen the cross? Does he mean to 'terrorise' her further, or is this the beginning of an awkward liaison, when they will discover a 'situation in common ... an inflection of mutual sympathy', the 'friendship' he offered, in his way ('be friends', he pleads), and she did not want in hers?

In these ways, I think, DeLillo's story comprises a counternarrative which extends meanings and, in some kinship with Richter's art, investigates the blur of disparate interior lives and motives, both of terrorists and a terroriser and his lone victim.

Eric Packer in *Cosmopolis* (the English edition shows the Empire State building on its cover) is a young, high-powered, stupendously rich and powerful asset manager and currency trader. He lives already 'in the future, in the utopian glow of cyber-capital' where 'there is no memory' and 'where markets are uncontrolled and investment potential has no limit'. For Packer 'skyscraper' is an obsolete word, 'office' is out of date, even 'computer sounds backward and dumb';[26] while another piece of technology, the spycam in his fabulously equipped stretch limousine, records his actions before he commits them. This is the American world narrative as DeLillo describes it in the essay 'In the Ruins of the Future', now usurped by the terrorist narrative. The novel's epigraph is a line from the poet Zbigniew Herbert, 'a rat became the unit of currency', from a poem DeLillo read in Oct 2001 after 9/11 at the New York Town Hall. The novel is set, however, *before* 9/11, on a day in April, 2000. DeLillo offers therefore to scrutinise the operation of capital markets, which defines America, before the attack. And if the American future has 'no memory' he does here bring one to it. For, the point must be, American capital had already collapsed, in the fall of the stock market on 14 April 2000, a collapse observers compared to the crash of 1929 and the slump of 1985.

In the novel Packer sets off on an apparent whim on this day in April 2000 to have his hair cut on the other side of town. The President is visiting the city and this delays the journey. And so, in an evident device, Packer's limo crosses the city along 47th Street, taking in the imprinted history of the city from East to West; passing through the area of the United Nations, the banking district, the diamond district, the theatre district, and so on, until he comes to the car breakers and the barber shop, a place of his boyhood which is his destination on 11th Avenue. On his route he witnesses an anti-

26. DeLillo
Cosmopolis, op. cit.,
pp9, 15, 66.

capitalist demonstration which wrecks his vehicle, and the state funeral, practically, of a black Sufi rapper, and joins a street installation composed of naked bodies. He calls in on his mistress; he consults with his money advisors and chief of theory; he is examined in his limo by his doctor; he meets and separates from his new wife, a poet and heiress; he loses her fortune; and he murders his bodyguard. For all along, on this day in the life of America in the global financial capital, the Yen has rocketed and shaken the markets and shaken Packer. He keeps buying, trusting that there will be a pattern, but there isn't. Not in the money markets at least, for the novel is itself plotted as if on a grid and moves Packer slowly and unstoppably towards his destiny. What awaits him, ensconced in an abandoned apartment building, is a vengeful former employee Benno Levin, as he calls himself, the enemy the system has itself produced. The novel ends with Packer facing Levin's gun and seeing his death in advance on his videowatch as we read it ourselves, also in advance, in Levin's earlier confessional diary.

Cosmopolis is not about 9/11 but brings a history and inner critique to America's self-identity which stalls any easy sense of the clash of civilisations, good and evil, which the event provoked. Reviewers of the novel, John Updike prominently among them, lamented the novel's lack of realism.[27] He had a point. 'Plots reduce the world', DeLillo had written[28] and his own pursues the reductive equation of Manhattan, money markets and America in deliberate street by street fashion. But *Cosmopolis* is not a realist novel but a fable. And Packer is a sufficiently complex stand-in for the abstract, self-motivating assimilative drive of capitalism: a self-made man, who knows five languages, whose egotistical sexuality matches his will to financial power, who reads serious poetry, who admires modernist art works, but wants to buy up not only all the Rothkos but the chapel which houses them in Houston, Texas. He is in short the face of American modernity DeLillo speaks of, riding the waves of the future, but sinking now in the hyperreal cityscape and risk society theorised for him by his Baudrillardian assistant. At the other end of this grid plan, Benno Levin is not a terrorist but a lone assassin, Packer's metaphorical, almost 'twin', most crucially in possessing like him an asymmetrical prostate.

This is crucial because the asymmetrical confounds the order of things. Jean Baudrillard himself suggests how 9/11 raised the stakes beyond America and Islam to the scene of globalisation itself, pitching the consummate global power against the global antagonists it inevitably produced, like a virus within the system. 'Terrorism is immoral', he writes, 'but so too is globalisation.[29] 'So it is terror against terror. But asymmetric terror', he says, and 'asymmetry … leaves global omnipotence entirely disarmed' (15). Eric Packer embodies this omnipotence and excess and is disarmed. His faith that the one world order is indeed ordered and patterned deafens him to the message of his own body and his other, his asymmetrical narrative twin, the powerless little man. *Cosmopolis* reaches out in this way for a public statement from the narrow gauge of 47th Street. Edward W. Soja adopts the

27. John Updike, 'One Way Street'. Review of *Cosmopolis*, *The New Yorker*, 31/03/03, <http://www.newyorker.com/critics/books/?030331crbo_books1>

28. DeLillo, 'In the Ruins of the Future', op. cit.

29. Jean Baudrillard, *The Spirit of Terrorism*, London, Verso, 2002, p12.

30. Spiegelman, op. cit., 'The Comic Supplement', Spiegelman has in mind poetry readings 'as frequent as the sound of police sirens' and the number of readings especially of W.H. Auden's 'September 1, 1939'. Aside from the poetry, the stories – and the comic strips – two prominent public

term 'cosmopolis' to highlight the globalised phase of cityspace, characterised both by transnational economic flows and the opportunity for new notions of citizenship, justice and democracy. DeLillo's *Cosmopolis* is dystopian by comparison. The complex inner life of *character* is neglected for a display of the uncontrolled rhythms of capital on one day in the life of Packer and the global city. The novel is therefore curiously abstract and local at once. But this situates it at the same time within 'the inner life of this *culture*' (my italics) and the localised national consciousness provoked by 9/11 into a new belligerence - the attitude which seems to come at us with unblinkered hubris in 'In the Ruins of the Future'. 'We are the astonishment' DeLillo writes there. These are the tones of an offended patriotism. Yet in the auto-critique of the fable *Cosmopolis*, the investment in futures, claimed as if it were America's own in DeLillo's essay, is shown as having already self-destructed.

SATIRICAL FANTASY AND GHOSTLY ECHOES

Both 'Meinhof' and *Cosmopolis* are examples of fiction's displaced, oblique reaction to 9/11. *The Body Artist* published before this event will seem even more plainly unconnected. I want to discuss this novel finally alongside Art Spiegelman's, *In the Shadow of No Towers*, and in that way reflect further on place and memory, and the problematic distinctions between direct reference and indirect resonance, and between the real and imagined.

In its reaction to 9/11, New York turned to 'culture', says Art Spiegelman, 'to reaffirm faith in a wounded civilisation'.[30] Finding nothing in the place of this culture himself he resorted to old comic strips, 'vital unpretentious ephemera from the optimistic dawn of the 20th century'. Here he discovers another contrary, subversive, upside down narrative, where fantasy invades the real and performs its own role in making an American and specifically New York identity. Ten full size plates tell the story as 'a slow-motion diary' of his own experience of 9/11 and its immediate aftermath and give vent to his political spleen. 'The Comic Supplement', comprising the later part of the book, reproduces full-size pages of *The Kinder Kids* (1906); *Hogan's Alley* (1893) featuring 'The Yellow Kid,' 'one shanty Irish guttersnipe in a bright yellow nightshirt' and a gang of street urchins in a Lower Manhattan ghetto; *The Upside Downs of Little Lady Lovekins and Old Man Muffaroo* (1904); and a story of *Foxy Grandpa* (1902) which includes Hans and Fritz, from the world of 'nihilistic vaudeville' as Spiegelman terms it. Hans and Fritz derive from the earlier strip of *The Katzenjammer Kids*, lambasted because of its violence (since they regularly blew up the adult world) and semi-literate immigrant idiom. Here, in the story of Foxy Grandpa, 'the little terrorists', as Spiegelman terms them, dynamite Grandpa's patriotic reading of the Declaration of Independence ('When in the course of human events ...'). Notably in this section of the book there is *Little Nemo in Slumberland* (1905), invented by the 'genius' Winsor McCay, says Spiegelman, at a 'moment of

examples of this 'turn to culture' appeared in Daniel Libeskind's proposed new memorial concept for ground zero and the reopening, after renovation and expansion, of MoMA, greeted with a warm sense of renewed self-definition in the city at the end of 2004. The first has been marked in the event by an attempt on the part of the developer and leaseholder of the site, Larry Silverstein, and his elected lead architect, David Childs, effectively to sideline Libeskind's aesthetic and ethical purpose. At MoMA, the exhibition of now 'classical' modernist works by Matisse, Van Gogh and early Picasso in Yoshio Taniguchi's breathtaking but self-effacing and itself modernist structure, combined to reaffirm New York's hold on the Western heritage of modernist art. The refurbishment at MoMA had been made possible by a donation of $500 million from members of the Board of Trustees towards the total cost of $858 million. Both monument and Museum embodied ideas of culture; in both, its public expression depended upon a contract, troubled in one and benign in the other, between art and money. The civilisation New York reaffirmed was thus rebuilt, we might say, upon its foundational relations between culture and capital.

open-ended possibility and giddy disorientation' which opened the century. Nemo here dreams his way into a baroque out-of-scale New York cityscape, accompanied by the ethnic stranger, the 'savage Jungle Imp'. 'Flip', their associate, scrambles across the buildings to catch up with them, knocking down buildings 'near where', as Spiegelman points out, 'the twin towers would fall 94 years later'.

What Spiegelman is doing, I suggest, is recovering a popular, unlettered idiom, a history from below and from the margins, of immigrants, slum kids, delinquent brats, of topsy-turvy escapades, of surrealism and dream in all its mayhem, anarchistic subversion and possibility. He reclaims this native comic terrorism as the vehicle for his own present mood of frustration and protest. Already scandalised by the Presidential election of 2000, 'equally terrorised' by Bush and Bin Laden, Spielgelman tells his own tale, here converting his image into that of Maus from the earlier volumes *Maus I* and *II*, and populates his real life story with characters from the early comics, including Hans and Fritz. He is brought to despair finally at the arrival of the Republican convention in New York in September 2004. Yet he comes nonetheless to feel that he is now 'a "rooted" cosmopolitan'; that he feels 'a pang of affection for his familiar, vulnerable streets'. Allegiance to 'the chaotic neighbourhood that I can honestly call home', he says, 'is as close as I can comfortably get to patriotism'. Crucially too, in a latent implication - the 'unstated epiphany' of the work, he says - he vows to take up the art of making comics once more.[31] Belonging to and reinvigorating this tradition - a popular form begun at the onset of American mass society - helps inspire the terms of an identity which can move across the abyss of 9/11: a dissident but patriotic, lower Manhattan, New York American-Jewish identity, 'rooted' but in a state of permanent agitation.

Spiegelman's *In the Shadow of No Towers* is a direct response to 9/11 but exceptional in its dissenting, satirical iconoclasm. DeLillo's *The Body Artist* is a ghost story, distant from 9/11, but exceptional in its analysis. 'Time seems to pass' the novel opens. '*Seems* to pass'; 'it all happens around the word *seem*', DeLillo writes later.[32] In the first twenty-five pages, Lauren Hartke and her husband, Rey Robles, move slowly through the domestic routines of breakfast in a rented house by the ocean; mis-hearing, repeating words and gestures, backing up, sidling forward through half-thoughts and actions. We learn that this was the last morning before his suicide in a Manhattan apartment and realise this episode is already a reconstruction. We know then that the novel is about time, about mourning and memory.

Before Rey's death, the two of them had heard noises in the house. And Lauren discovers a manifestation of this disturbance, a figure who is at once child-like and a man, a 'gnome like' puppet whose speech and movement come in jerky, eerie echoes of the real thing. He exists 'in a kind of time that had no narrative quality', says Lauren (65); at an empty crossroads, says DeLillo, where 'time is something like itself, sheer and bare, empty of shelter'[33] - and in this stranger's own alien idiom in the novel, 'If I am

31. All statements from the opening prefatory section 'The Sky is Falling!' and Plate IV.

32. DeLillo, *The Body Artist*, op. cit., pp7, 31.

33. DeLillo, Interview with Michael Silverblatt, *Bookworm*, KCRW Radio, Santa Monica USA, Part One, 19/06/2003; Part Two, 26/06/2003b, <http://www.kcrw.com>

where I will be. Because nothing comes between me' (74). Lauren records their conversations, if this is what they are, when he speaks sometimes in broken spasms and at times, in a rush, sounds like herself or like Rey, repeating verbatim snatches he had perhaps overheard. She calls him 'Mr Tuttle', a name from her past. And he is, from one view, not simply under her care but her creation: a figment of her grief who seems to mimic Rey because she is mimicking Rey as she speaks into a tape recorder. Mr Tuttle's non-linear time is her time, attenuated out of joint, as she tries to defy the passage of past into present and deny the fact of Rey's death.

DeLillo insists that Mr Tuttle is 'real'. He is 'totally lost in the world', he says, 'in the real world, not in the world we have build with our self-protective mechanisms'.[34] But this is a real without co-ordinates at 'a kind of dead-end, or one step beyond all human striving towards expressibility'.[35] DeLillo himself is 'on the verge of stuttering', he says, in trying to describe this 'pre-human' figure and the raw 'unprotected' real time and no-place he exists in.[36] Mr Tuttle is the invasive 'Real', then, once more, of Lacan and Zizek, the embodied uncanny, the ghost or spectre who enters the house and the house of fiction from a realm at the edge of comprehension. Lauren we understand, in this respect, is 'working-through' trauma in the realm of the imaginary.

In this respect too, Lauren, the body artist of the title, prepares for a performance in town. She disciplines and meticulously scours her face and body, stripping herself back to a kind of transparency so as to remake herself as many selves. Like Mr Tuttle she employs mimicry to perform other selves, in voice and gesture, including himself. She wants to 'stop time, or stretch it out, or open it up' (107). And when she returns to the house thinking to find Mr Tuttle or Rey, (the two are confused) both are gone; one disappeared, one now finally dead. The novel ends with her looking outwards, beyond the window to feel 'the flow of time in her body to tell her who she was' (124).

None of this is about 9/11, nor even about New York City, but in another way it surely is. For *The Body Artist* resonates with the themes and motifs of this episode: of loss and mourning, dislocated time, the encounter with the Lacanian 'Real', and how this outside comes inexplicably to inhabit the inside and familiar. Tuttle has 'no protective surface', he drifts painfully across realities and is 'scared … here in the howl of the world' (90). In this no-place, DeLillo writes, 'was the howling face, the stark, the not-as-if of things' (90). We are reminded of the chasm of absence and loss which is the 'howling space' he speaks of in the essay 'In the Ruins of the Future', but reminded too of this essay's haunted naming of the 'medieval' 'pre-modern' terrorist. In *The Body Artist* the disturbance of the alien, 'pre-human' other is acknowledged; neither accommodated not abjected. In the ambiguity of the tale Lauren both projects and incorporates Mr Tuttle's alterity. He is the stranger and revenant, the ghost of Rey, conjured somehow out of the need to slow, to replay, and re-enter time. And 'Time', we are told, 'is the

34. Ibid.

35. Ibid.

36. Ibid.

37. Andreas Huyssen underlines the temporality of the urban imaginary which 'in its temporal reach may well put different things in one place: memories of what there was before, imagined alternatives to what there is', *Present Pasts, Urban Palimpsests and the Politics of Memory*, California, Stanford University Press, p7.

38. In the words of the then Mayor of New York City, Rudy Giuliani, the fact that the World Trade Centre was occupied by 'individuals of every race, religion and ethnicity' confirmed that the attack 'was not just an attack against the City of New York or the United States of America,' but an attack 'against the very idea of a free, inclusive, and civil society … We have emerged stronger and more united,' he

says, 'We are more determined than ever to live our lives in freedom' (Joel Meyerowitz exhibit <http://www.911exhibit.state.gov/>). At the Republican convention held in New York in August 2004, the audience began to chant 'USA! USA! USA! USA!' It sounded, writes Andrew O'Hagan, 'like words of anger and threat pressed into the New York night', London Review of Books, 23/9/2004, p9.

39. Ash Amin, and Nigel Thrift, Cities. Reimagining the Urban, Cambridge, Polity, 2002, p4.

40. Iris Marion Young, 'The Ideal of Community and the Politics of Difference' in L. Nicholson (ed), Feminism/Postmodernism, New York, Routledge, 1990, pp303, 301.

41. Perhaps, also, this thinking is not actually so distant from the direct experience of 9/11. A contributor to the collection 110 Stories, for example, thinking of the images of 'the missing' posted around Lower Manhattan, alludes to D.H. Lawrence's words in his essay on Edgar Allan Poe: 'There are terrible spirits, ghosts, in the air of America', in Baer (ed), pp238-9; D.H. Lawrence Studies in Classic American Literature, 1965, [1924], p71. More generally I have in mind on these themes texts

only narrative that matters', 'It stretches events and makes it possible for us to suffer and come out of it and see death happen and come out of it' (92). The story speaks in this way of strategies of survival and reinvention, or of 'working through', and speaks from the distance of its small story and personal trauma to the 100,000 stories and collective trauma of 9/11.

Finally it is also about art and what art does. For Lauren is the body artist who absorbs the otherness of her experience to remake herself; and DeLillo is the novelist who tells her counternarrative: a woman's story which 'in time' overcomes loss and at its heart deconstructs the underlying binaries of self and other upon which the series of binaries detailed here - of novelist and terrorist, the real and unreal, America and its critics, America and the world - depend.

RECONFIGURING THE URBAN IMAGINARY

Edward W. Soja, once more, defines the urban imaginary essentially in terms of our cognitive grasp upon urban experience. We need to refine this, even in general terms, so as to recognise how the urban imaginary comprises an internally differentiated set of representations and ideological shadings and how these are joined by a range of psychic or affective tones, lived in the mind and the body, across both space and time.[37] We need to recognise too that the urban imaginary will be particular to individual cities and how New York's physical and visual regime has given a distinctive base to its cognitive and affective rhythms, producing a kind of jazzy opus of regularity and extravagance in which the real and not so real are played off against each other.

9/11 interrupted the taken-for-granted weave of the material, mythic and psychic threads in the City's fabric. In foregrounding loss and absence, it forced up a nostalgic and more fervent attachment to the City, embodied in its cultural iconography and the chequered moods and manners of its populace. What was loved afresh was the routine life which had been unseen until it was demolished. Everyday life and times in the City were, in short, estranged. This fed a sense of solidarity and belonging to a neighbourhood, a sharpened sense of the City's ethnic diversity which prompted the combative, protective sense of New York as global city, not of financial flows, but of peoples and values. Politicians, comic books, and New York novelists joined in this re-affirmation.[38]

This besieged re-territorialisation of community and patriotism echoes the quest for a 'lost territorial identity' referred to earlier. It does not sound like the urban imaginary of postmetropolitan global cities described by recent cultural geographers. For Amin and Thrift in their thoughts on 'reimagining the urban' we must 'move on from a politics based on a nostalgia for a lost past of tightly knit and spatially compact urban communities'.[39] The new urbanism is based rather on the 'transhuman ... the distanciated ... the displaced and the intransitive' (5). The evocation of neighbourhood, of local and national unity in response to 9/11 confound this and earlier arguments, by Iris Marion Young (1990) and others, for an urban 'politics of difference' comprising an 'openness to unassimilated otherness'.[40] The new-found sense of solidarity expressed by many New Yorkers should bring us to think again about how notions of community, home, and belongingness continue to be articulated.

DeLillo's question is whether fiction any longer reaches effectively into 'the inner life of the culture'. What we have to assess, so he teaches, is whether these texts 'increase the flow of meaning' of, for example 'terror', 'capitalism', 'time', 'grief' and the 'real' - or of 'patriotism' or 'freedom'. Art Spiegelman's graphic novel answers to this, I believe, with all the specificity of a locally based, oppositional imaginary, as do, in their different ways, DeLillo's 'Meinhof' and *Cosmopolis*. My question has also been about how fiction takes the measure of an inner culture when it is removed from its immediate public drama. If *The Body Artist* does this, it also joins company with other trains of thought. For the tropes which accrue around 9/11, and which this text addresses - of absence and mourning, the self and other, memory, the real, the uncanny and spectrality - have formed the agenda for much recent theory and cultural criticism.[41] Often, too, this work has had the holocaust as its specific, iconic point of reference, and this has set these themes in a longer history as Spiegelman's earlier graphic novels *Maus I and II* remind us. That these have emerged as 'our' contemporary cultural topoi, speaks of a broader common discourse and consciousness. And if 9/11 has given a newer focus to this thinking, this can in its turn stretch the meaning of New York another way. I mean that these texts, *The Body Artist* included, might open New York to a different set of identifications within and outside itself: an imaginary which does not stack up to the equation New York = America = the World. A fundamentalist USA sees only enemy aliens outside itself. A fiction which voices the 'pre-human', which sees the alien in the mirror, which finds the asymmetric and irregular in the body of the host, might pose a different set of relations, a counter urban imaginary, in short, of the self and other in a differently configured setting of the local and the global.

First delivered as a lecture at the symposium 'Cinematographies: Fictional Strategies and Visual Discourses in New York City' at the Centre for Literary Study, Humbolt University, Berlin, March 2005.

such as the following: Jacques Derrida, *Spectres of Marx* (1994), *The Work of Mourning* (2001); Jonathan Dollimore, *Death, Desire and Loss in Western Culture* (1999); Andreas Huyssen, *Twilight Memories* (1995), *Present Pasts. Urban Palimpsests and the Politics of Memory* (2003); Cathy Caruth (ed) *Trauma. Exploration in Memory* (1995); Mieke Bal et al, *Acts of Memory* (1998); Svetlana Boym, *The Future of Nostalgia* (2001). Derrida's *Spectres of Marx* also posited a 'new international' which would rigorously interrogate questions of law, 'the concepts of state and nation, and so forth'. He detects an alliance of this kind, joined 'without coordination, without party, without country, national community … without co-citizenship' which recognises its debt to 'the' or 'a' spirit of Marxism in maintaining the practice of critique and 'interminable self critique'. He is speaking of those who 'have ceaselessly proceeded in a hyper-critical fashion … in a deconstructive fashion, in the name of a new Enlightenment for the century to come', 'Spectres of Marx' *New Left Review* 205, (May/June 1994): pp53, 55. We might set the question of a newly configured cultural or urban imaginary in the context of debates upon this new internationalism.

Practical Deleuzism and Postmodern Space

Ian Buchanan

1. Edward Casey,
*Getting Back into
Place: Toward a
Renewed
Understanding of the
Place-World*,
Bloomington &
Indianapolis,
Indiana University
Press, 1993, pxiii.

'We pay a heavy price for capitalizing on our basic animal mobility' writes Edward Casey and that price is 'the loss of places that can serve as lasting scenes of experience and reflection and memory'.[1] This loss is usually blamed on the proliferation of generic spaces - or, to use Marc Augé's phrase, 'non-places' - like malls, airports, freeways, office parks, and so forth, which prioritise cost and function over look and feel. Even so, Casey still wants to argue that transitory spaces like airports retain a certain 'placial' quality that gives meaning to contemporary existence. In contrast, writers like Augé (and he is by no means alone - Augé himself attributes the key elements of his idea of non-place to de Certeau and Foucault) have in much recent writing on space sought to elucidate this new type of generic space's distinct lack of placiality. These two positions are, however, simply two sides of the same conceptual coin - Augé does not conceive of a new type of place, he uses a traditional model of place to decry the seemingly soulless transformations to the built environment he witnesses everywhere in the developed world. By the same token, Casey acknowledges that these new spaces appear placeless, but that is only because one isn't looking at them in the right way. His work then seeks to restore their seemingly lost placiality. The interest of bringing Deleuze and Guattari into this debate resides in the fact that they do not hold that the idea of place continues to be relevant.

Taking this as my starting point, I want to advance three propositions relating to the analysis of contemporary space. These three propositions will not by any means exhaust what can be said about this subject, but my hope is that they will inflect discussion about it in a useful way.

1. Alfred Hitchcock's cinema anticipated the affect of postmodern space - a kind of anxious mourning for the loss of place.

2. The suburban shopping mall was the harbinger of postmodern space - it is the form of content proper to postmodernism as form of expression.

3. The transformations that have made postmodern space what it is can be understood in terms of deterritorialisation.

BODY WITHOUT ORGANS

'The modern fact', as Deleuze put it, 'is that we no longer believe in this world. We do not even believe in the events which happen to us, love, death, as if they only half concerned us. It is not we who make cinema; it is the world which looks to us like a bad film'.[2] The world Deleuze is speaking of is post-war Europe, a world of rubble, housing shortages, refugees and bold reconstructions. He is also speaking of the cinematic or virtual worlds created in this period, signalling their radical difference in construction and operation from the cinema that preceded this moment. Pre-war cinema was a cinema of belief, or better, a cinema that could be believed in; in the post-war period this was no longer true, the cinema had to confront a world that exceeded what cinema up to that point could contrive to present, it went beyond its limits.

2. Gilles Deleuze, *Cinema 2: The Time-Image*, H. Tomlinson & R. Galeta (trans), London, Athlone, 1989, p171.

> Why is the Second World War taken as a break? The fact is that, in Europe, the post-war period has greatly increased the situations which we no longer know how to react to, in spaces which we no longer know how to describe. These were 'any spaces whatever', deserted but uninhabited, disused warehouses, waste ground, cities in the course of demolition or reconstruction. And in these any-spaces-whatever a new race of characters was stirring, a kind of mutant: they saw rather than acted, they were seers.[3]

3. Ibid., pxi.

It is a world that has been emptied out, a world in which the people are missing. A world of any-space-whatever not place.

What Deleuze is attempting to describe here is something he would in other works call the body without organs. So what is the body without organs? It is well known that the phrase itself is lifted from a poem by Antonin Artaud, but it is in vain that we look there for an explanation of the concept. Instead we must look to two quite distinct sources: Marx and Lacan. The first accounts for how the body without organs (BwO) functions, while the latter explains how it is possible for it to function that way. In *Anti-Oedipus*, Deleuze and Guattari say if we want to have some idea of the forces exerted by the BwO then we must first establish a parallel between desiring-production and social production. Forms of social production, like those of desiring-production, involve, they argue, 'an unengendered non-productive attitude' or what they call a 'full body' which functions as a *socius*. 'This socius may be the body of the earth, that of the tyrant, or capital. This is the body that Marx is referring to when he says that it is not the product of labour, but rather appears as its natural or divine presupposition'.[4] This is the body without organs. It is an active form of presupposition that inserts itself into a given context and in so doing smothers its origins so that it always appears as naturally occurring. 'It falls back on (*il se rabat sur*) all production constituting a surface over which the forces and agents of production are distributed, thereby appointing for itself all surplus production and arrogating to itself both the whole and the parts of the process, which now seem to emanate from it as a quasi cause'.[5] It defines not what we think and feel about something, but the unthought set of presuppositions we utilise to compose

4. Gilles Deleuze and Felix Guattari, *Anti-Oedipus: Capitalism and Schizophrenia*, M. Seem et al (trans), Minnesota, University of Minneapolis Press, 1983, p10.

5. Ibid.

our thoughts and feelings without them ever being intelligible to us.

I want to suggest that the body without organs of postmodern space is precisely the unintelligible fear that we have that it is placeless. Cinema's attraction, I would further suggest, stems from the fact that it is able to make this body without organs tangible. While it is true American cinema did not go down the same pathway as European cinema, it nevertheless ended up confronting its own kind of placelessness, or rather it generated its modulation of the same anxiety: that place had been destroyed. At this point in his history of cinema, Deleuze gives centre stage to the European directors. But even if Deleuze's implication is true that no new aesthetic developments were occurring in Hollywood at this point, that doesn't mean that nothing of interest was happening. Indeed, it is widely agreed that the films Hitchcock made in this period are among his best, to which judgement I want to add that these films are also films about a very different kind of landscape. As Joan Didion put it: 'It was a peculiar and visionary time, those years after World War II to which the Malls and Towns and even Dales stand as climate-controlled monuments [...] The frontier had been reinvented, and its shape was the subdivision, the new free land on which all the settlers could recast their lives *tabula rasa*'.[6] Hitchcock's cinema helped shape the unsettling feeling tone of this new unhomely era by perfecting what Deleuze calls a cinema of the 'mental image', that is, a cinema of the closed universe of the monad and the bunker.[7] The worlds Hitchcock constructs in his films, especially the later ones, do look like 'bad films', but in that precise sense they anticipate the postmodern landscape of glitzy but standardised façades. It is a cinema of a 'global style' that could be anywhere and as Rem Koolhaas puts it has spread everywhere like a virus.[8]

Hitchcock's films operate within highly contrived and closely observed buildings: the apartment block, the motel, the mansion, the terrace house at the end of the street (the ensuing claustrophobic atmosphere of constant surveillance is doubtless the element of his work that retains the most potent resonance in contemporary society). Hitchcock's famous preference for sound stages over locations, back-projections and mattes instead of the 'real' thing, created a cinema of what (after Eco and Baudrillard) and in contrast to Rossellini's neo-realism might be termed hyperrealism.[9] That is an aesthetic of the 'realer than the real'. There are any number of examples one could point to, but one of the more ironic (because of its 'ruse of history' undertone) is the filming of (1955) *The Trouble with Harry* - according to biographer Donald Spoto, Hitchcock deliberately set it in Vermont to capture the striking autumn colours. However, when he got to East Craftsbury in October 1954 to photograph it, he found he had been preceded by a storm and had to film indoors in a converted school-gym prepared in case of inclement weather. The finishing touches were done on a soundstage in Hollywood using East Craftsbury leaves hand-pasted onto plaster trees.[10] Here and elsewhere, the outside world in Hitchcock is literally a simulacra of a simulacrum. Hitchcock's disdain for actors (he notoriously used to fall

6. Joan Didion, *The White Album*, New York, Farrar, Straus & Giroux, 1979, pp180-1.

7. Gilles Deleuze, *Cinema 1: The Movement- Image*, H. Tomlinson and B. Habberjam (trans), Minnesota, University of Minneapolis Press, 1986, pp200-5.

8. Cited in Fredric Jameson, 'Future City', *New Left Review* 2, 21(2003): 65-79.

9. I take the term 'hyperrealism' from Umberto Eco, *Travels in Hyperreality*, W. Weaver (trans), London, Picador, 1986.

10. Donald Spoto, *The Dark Side of Genius: The Life of Alfred Hitchcock*, London, Plexus, 1983, p355.

asleep during the actual filming of scenes) which Deleuze charitably describes in terms of an opposition to the Actor's Studio is clearly of a piece with this.[11] If one must speak of a break between Hitchcock and Rossellini it is because Hitchcock could not reconnect the severed link between man and world; his characters persist 'in the world as if in a pure optical and sound situation'.[12] His worlds, like shopping malls, are interiors whose aim is to eliminate the desire for the outside by reproducing it in facsimile: everything within is related at the price of their being no relations without.[13]

11. Deleuze, 1986, op. cit., p201.

12. Deleuze, 1989, op. cit., p172.

13. Deleuze, 1986, op. cit., p204.

This closed-off world is difficult to sustain and as Deleuze argues some of Hitchcock's best films give us a glimpse of the ways in which the mental image would be pushed into a crisis.

Vertigo [1958] communicates a genuine image to us; and, certainly, what is vertiginous, is, in the heroine's heart, the relation of the Same with the Same which passes through all the variations of its relations with others (the dead woman, the husband, the inspector). But we cannot forget the other, more ordinary, vertigo - that of the inspector who is incapable of climbing the bell-tower staircase, living in a strange state of contemplation which is communicated to the whole film and which is rare in Hitchcock.[14]

14. Deleuze, 1986, op. cit., p204-5.

The Bates motel is a relic of an older 'placial' mode of spatiality, one that is nostalgically filled with all the qualities supposedly lost to us now that motels belong to freeways not towns, now that they are part of a spatial network, which may span the globe, rather than places in their own right. Chain motels like Howard Johnson's began to take a hold of the American landscape in this period, too, precisely by promising an end to particularity, to place-specific motels with idiosyncratic characteristics. The new chain motel guaranteed an end to the variations in motel fittings and fit-out old-style travellers like Humbert Humbert speak of, at once knowingly and ironically.

We came to know - *nous connûmes*, to use a Flaubertian intonation - the stone cottages under enormous Chateaubriandesque trees, the brick unit, the adobe unit, the stucco court, on what the Tour Book of the Automobile Association describes as 'shaded' or 'spacious' or 'landscaped' grounds. The log kind, finished in knotty pine, reminded Lo, by its golden-brown glaze, of fried-chicken bones. We held in contempt the plain whitewashed clapboard Kabins, with their faint sewerish smell or some other gloomy self-conscious stench and nothing to boast of (except 'good beds'), and unsmiling landlady always prepared to have her gift ('...well, I could give you ...') turned down.[15]

15. Vladimir Nabokov, *Lolita*, Harmondsworth, Penguin, 1995, pp145-6.

Lolita (1955) is, among other things, an ironic paean to a rapidly disappearing kind of place, namely the kind of place the Bates' motel is, a spatial native, a highly localised, albeit still generic, species of place. At least part of the thrill of *Psycho* is the familiar fear it evokes of the unexpected that dominated travel in the age before chain motels. It confirms the suspicion 'we moderns' have been taught to harbour that such unbranded places are at best uncongenial and at worst unsafe. Humbert is in this respect perfectly modern: he is not the least sentimental about the out of the way places he goes to, although he is occasionally moved to regret not really remembering where exactly he'd been to, nor what he'd seen - 'We had been everywhere. We had really seen nothing'.[16] He is not a tourist as such, but a nomad moving ceaselessly in order to stay put in the smooth any-space-whatever of the cloistered motel room. Like Norman Bates, he has a horror of the family home because he knows full well his particular fantasy cannot be enacted there. Not surprisingly, Humbert expresses a strong preference for the streamlined spaces that were even then replacing the eccentric places described above. 'To any other type of tourist accommodation I soon grew to prefer the Functional Motel - clean, neat, safe nooks, ideal places for sleep, argument, reconciliation, insatiable illicit love'.[17] What he looked for were spaces where the idiosyncrasies of place (noises, smells, and assorted other discomforts and distractions) did not intrude on his designs.

16. Ibid., p175.

17. Ibid., p145.

As Deleuze narrates it, then, what emerges in the years following World War II are two separate but dialectically connected cinematic traditions: a European tradition of any-spaces-whatever and (by implication) a Hollywood tradition of non-places; or, to put it another way, a neo-realism of the bombed-out city and a hyperrealism of suburban monoculture. This hyperrealism should not be read as a kind of intensified verisimilitude or cinematic equivalent of photorealism. I'm not suggesting that Hitchcock's cinema captures the truth of postmodern space in a representational sense. On the contrary, I'm suggesting his cinema has helped create the unthought recording surface on which much writing about, and indeed film-making in response to, postmodern space takes place - it was his cinema that taught us to think of the motel, the suburban family home and so on as places of anxiety; and he did so precisely by showing us that these places aren't as homely as we'd like to assume. Of course, Hitchcock didn't act alone, but we find encapsulated in his work the potent feeling that place isn't placial anymore: it is unsettling, un-homely, fearful, empty, lacking human dimension.

ABSTRACT MACHINE

At least part of the shock of Fredric Jameson's programme essay on postmodernism stemmed from its willingness to pronounce this new space of hotels and malls uninhabitable.[18] His entire argument can be understood as an attempt to describe a new kind of space that puts the old, or received spatial sense in question, leaving us unsure of how to act or feel in the face of such radical transformations in the built environment as the Bonaventure

18. Fredric Jameson, *Postmodernism, or, the Cultural Logic of Late Capitalism*, London, Verso, 1991, p40.

Hotel appeared to betoken. While much of his discussion of this space centres on its architectural attributes which are to him in equal parts striking and banal, it is the emergence of a total space of shopping that he is at most pains to document.[19] The Bonaventure Hotel, which sits on top of a six storey shopping mall, plus ubiquitous food court, offers a telling example of the way in which the built environment follows the postmodern dictate that all aspects of everyday life can and should be made to generate surplus value. Every aspect of life - eating, sleeping, shitting, fucking, and so on - can take place within its confines for a price. As Sharon Zukin argues in her history of this transformation of the American landscape, although no-one had eyes to see it at the time, the spread of the suburban shopping mall previewed the post-boom landscape inasmuch that - as we now know - spaces of consumption (rather than manufacturing, growing, or indeed simply living) would dominate and indeed determine our sense of place.[20]

In Deleuze's terms, the mall is an abstract machine - it is an ideal form that is actualised in a variety of formats. Central to the abstract machine is the distinction between form of content and form of expression Deleuze and Guattari draw from Hjelmslev. Deleuze and Guattari refer us to Foucault's analysis of the prison for an example of how this kind of analysis works. The prison is a form of content and is related to other forms of content (schools, barracks, hospital, factories and so on). But this form does not refer to the word 'prison' for its sense, but to an entirely different set of statements to do with the discourse of 'delinquency'. Delinquency is a form of expression articulating a new way of translating, classifying, stating and ultimately even committing criminal acts. The form of expression cannot be reduced to words - it refers to statements arising in the social field (the realm canvassed by Deleuze and Guattari's concept of the regime of signs). By the same token, the form of content is not reducible to a thing, or set of things; it refers to an assemblage (rather than to a state of affairs) comprising of architecture, discipline, and so on. Ultimately, we can say that there are two constantly intersecting fields here, one, a discursive multiplicity of expression, and the other, a non-discursive multiplicity of content. But, 'it is even more complex than that' because these two terms each have their own micro-histories, but also they make other kinds of connections to other kinds of formalisations. At most, Deleuze and Guattari say, they share an implied state of the abstract machine.[21]

Writing about postmodernism has tended to concentrate on the form of expression - the very word 'postmodernism' is an example par excellence of a form of expression. Expression refers to the production of what Deleuze and Guattari call (following Foucault) statements. Theorists as diverse as Meaghan Morris, John Fiske, Rob Shields, Anne Friedberg, as well as many others, have tended to focus the debate around the question of what is the proper statement for the mall - banality, resistance, panopticism, etc. What makes Jameson's approach different is that he not only discusses the form of expression, he also attempts to isolate the form of content of the mall,

19. For a longer discussion of Jameson's account of the Bonaventure see Ian Buchanan, *Deleuzism: A Metacommentary*, Edinburgh, Edinburgh University Press, 2000, pp143-74.

20. Sharon Zukin, *Landscapes of Power: From Detroit to Disney World*, Berkeley, University of California Press, 1991, p20.

21. Gilles Deleuze and Felix Guattari, *A Thousand Plateaus: Capitalism and Schizophrenia*, B. Massumi (trans), 1987, p67.

namely the creation of a new total space of consumerism that not only seeks to incorporate everything under one roof, but actively seeks to exclude or denigrate the world beyond its walls. The mall is a supreme example of what Rebecca Solnit has aptly described as the propagation of monoculture.[22] Her analogy is derived from agriculture and essentially depicts a situation in which a single 'cash' crop is grown to the exclusion of all other crops and ruthlessly defended using every available means. All the available evidence now suggests that in spite of its appearance of high productivity the monocultural approach is not only ecologically disastrous it is also commercially disastrous too since it is overly prone to bacterial and insect infestation and therefore too reliant on increasingly expensive pesticides. As a form, the mall promotes a single objective: the sale of consumer goods and services. Unlike the city, the mall is not a shared space - it has a single governing body reporting to a corporation which in turn reports to shareholders; unlike the city it is not a mix-use space - it is a single-use space, shopping and not-shopping are simply opposite sides of the same coin; unlike the city, the mall has no residents - it is a space for customers and employees only; unlike the city, the mall does not command our love and pride, it only wants our business. It is the proliferation of this form that I am suggesting has been a primary shaping force with respect to the shape and feel of contemporary space.

Despite the naïve celebrations of the 'pleasures' afforded ordinary citizenry by shopping malls and the still more naïve accounts of the possibilities of resistance to be found within their windowless walls, the reality is that their triumph came at the expense of previous models of coherent connection between population and place. They are not the organic product of economic growth in a community, but transplants from afar that settle into an area with no more care for the local than any foreign invader has. 'The regional shopping centre looks in retrospect like the inevitable outcome of mass automobile ownership and suburban growth, but its emergence in the 1950s was a dramatic event. Newspapers wrote glowingly about the advantages of "markets in the meadows": places totally planned for the consumer that made more sense than the helter-skelter competition of the average Main Street'.[23] As Baudrillard astutely observed, the mall-form functions as a nucleus around which the new, still to be built, suburb eventually settles like so much kipple.[24] Wal-Mart, currently the largest corporation in the world (its 2003 net worth was a staggering $US258 billion, its revenues amounting to 2 per cent of US GDP) took this strategy a step further in the 1950s and concentrated on towns with populations under 5,000, effectively turning them into satellites of its superstores.[25] With no other competition in sight, these stores effectively sucked the life out of the town's commercial districts, as small and fragile as they were, and refocused the flow of traffic and funds in the direction of an ugly bunker situated in an airfield-sized car park at the outer edge of the town.

The advent of the freeway system brought an end to point-to-point travel,

22. Rebecca Solnit and Susan Schwartzenberg, *Hollow City: The Siege of San Francisco and the Crisis of American Urbanism*, London, Verso, 2000, pp153-72.

23. Bernard Frieden, and Lynne Sagalyn, *Downtown, Inc. How America Rebuilds Cities*, Cambridge, MA, The MIT Press, 1989, p62.

24. Jean Baudrillard, *Simulacra and Simulation*, S. Faria Glaser (trans), Ann Arbor, The University of Michigan Press, 1994, p77.

25. Simon Head, 'Inside the Leviathan', *The New York Review of Books*, 51, 20 (2004): 80.

journeys no longer plotted a route from town to town, but instead pursued a transversal line of pure speed. The mall was an integral part of this system, displacing the town centre almost completely within a few years. It reappeared in fantasy form in Walt Disney's homage to an America that had disappeared, Disneyland. Malls occupy those spaces in the city where the factors we associate with place have either ceased to operate, or (more usually) are vulnerable to predatory reinterpretation. The mall took the beating heart of the city - the crowds, the big variety stores, the small specialty stores, the eclectic eateries - and transplanted it in greenfield sites sure in the knowledge that the people would come. But not all people, since one of its most potent attractions was and continues to be its promise of social homogenisation. As a privately owned space, the mall is, in contrast to the city, selective about who it permits to use its space. So although its use may appear public in character, the mall is not given to the public to use; it is rather 'open' to the public, providing they agree to abide its rules - no skating, no chewing gum, no smoking, no drinking, no loitering, and so on. Its commercial success is built on a series of what Zukin calls 'abstractions'. She has in mind both architectural abstractions - visual adumbrations of the city's iconography - and what might be thought of as abstractions of some, at least, of its more typical sensual pleasures, particularly those of the palate.

I specified the visual here because the mall's real breakthroughs in architectural terms lay elsewhere.[26] Rem Koolhaas claims the mall as apparatus hinges on three innovations for its efficacy: air-conditioning; the escalator; the automatic fire-sprinkler. To which one may add the bar-code and the brand, which although not architectural in themselves, have had an enormous impact on the architecture of the mall. The bar-code revolutionised inventory control; while the brand means products display themselves - the old idea of the department store, modelled on the museum, was that spaces had to be created to display goods in an attractive light. The buildings themselves had to be magnificent to compensate the shabby mercantilist dealings within (for example Harrods in London, Magasin du Nord in Copenhagen). This is patently not the way of postmodern supermarkets, which stack products floor to ceiling. Their display occurs in the virtual space of TV and billboards, their branding functioning then as a synecdoche of these images. The mall's success as an apparatus of consumption hinges to a large degree on the canny way in which it has created a form that can be decorated in such a way as to recollect the city minus its actual grittiness, smells, noise, in short, any of its typical characteristics. In this sense, it is perhaps more precise to say it recollects a movie of a city, rather than an actual city, and doubtless part of its appeal lies in the fact that to walk through a mall is like walking through not a movie set as such, but the virtual world the movie projects as a necessary condition to its cognition. The mall is the after-image of the city.

Abstraction, of the type Zukin talks about, can be seen in the Trafford

26. Jameson, 2003, op. cit..

Centre mall John Urry discusses in *The Tourist Gaze*. As can clearly be seen in the image he reproduces, it encases within its featureless walls a facsimile New Orleans streetscape replete with iron balustrades, French windows, gas lamps and ivy cascading from balcony planter boxes, but without the litter, horse dung, stale urine, drunks passed out in doorways, panhandling bums, and prostitutes of the real French Quarter before Hurricane Katrina. One cannot help but note in Urry's photo the ubiquitous presence of Starbuck's, which was also very much at home in the real New Orleans.[27] If one were to revive an outmoded critical discourse and ask which of the two spaces - the mall or the city - is the more authentic, the answer wouldn't be as easy to determine as one might expect. The French Quarter, although it continued to exude many of the same smells as it had when it was playground to the thousands of boilermakers and stevedores labouring in its shipyards and wharves, was nevertheless a Disneyfied facsimile of itself - an 'adults only' theme park. Indeed, Jackson's Brewery was literally a shopping mall. The waterfront had been converted into a bicycle path and the eateries in the Quarter had gone so far upmarket that none but the middleclass could afford an 'authentic' poughboy. The Quarter was girded by the postmodern equivalent of the Maginot line, a vast grey curtain of dour concrete superbunkers variously kitted out as a convention centre, casino, this or that chain hotel, and last but not least the superdome. The only people who visited the Quarter were middleclass tourists of that peculiarly American kind: conventioneers, sports fans, and salesmen. In that sense, New Orleans represented the apotheosis of the logic of the mall.

ASSEMBLAGE

How does an entire city become monocultural? How do malls work in other words? What follows is an attempt to show how the terms 'deterritorialisation' and 'reterritorialisation' might be used to understand, for example, that what makes the Bonaventure a postmodern building is precisely the fact that it was built as part of an earnest programme to transform Los Angles into a business centre to rival San Francisco and not simply its architecture.[28] It isn't the look of the building that is postmodern, so much as the willingness to displace the 'wild' city in favour of a 'monoculture'. Although Jameson doesn't put it this way himself, his later reading of the transformation of New York City's downtown makes essentially this argument: it is not the buildings, finally, that are postmodern; what is postmodern is the willingness to transform a city (to creatively destroy it) as a whole in order to revitalise it as a source of surplus value. While it is customary to celebrate the architects for their creative work, it is not the architects, but the city-planners (the regulators who make and police zoning laws, land taxes, and so on), and behind them the financiers who reap value from these laws, who are the real visionaries, the true mechanics of space, for they are the ones who create the context in which the new structure will work.[29]

27. John Urry, *The Tourist Gaze*, London, Sage, 2002 [2nd ed], p112.

28. In other words, one shouldn't read Davis against Jameson, but rather read them together.

29. Fredric Jameson, *The Cultural turn: Selected Writings on the Postmodern, 1983-1998*, London, Verso, 1998, pp183-5.

In spite of what many people (Deleuzians among them) seem to think, reterritorialisation and deterritorialisation are not a binary pair: reterritorialisation is not the opposite of deterritorialisation. As such, one must be wary of shorthand attempts to define them with reference to either a logic of opening and closing or detachment and reattachment because intended or not this cannot but instil the idea that they are a binary pair after all.[30] It is true Deleuze and Guattari do say that every deterritorialisation is followed by an accompanying reterritorialisation, but the one (deterritorialisation) does not spontaneously give rise to the other (reterritorialisation) as Keith Ansell Pearson implies.[31] To suggest that one kind of process can give rise to another is tantamount to smuggling dialectics back into a philosophy that is famously anti-dialectical. Even more wrongheaded, though, is to suggest as Charles Stivale does, that territory, deterritorialisation and reterritorialisation form a ternary structure. If this were indeed the case, then we would be compelled to concede that Deleuze and Guattari do indeed practice dialectics.[32] Also to be resisted, even though it is in fact very close to the spirit of Deleuze and Guattari's intent, is Jameson's claim that 'its first and as it were foundational meaning lies in' the emergence of capitalism itself; this was, he continues, 'the first and the most fateful deterritorialisation'.[33] This definition hypostatises deterritorialisation as an event, when in fact it is an ongoing, continuous process, a constant force (to use the not unrelated Lacanian language of the drives); deterritorialisation is not something that can be caused: one can unleash it, accelerate it, decelerate and contain it, but never engender it.[34]

What Deleuze and Guattari actually say is that capitalism is 'the thing, the unnameable, the generalised decoding of flows that reveals *a contrario* the secret of all [social] formations' that stands at the end of history enabling us to read history retrospectively in its light. It is not the first deterritorialisation, but the last. The first was in fact the coming of the State form, but in one respect Jameson is right in saying capitalism was the first because, as Deleuze and Guattari put it, it 'cannot be said that the previous formations did not foresee this Thing that only came from without by rising from within, and that at all costs had to be prevented from rising'.[35] Before Derrida coined the word 'hauntology' the concept was already - albeit namelessly - operating in Deleuze and Guattari's work.[36]

Capitalism is synonymous with the breakdown of the social conceived as a 'territorial machine' which connects a people to an earth (BwO) by means of inscription, but not the actual cause. Capitalism was able to come into being because of the propensity for deterritorialisation inherent in every social system: it is in effect the product not the cause of deterritorialisation. 'In a sense, capitalism has haunted all forms of society, but it haunts them as a terrifying nightmare, it is the dread they feel of a flow that eludes their code'.[37] In this respect, Jameson is also correct to describe it as fateful, for in its dissolute, decoded state, it is the end primitive societies feared and worked consciously to avoid. The coding of desire and the fear of decoded

30. See for example Eugene Holland, *Deleuze and Guattari's Anti-Oedipus: Introduction to Schizoanalysis*, London, Routledge, 1999, p20.

31. Keith Ansell Pearson, *Germinal Life: The Difference and Repetition of Deleuze*, London, Routledge, 1999, p177.

32. Charles Stivale, *The Two-Fold Thought of Deleuze and Guattari: Intersections and Animations*, New York, The Guildford Press, 1998, pp22-3.

33. Jameson, 1998, op. cit., p152.

34. Deleuze and Guattari, 1983, op. cit., p35.

35. Ibid., p153.

36. Jacques Derrida, *Spectres of Marx: The State of Debt, the Work of Mourning, and the New International*, P Kamuf (trans), London, Routledge, 1994.

37. Deleuze and Guattari, 1983, op. cit., p140.

38. Ibid., p139.

39. Ibid., p142.

40. Ibid., p145.

41. Ibid.

42. Ibid., p154.

43. Margaret
Crawford, 'The
World in a Shopping
Mall', in M. Sorkin
(ed) *Variations on a
Theme Park: The New
American City and the
End of Public Space*,
New York, Hill and
Wang, 1992 p8.

desire 'is the business of the socius'.[38] The 'essential thing is to mark and be marked', Deleuze and Guattari say, and what they mean by this is that all 'organs' (anything capable of producing or interrupting a flow - signs, status, women, children, herds, seeds, sperm, shit, menstrual blood, can all be conceived as 'flows') must be subject to a collective investment that 'plugs desire into the socius and assembles social production and desiring-production into a whole on the earth'.[39]

It should be clear enough from the foregoing that deterritorialisation cannot be understood independently of territoriality; what is perhaps less clear is that territoriality (or territory, these terms are used interchangeably) is not a 'placial' concept. Deleuze and Guattari quite explicitly rule this out. If territoriality 'is taken to mean a principle of residence or of geographic distribution, it is obvious that the primitive social machine is not territorial'.[40] The territorial machine does not divide land, it divides people, 'but does so on an indivisible earth where the connective, disjunctive, and conjunctive relations of each section are inscribed'.[41] The earth, a great, immanent, unengendered unity, is the space where our soul (in Foucault's sense of the term) circulates; it is the thing to which we pledge allegiance and attach ourselves and more especially our organs by means of ritual and bodily marks; but it also appears to us as our origin, where we came from, our mother, our memory. 'These are the two aspects of the full body: an enchanted surface of inscription, the fantastic law, or the apparent objective movement; but also a magical agent or fetish, the quasi cause'.[42]

Let me try, then, to give deterritorialisation and reterritorialisation a more concrete meaning: land value and ground rent create a powerful, contradictory motor for urban development. Zoning laws are designed to protect land values, but their efficacy is dependent upon ground rent, which is where the problem lies. If ground rent is a form of value mortgaged on the future surplus value of the labour performed on that site, it is essentially a highly coded form of value dependent upon a structure of equivalence that in an era of such rapid technological change as we are in now is a very uncertain proposition indeed. Futurists are constantly predicting that most or all of the jobs we'll be performing two or three decades from now have yet to be invented. But if that isn't risky enough, ground rent also faces competition from land value itself, which isn't tied to labour in any determinate fashion and may rise or fall according to its own inner logic. Land value is, in this sense, the classic example of a deterritorializing force - if it is allowed to run free it can literally destroy a city, whereas ground rent is a steady engine of growth (the shopping mall is the example par excellence of this, and for this very reason its rapid rise to prominence as a new cultural form was largely financed by pension funds in search of stable, non-speculative investments).[43]

Capitalism has at its disposal two means (axioms) of 'overcoding' the free flow of ground rent: (1) zoning laws; and (2) land tax. Zoning laws exert pressure on land value by regulating the supply (increasing the residency rating of a suburb increases the number of houses or dwellings that may be located there - the effect of this on price varies because in a poor suburb it may provoke the view that it is tending towards a slum, whereas in a middleclass suburb it will increase the value of the land because it enables 'development'). Land taxes, on the other hand, exert pressure on land value by regulating demand (reducing the taxes generally increases demand, while raising taxes will tend to slow demand). These two instruments are used in combination by city governors to at least preserve value, but more importantly to maintain structural equilibrium. If production is profitable and property values fall, this can be a serious problem if the production process is underwritten by loans guaranteed against the land value of the factory site itself. By the same token, if land values appreciate too much the economics of production itself ceases to make sense - if the land turns a profit without producing anything, why continue to produce? In both instances, the company involved may choose to exit the city, which if the company is big enough or it occurs on a sector-wide scale can be disastrous for the city.

The point I want to make here is that deterritorialisation isn't a placial concept, but rather an inherent property of the notion of value itself. But more importantly, the example above brings to our attention the essential matrix of Deleuze and Guattari's thinking: on the one hand, property value in isolation is an intensity, it moves up and down a sliding scale seemingly of its own accord; but on the other hand, when viewed in the context of a city as a whole, its effects are felt in extension, even though it remains an intensity. Supply and demand are tensors of value, not creators of value. Value is like wind velocity, air pressure, temperature, and so on, indivisible: if a bucket of water is 40 degrees Celsius and you tip half out, you'll have half a bucket of water left, but it will still be 40 degrees Celsius. Or, to give a different example, if you take a five dollar note and tear it in half you won't get two times two fifty; indeed, if you set fire to it, you don't necessarily end up with zero either. The value of money is an intensity. This doesn't mean, however, that intensities are not subject to change or somehow protected from the effects of their environment. Water can obviously be heated up and cooled down by a variety of means and likewise one can heat up an economy and thereby affect the value of money. Hot water in an airtight container isn't dangerous, but spilled on unprotected flesh it can scald and even kill; money in a closed economy (such as China used to have) is similarly benign, but when placed in an international exchange context it becomes vulnerable to fluctuation and in turn jeopardises the livelihoods of the people who rely on it - if the value falls too far or worse too fast, it leads to impossible trade deficits and debt burdens; yet if it rises too far or too fast it can cripple exports and trigger an import bonanza.

SCHIZOANALYSIS AND THE CITY

We are still a long way from being able to say what a Deleuzian analysis - that is, schizoanalysis - of space might, much less should, look like. There are literally dozens of books on Deleuze and Guattari, but not one of them can tell you how to read a text in a manner that is recognisably Deleuzian. Even if one accepts Deleuze and Guattari's injunction against interpretation, it should nonetheless still be possible to reliably identify a body without organs and distinguish that from an abstract machine and so on. Otherwise, Deleuze's famous toolbox is useless to us in much the same way as surgical instruments are useless to the non-surgeon. And yet, given the wide differences in definitions to be found in the secondary literature, one can safely say we have not yet reached that stage. As cultural critics we are the poorer for this because it means the rich critical language Deleuze left us is not being utilised to its fullest extent. We need to return to Deleuze in the Lacanian sense, that is, return to the analytic situation itself. This gesture is not at all foreign to Deleuze. His frequent insistence that we should start with problems, that philosophers must be allowed to ask their own questions, and so on, means nothing other than this: the analytic situation of the philosopher is precisely the creation of problems and their associated concepts. The parallel with Lacan can be brought a little closer too. In his book on Bacon, Deleuze writes of the clinical underpinnings of concepts, thus nudging us in the direction of the analytic situation as Lacan conceives it. Is this not what Guattari brought to the collaboration? Many readers of Deleuze object to the very idea that some kind of analytic program of action might be elaborated in his name. While I am sympathetic to the anarchic spirit underpinning this view of Deleuze, it is not supported in Deleuze's own work. He is quite explicit in saying that he wanted to create a practical, useful form of philosophy. This is what he meant when he said *Anti-Oedipus* is an experiment in writing Pop Philosophy.

AFTER THE FACT: SPATIAL NARRATIVES IN THE CANADIAN IMAGINARY

Jody Berland

YOU ARE HERE
The labyrinth holds me,
Turning me around ... a spiral
Margaret Atwood[1]

At that point you realize that Canada is the answer to its own question ... which in the end is its great trump card. We all need a form and Canada is ours, having, in the course of its relatively young existence, drawn boundaries around a land ... Imagine Canada: the first post-modern state willing to do something about post-modernity. Imagine Canada: a country willing in part to be the imaginary country it actually is.[2]

An important tradition in Canadian writing has been its investment in and innovative approach to the subject of space. Canonical texts in fiction and poetry, literary theory, history, cultural studies and communication theory are replete with commentaries on the importance of space to Canadian identity. This trajectory was consolidated by the work of two postwar thinkers who separately and together defined twentieth-century thought on Canadian nationhood. Harold Innis was an economic historian who extended his research on the resource-intensive economy of dependent economies (the staples theory) to the field of technology and history. He argued that media's material properties encouraged space and time biases that were central to the formation of monopolies of knowledge, centres and peripheries, and the rise and fall of empires. Canada, he concluded, had gone from colony to nation back to colony of the new American empire, which was built on the space-binding properties of media designed to conquer space at the expense of time, memory and continuity.[3]

In a 1965 essay on Canadian literature, Northrop Frye noted that the Canadian sensibility is 'less perplexed by the question, 'Who am I?' than by some such riddle as 'Where is here?''[4] Frye's words translate the 'identity' question into a commentary on 'paradoxical' social-spatial relations evidenced in poetry and fiction and more broadly in commentaries on Canadian nationhood. Commenting on the 'geografictional' imperative in Canadian writing, Barbara Godard suggests that 'Where is here?' and its continuing elaboration in fiction and poetry should be read as 'the consequences of specific colonial relations of power instantiating Canadian economic and cultural dependency.[5] For Richard Cavell, on the other hand, Frye's contention that 'Canadian space is a space without place' corresponded

1. Margaret Atwood, 'A Night in the Royal Ontario Museum' cited in Godard, 'Notes from the Cultural Field: Canadian Literature from Identity to Commodity', in *Essays on Canadian Writing*, Winter, 72, (2001): p212.

2. Steven Schecter, *Zen and the Art of Postmodern Canada*, Montreal-Toronto, Robert Davies, 1993, p102.

3. Harold Innis, *Empire and Communications*, Toronto, University of Toronto, 1951. See H. Innis, *Staples, Markets and Cultural Change: Selected Essays*, Daniel Drache (ed), Montreal and Kingston, McGill-Queen's University Press, 1995; Charles Acland and William Buxton (eds), *Harold Innis in the New Century: Reflections and Refractions*, McGill-Queen's University Press, 1999.

4. Northrop Frye, *The Bush Garden: Essays on the Canadian Imagination*, Toronto, Anansi, 1971, p220. Cf. Alan Morantz, *Where is Here? Canada's Maps and the Stories They Tell*, Toronto and London, Penguin, 2002.

5. Barbara Godard, op. cit., p212.

6. Richard Cavell, 'Theorizing Canadian space: Postcolonial articulations' in Terry Goldie, Carmen Lambert and Rowland Lorimer (eds), *Canada: Theoretical Discourse / Discours theoriques*, Montreal, Association of Canadian Studies, 1994, p81.

7. Northrop Frye, op. cit., p221.

8. W.H. New, *Land Sliding: Imagining Space, Presence, and Power in Canadian Writing*, Toronto, University of Toronto, 1997.

9. Stephen Slemon, 'Unsettling the Empire: Resistance Theory for the Second World', *World Literature Written in English*, 30, 2 (1990): 30-41.

10. Donna Palmateer Pennie, 'Looking Elsewhere for Answers to the Postcolonial Question' in Laura Moss (ed), *Is Canada Postcolonial?* Waterloo, Wilfrid Laurier University, 2003, p82.

11. George Elliott Clarke, 'What Was Canada?' in Laura Moss (ed), *Is Canada Postcolonial?*, Waterloo, Wilfrid Laurier University, 2003, p33.

12. See for instance, W.H. New, *Landsliding*, op. cit.; Rob Shields, *Places on the Margins: Alternative Geographies of Modernity*, London,

to the appropriation of various indigenous cultures (more easily conflated with their natural environment) that was itself an act of cultural colonisation.[6] In both instances the emphasis on space and landscape provides an ordering principle for an emerging sense of national identity located, as Frye puts it, in 'next year country'.[7] As W.H. New suggests in the title of a recent book, however, the 'land is sliding'.[8] Changing geopolitics introduce painful questions about what makes this land Canada; about who is colonist, who colonised; about whether the focus on 'space' advances or contains the interrogation of power; and about the adequacy of these questions for the analysis of the nation state in the global arena.

In Canada, the emphasis on land and space has both expedited and resisted forces of colonial power. It is precisely this ambivalence that characterises post-colonial literature of what Stephen Slemon calls the Second World.[9] Slemon defines the 'Second World' as a 'neither/nor' grouping of invader-settler cultures that are grounded in 'a confused, contradictory, and deeply ambivalent position within the circulations of colonialist power and anti-colonialist affect [which] present significant and enormously difficult problems for the field of postcolonial critical studies'.[10] Both colonisers and subjects of colonisation, these geopolitical entities (Canada, Australia, New Zealand, South Africa) cannot draw on prior linguistic, aesthetic or cultural traditions to articulate their dilemma. Their nations can never be more than a fusion of multiple identities. However strongly the land occupies the imaginary, Canada is 'never homogeneous, never "pure," but constructed, partially, by First Nations peoples, francophones, other European groups (from Russians to Italians), Asians (Chinese, Japanese and Indian), and yes, Africans (primarily African American and West Indian)'.[11] The ambivalence of identity combined with the ambivalence of power relations prevent the achievements of Second World countries from registering in the canon of First-World post-colonial writing, with its fundamentally binary model of the West and the Rest.

In this context, cross-disciplinary writing on political and literary space has frequently turned to the work of Henri Lefebvre, whose trenchant model for the production of space demonstrates that space is not a thing but a social, physical and mental process, in which imaginary space interacts with the production of social space just as the historical production of social space informs and elaborates discursive space.[12] Canada's 'spatial production' relies on and yet complicates Lefebvre's formula, for no one is sure what kind of space Canada is. Canadian inscription produces a national space and reflects on its actions in doing so; as a result the political, technological and/or narrative apparatus remains visible. The continuing efficacy of this discursive practice, so busily navigating space, place and nation, suggests that it can be understood in the context of a narrative archive. Like Keith Belton, I am interested in how the production of a regional space (central English-speaking Canada, in this case) interacts with 'the production of knowledge about that space' in light of 'the interaction of a literary system of scientific, academic, and novelistic narratives with global systemic capitalism'.[13] In this process the archive 'becomes a repository of images about the region and the *topos* becomes the cultural site of those images when they are projected onto geographical space'.[14]

Belton defines the *topos* as the product of local narratives and images circulating within the cultural sphere of capital development. It is 'an ideal representation of a place - a fantastic place, but a place nonetheless ... Using different sets of elements, different *topoi* may be constructed around a place, and form different "filters" for how that place is projected and perceived. The *topos*, abstract and imaginary, becomes, in [Fredric] Jameson's formulation, the narrativization of that imaginary geography in the political unconscious'. The *topos* thus represents the layering of historically and chronotopically diverse narratives over a topography that shapes and is shaped by such narratives. In the case of English Canada, such 'narrativisation' is intermixed with chronic questioning of the possibility of itself. 'Ours is a history written in terms of 'colonial status', 'imperial connection' and 'continentalism', rather than 'Canadian Revolution', 'self-determination' and 'national independence', Wallace Gagne argued in 1976. As a consequence, Wallace Gagne suggests, 'we must be open to the nature of technique and what it implies for man'.[15] The narrative continuously circles around this theme, so that the 'problem' of Canada, the 'problem' of technology and the 'problem' of space are imbricated and perpetuated in the narrative strata forming Canada's *topos*.

What is the relationship between this self-querying *topos* and the contemporary question of (post)colonial space? Is this geografictional imperative' a 'structural allegory' of postcolonial space, as Jameson suggests with respect to third world literature?[16] Canada complicates this model as well, for the Canadian *topos* represents not so much a (post)colonial third world national geopolitics but rather the complicated imaginary spaces of the second world, the world of settler economies whose subjects are simultaneously subjects and objects of colonial power. If an archive is produced by the layering of stories atop one another, telling some of the stories offers an interesting archaeological entry to this *topos*. It is my starting point for understanding the interaction of land, space and narrative in terms of the political subjectivities of those who, like myself, inhabit this middle-ground of (post)colonial space.

TELLING STORIES

I am sitting in the car listening to the radio. It is 23 degrees below zero, the coldest March day since 1868, and I have reached my destination, but I am listening to Cedric Smith reading a story by Leon Rooke, *The Last Shot*, on the CBC (2002). It is a recent exemplar of a narrative classic, the young girl with tough demeanour and heart of gold, who lives at the border between country and town, at the edge of convention and civility. I am interested in

Routledge, 1991; Jody Berland, 'Space at the Margins: Colonial Spatiality and Critical Theory After Innis', *Topia* 1 (Spring 1997): 55-82.

13. Keith Belton, *Orinoco Flow: Culture, Narrative, and the Political Economy of Information*, Lanham, Scarecrow, 2004, p2.

14. Ibid., p10.

15. Wallace Gagne, *Nationalism, Technology and the Future of Canada*, Toronto, Macmillan, 1976, p1, p3.

16. Fredric Jameson, 'Third-World Literature in the Era of Multinational Capitalism', *Social Text* 15 (1986): 65-88.

17. Cecily Devereux, "'Canadian Classic" and "Commodity Export": The Nationalism of "Our" *Anne of Green Gables*', in A. Gedalof, J. Boulter, J. Faflak and C. McFarlane (eds), *Cultural Subjects: A Popular Culture Reader*', Toronto, Thomson Nelson, 2005, p180.

18. Ibid., p185.

19. One of the poems set to music by PCC:

I spun you out
Of my eyes'fire;
It wasn't you
But my desire

For the pure vein
Of silver
Running there
Even if not mine;

But I have it now,
Out of my wish
I created it
And can slough

Off the idiocies
I constructed of you,
Can look through
My hopeful lies

To your sorry
Hopes of yourself,
And your mysterious
Flawed glory.

Milton Acorn, *I've Tasted My Blood* McGraw-Hill Ryerson, Toronto, 1969. Reading it in this context I am struck by the re-othering that takes place in this poem, by the proximity of the narrator's words to the positive 'abjection' Ian Angus (1997) describes in the Canadian subject's recognition of the other.

20. Laura Moss, 'Is Canada Postcolonial?

the prominence of this narrative in Canadian culture, and in the possessive fondness I feel for that tough girl, her indomitable spirit, her ability to stand for a century of story-telling, just by hitting her brother and hitch-hiking down to the corner store to weasel some groceries.

A harsh environment, authority figure or social institution pushes this orphan toward the wild zone, beyond civility and potentially beyond salvation. An alternative figure, model or ideal, perceptive, compassionate, friendly with authority but indifferent to its routines, pulls her toward culture and the fulfilment of herself. In this narrative topography of living at the edge, no simple resolution is possible. Judging from how often her story recurs, she performs an iconic function for Canada.

This narrative role can be traced back to the publication of Suzanna Moodie's *Roughing It in the Bush* (1852), but it enters a more dispersed imaginary with *Anne of Green Gables (1908)*, a novel about an orphan who enters a farm family in Prince Edward Island and stirs up the neighbourhood. Anne is by far 'the best known fictional character in Canadian history ... [and is] read by more people than any other Canadian book;' she is also a major cultural export embraced and 'domesticated' in national cultures worldwide.[17] Thousands of tourists visit Prince Edward Island every year to visit 'the land of Anne'.[18] Anne is a rebellious girl who triumphs over adversity by making a useful and happy life without sacrificing her insistent self. Her achievement reconciles pre-war communal rural values with modern individual aspirations of a young woman from town. Countless instances of a female adventurer's homecoming - from wilderness/civilisation to a reconciliation of the two - can be retrieved from the archives of fiction, film, and television, usually with ambivalent endings. Even the feisty Anne cannot escape their shadow, for so fraught is the struggle for copyright income arising from her story that new legislation had to be passed just for her.

But I am focused now on the voice of the reader, Cedric Smith, formerly singer in the band Perth County Conspiracy. Like the writing of Milton Acorn, Canada's 'people's poet', whose writing covers their live album and provides lyrics for some of their songs,[19] the Conspiracy's music enacted and commemorated the magic of story-telling in ordinary locations. In the 1970s, writing was 'pointedly located in a Canadian cultural, political, historical, and geographical landscape, sometimes presumably in response to the teaching of colonial models',[20] as we just saw with Walter Gagne. At the same time 'the local' was acquiring a charismatic aura in the global musical marketplace. In this formative moment of global-local spatiality, music and story-telling brought local landscapes to life and inscribed Canadians' memories of them as singular places. Smith's voice occupies each character as though it were a familiar place of residence. He gives each voice equal dignity and temerity; whatever the age or gender, he knows it, he has been there, and he is moving right in and taking us with him. At the same time, his voice tells us, we can't be sure what is going to happen. There is some uncertainty in this growing-up. The voice, the girl, and the uncertainty together constitute a familiar sense of place. The voice is replete with story-telling pleasures and the sound of the CBC; it is radio, and I am in the car, where my first thoughts about radio arose some fifteen years ago.

These mythic echoes remind me that the earliest mobilisation of a national imaginary - not just my own, but according to records, Canada's - was through (and about) mediated communication; first the railway and later the radio it carried westward across the country. The country's vast geography, regionalised settlement and ethnic diversity, together with its vulnerability to US expansionism, presented acute challenges to policy makers concerned with nation-building. Commercial (mainly US) radio threatened to enhance north-south connections at the expense of east-west solidarity. Sound is characterised by its ability to travel across space and to create a shared sonic landscape in 'real time'. Whatever the local organisation of space, sound promises to exceed it.[21] Radio's ability to create shared spaces proposed different implications for residents on the two sides of the border. US radio was designed to cross the border and circumvent its intent; Canadian radio, in response, to mark the border and strengthen the nation. Its imbrication of space-binding and boundary-making established a profound resonance in Canadian history and myth.

First routed along the railway, public broadcasting seemed the ideal medium of national self-realisation. Radio established a new *topos* whose participants could transcend their isolation and join in the realisation of this political ideal, making explicit the technical process of their own construction as a geopolitical entity. This origin myth sidesteps the tales of frontier and conquest (not always with salutary effect, for conquest is not best forgotten) in favour of an inclusive space-binding magic. For the first time, dispersed residents of the Dominion were the subject of common rhetorical address in shared temporal space: addressed, celebrated and circumscribed, or in more contemporary terms, constituted as national subject. Stories of the time are replete with memories of rural listeners, train conductors, local orchestras, adult education cooperatives, activist women's associations, amateur inventors, radio league activists, journalists, and politicians, welcoming and celebrating the train-radio as a triumph of collective will as it chugged and fiddled across the country. It required only proximity, hardware, and the willingness to listen as constituents of citizenry. Citizenship arose then from the imbrication of space and hardware, locked in an indissoluble embrace.

Insofar as this narrative is transmitted through pictorial histories, school textbooks, cultural policy documents, public broadcasting archives, travel agents, and fiction, the story of radio participates in the formation of the national archive.[22] The narrative emphasises the autogenetic character of the country, and the way Canada was brought into subjectivity when its inhabitants heard themselves (virtually) talking in the sonic mirror of the public broadcast. Rather than promoting a genealogical or ethnic lineage, such stories emphasise a performative, political, technologically mediated

Introducing the Question' in Moss (ed), *Is Canada Postcolonial? Unsettling Canadian Literature*. Waterloo, Wilfrid Laurier University, 2003, p9.

21. It is interesting how often the promise to transgress or exceed boundaries is valorized in contemporary criticism. Visual theorists claim that the internet does this for images whose power will explode global politics. Internet theorists claim the web does this for the body. Music theorists argue that sound does this for the subject. Political theorists claim that immigration does this for geopolitical identity. 'It is clear that each successive migrant group represented a rupture in the myth of the nation', Rinaldo Walcott suggests; 'It is the migration of non-whites that has continuously disrupted the fictions of the nation-state'. But the Canadian 'fiction of the nation-state' is all about migrant groups. Rinaldo Walcott, 'Keep on Movin', in Lynne Van Luven and Priscilla L. Walton (eds), *Pop Can: Popular Culture in Canada*, Scarborough, Prentice-Hall, 1999, pp 27-41, p29.

22. 'Another nice thing about radio is you really feel hooked up to the country, can understand what it must have meant in

the thirties if you lived in some rural outpost and only the wireless to keep you in touch. In the long historical perspective, radio really brought about the transformation', in Schecter, op. cit., p103.

identity (if this is the right word) that must be continuously renewed through the reiteration of specific practices. These practices, together with the railway tracks, the radio broadcasts, the changing technological infrastructures, the memories, the physical archives and the values attached to them are part of a 'concrete assemblage', in which the spatial-narrative archive plays a principle role. In the logic of this archive, the medium structures the *topos*, so that medium and *topos* - rather than any specific symbolic form or convention - are forever imbricated with the politics of space. Cultural policy and critique further the idea that it is not identity that produces national culture, but rather cultural and political activity that produces - or conversely, threatens - the nation. This logic reverses the customary logic through which European thought has addressed nation-building. With this reversal the social processes of conceiving, ordering, and living space are at once more ambiguous and more transparent.

THE SPATIAL IMAGINARY

'In a country of the vast geographical dimensions of Canada', wrote Canada's first Royal Commission on Broadcasting in 1932, 'broadcasting will undoubtedly become a great force in fostering a national spirit and interpreting national citizenship'.[23] Radio programmes, broadcasters and manufacturers were then almost exclusively American, and broadcasts were directed to the long chain of towns and cities along the border. The public system created a counter-radiophonic space/time, structured to unite people east-west rather than to fragment them through commercial logics of currency and demographics.[24] In pursuing the anti-colonial development of the national subject, Canada's government emphasised geographical inclusiveness; it promised to reach all of Canada through radio, and accrued substantial political legitimacy from fulfilling this mission. This privileging of dissemination across space (arguably analogous to the privileging of trade and transmission over labour and capital in Innis's work[25]) carried its contradictions forward into the present, for each successive medium, built with public funds and disseminated in the name of national interest, has become the vehicle for aggressive, primarily American commercial expansion with its famous 'dumping' policies and its voracious economies of scale.

On a positive note, this conjuncture brought into view what has been a lasting theme in Canadian society, a construct best envisioned as a semiotic square connecting space and time, citizenship and justice. A semiotic square shows that each term in each binary set achieves meaning only in relation to the other set of terms. Broadcasting's important role in the emerging discourse of citizenship was based on (and helped to constitute) the view that justice derives from a balance of space and time, while rights of citizenship determine (and are determined by) how time and space are mapped. Too vast a space joins with too fast a tempo at the expense of memory, continuity, democracy and justice. This construct reinforces the

23. *Documents of Canadian Broadcasting*, Roger Bird (ed), Ottawa, Carleton University, 1988, p43.

24. Cf. J. Berland, 'Radio Space and Industrial Time: The Case of Music Formats', in Justin Lewis and Toby Miller (eds), *Critical Cultural Policy Studies: A Reader*, Oxford, Blackwell, 2003.

25. See B. Drache, 'Introduction' to Innis, 1995, op. cit.

topos' deconstruction of the identity question through the critique of media technologies mediating space and culture. This reformulation continues to matter in the struggle to eradicate colonialism from the Canadian social fabric.

Postmodern space theory began by positing the death of place, writing of 'non-place' and 'placelessness', the end of the local, and the much over-stated end of the nation state. In documenting the ascendancy of global space such thinkers were unable to imagine that place and (national/global) space might coexist even as their interdependencies shift in response to changing geopolitics and mobilities. For Canada the local, the national and the transnational are always-already constituted in relation to the power dynamics of their interaction. The railway and the public broadcasting system materialised and confirmed the marginal location of the national *topos*. This project was fundamentally shaped by its relations to, and attitude towards, the British, the Americans, the indigenous First Nations, and Canadian settlers who chose to be here. But 'where is here?' Why here and not there?[26] The convergence of railway, radio and citizenship in Canada in 1927, the girl endlessly navigating between wilderness and metropolis, and popular scepticism toward the 'reactionary utopia' of globalisation variously (and with variable success) materialise links between the archive, the spatial imaginary and the politics of space. Through such materialisation, space is both product and producer of the social process.

The national *topos* begins then on a voluntarist myth of origin. Let us look more closely at the history of the railway, the medium designed to carry people, natural resources, and then radio westward from central Canada. In 1871 British Columbia agreed to join Confederation on condition that the Dominion government would build a railway linking B.C. with eastern Canada. Beginning in 1880, 17,000 Chinese workers arrived from China and California to build the Canadian Pacific Railway (CPR) through the Rockies to the Pacific Ocean. At least 1,500 of them died in the process. These workers lived in tents that were vulnerable to falling rocks and were paid one dollar a day while white workers earned five or six times that amount. The Chinese who built the railways were subject to 'absurd laws like tax on rice; special taxes on laundries; Chinese restaurants could not employ white women; segregation of schools; Chinese were denied welfare during the depression; and in Vancouver, a by-law was passed to forbid the selling of vegetables brought into the city by a shoulder pole with two baskets hanging on either end'.[27] The Head Tax and the Chinese Exclusion Act combined with other racist regulation to contain the Chinese community and to exclude its memories of nation-building from the archive.[28]

'Our community's history is entwined with Canadian history in more ways than one', states one historian. 'We all know about the Chinese railway workers. What else is written in the history books about Chinese Canadians? Do we know any of the names of the Chinese railway workers, the Chinese shipbuilders who settled on Vancouver Island, or the names of the Chinese

26. Frye's answer to this was that Canadians were Americans who had rejected the American Revolution. They wanted something different. Frye, op. cit.

27. <http://www.asian.ca/redress/sp_19951205.htm>

28. Thanks to Sarah Sharma for her help in locating these histories.

29. William Ging Wee Dere, *Presentation to the Nova Scotia Human Rights Conference,* United Nations and Human Rights, Halifax, Saturday, 9 December 1995. Transcripts at <http://www.asian.ca/redress/sp_19951205.htm>

farmers who applied their peasant skills in the interior of BC?'[29] The writer draws our attention to the conventional mapping of this history, much as I have related it: a long, lonely railway across the frontier; a community of labourers strung across the landscape; a city at the end with markets and ship-builders. This map does not recall the land through which the train was built, or commemorate the tribes whose lands were stolen and livelihoods, languages, and stories destroyed. The story does not relate the tales of chiefs who sold tribal land in exchange for lifetime railway passes, the towns bypassed by the railway and conniving to induce businesses and children to return, the homeless hobos railcar-hopping across the country. Such memories require a kinetic mobilisation of a map petrified by myth, and acknowledgement that communities defeated by history are conquered again and again through the telling of it. This is a familiar challenge now, a story that cannot end.

COMMUNICATION AND DEPENDENCY

While Canada shares in many of the industrial, cultural and managerial practices of advanced capitalist countries, it is shaped by its history as a colony, first within the British Commonwealth and later as periphery to US geopolitics. Innis's research emphasised the degree to which global trade was built on extracting and exporting natural resources from the peripheral territory (Canada) to the homeland, from the 'frontier to the back tier', which served to perpetuate economic and political power for the countries who purchased the resources, manufactured the products, and sold them back to Canada. The imperial countries built industrial empires; Canada dug, ploughed, chopped, and transported. This account of the 'staples' economy forms the basis of dependency theory in Canada.

Dependency theory has been a central influence in Canada's critical and symbolic culture. Its descriptive capabilities are affirmed daily by statistics on ownership patterns in the cultural and resource industries, and by images of huge, beautiful, recently logged, mined, or otherwise excavated terrain. This paradigm depicts an economically disempowered, culturally indefinite national culture juxtaposed against the all too definite economic structures and cultural strategies of foreign-owned communications media. Its left-nationalist predilections may have been trounced by contemporary theory, but its shape is indelibly printed on the Canadian *topos*.

At the centre of this media/culture/nation imbrication stands the problem of the nation state. In the trajectory of this intellectual history, the state is both central and absent. It is not hard to discover the logic of this ghostly presence. If Canada cannot be described as an identifiable *nation*, at least as nineteenth-century political theorists defined it, namely a group of citizens united by common history, language, ethnicity, and/or religion, there was always a *state* that advanced itself as speaking on behalf of a bounded territory that would be nation. With the state and its various social policies committed to defending a country that had not yet come into being (in cultural and constitutional terms at least), and given the peculiar economic logic of a country embedded in and sometimes fighting against service relations to a powerful global economy, the problem of the state has been implied every time culture, communication, identity, or nation appear on the agenda.

What comes from this ambiguous bond between local cultural trajectories and the state which appears to speak on their behalf? When 'the state' speaks, whose voices are heard? Is this state best understood as an instrument for the expansion of subjectless, nationless capital, as a dependent margin of the American empire, or as a player in global capitalism? Is it primarily an agent acting on behalf of class domination or an instrument of national dependency? This debate accumulates and turns back on itself, adding to the archive while proliferating the links between politics and political economy, literature and music, the cultural industries and the arts. Policy analysts influenced by Nicos Poulantzas analyse the state as a semi-autonomous, internally conflicted structure mediating between contradictory aims. This approach envisions government as a site for continuous but unequal negotiation between legitimation (whereby the state secures public loyalty by protecting its citizens against the excesses of the market) and appropriation (whereby the state facilitates the ever-expanding stranglehold of transnational cultural industries, for instance, as a way of securing the accumulation of capital). Canada's history offers itself easily to such a reading.[30] It confirms Miller's typification of the modern nation in that 'The state's legitimacy is often drawn from its capacity to speak for its citizens, to be their vocalising agent. This is achieved, depending on the type of society, at least in part through the doctrine of nations, the concept of particular space defined by the state itself but informed effectively by a sense of cultural belonging'.[31]

The Foucauldian turn encouraged critics to view government policies more sceptically as part of a broader field of 'specific, bounded rationalities inscribed in culturally particular "technologies of the subject"'. From this perspective, 'The aim of the modern art of government [is] to develop those elements of individual lives in such a way that their development also fosters the strength of the state'.[32] Whilst campaigning against imperial power, activists and writers enact a rationalised subjectivity - the 'citizen', the 'artist' - that inadvertently reinforces the strength of the (post)colonial state, which, like its collaborator the tourist industry, builds on the strategic production of difference. Here the 'legitimacy' process is reversed and internalised as part of the subject formation of the loyal citizen. Canada's history reiterates these analyses to some extent, yet again the theories simplify the history. The Canadian archive reflects directly on the ambiguous political implications and effects of such 'technologies' of culture. Its reflexivity is not (simply) the complacent reflexivity of a universal (European) bourgeois culture elevating itself above the crudeness of the popular. It does not straightforwardly reproduce the conventional distinction between a

30. See Rianne Mahon, 'Canadian Public Policy: The Unequal Structure of Representation' in Leo Panitch (ed), *The Canadian State: Political Economy and Political* Power, Toronto, University of Toronto, 1977.

31. Toby Miller, *The Well-Tempered Self,* Baltimore, Johns Hopkins, 1993, p10.

32. Colin Gordon, 'Governmentality: An Introduction', in Graham Burchell, Colin Gordon, and Peter Miller (eds), *The Foucault Effect: Studies in Governmentality,* London, Harvester Wheatsheaf, 1991, p10.

bourgeois culture which separates itself from its desire, and a common culture subsumed by it. Both familiar tropes - the governmental subject, the bourgeois subject - narrow this history and its contemporary implications.

In seeking to constitute a nation state in a space of non-identity, both 'cultural technologies', the media and the administration of subjects, are approached as motivated practices which oscillate between opposing terms: citizenship and consumption, national and international, coloniser and colonised. These terms are opposed, but (as usual when binary terms start to collapse) also foundationally interdependent. Poulantzas's model helps to explain how such opposition is materialised in state organisation, but it cannot show how this oscillation establishes itself in the core of citizen/consumer subjectivities. Canada's divided location in this field of combat *is* its culture. It is the ambiguous culture of a second-world power inhabited by settler populations and suffused with unequal power relations both internal and external to the nation state. It has never been other than an 'assemblage' of ethnicities, regions, communication and transport technologies, pedagogies, symbols, affinities, agencies, and corporate and social policies together comprising a national space. Foucault's followers invite us to identify all these as the product of transformative governmentalities within broadly conceived and apparently seamless state regimes. But Foucault dissuades us from seeking any essential theory of states in general, and if read properly permits us to retain our ambivalent feelings of love and horror towards our own state in particular. Needless to say, there are political as well as narrative and aesthetic consequences to how one addresses these questions.

What if the state and its broad tapestry of social policies and communal values (now being eroded by continental agreements, regressive budgets, and changing 'cultural technologies') is all Canada can claim as the specificity of its culture? How necessary is a traditional evocation of culture to the (post)nation Canadians inhabit as difference? Can a cohesive culture be created from a multitude of differences? What are the ramifications of this dilemma for any theory of the nation state? Is a post-nation state fundamentally different from a nation-state or was the nation-state always an unstable construct? Has the Canadian state seemed relatively benign with respect to multiplicity and the common good because of its own historical imaginary, or because of its marginality to the country that stands adjacent? Is this in any way a valid distinction? Is the struggle to retain sovereign powers and human rights, in this context, nationalism? Whose is this state, anyway?

MORE STORIES

How do such questions play out in the spatial imaginary of literary culture? You would hardly know, looking at Canada's canonical written and visual texts that nearly 80 per cent of them live in cities. Students read the pioneering stories of Susannah Moodie and Catherine Parr Traill, the tender small-town stories of Alice Munro, and the acerbic urban wilderness tales of Margaret Laurence and Margaret Atwood. These writers are drawn to rural life but reject a sentimental view of it. Theirs is a countryside that bites. Caught parentless and compass-free between wilderness and civilisation, the heroine looks for home. She has more knowledge than power, she is displaced from her origins, she thrives on the edge of the community, and she is naughty. She and Canada's national imaginary are caught in a longstanding symbolic embrace. The figure moves more or less effortlessly across genres, inciting readers and viewers to embrace this heroine so many times that she remains a symbol of the space called Canada long after Queen Victoria (and much of the countryside) has disappeared from the scene.

This narrative floats in its own reflexive frame. The narrator relates a story of personal struggle from the sympathetic vantage point of someone more knowing. What does this narrator know? It appears to be something about absence. The listening farmer is absent from her radiophonic interlocutor, the girl is absent from her parents; the centre of things is absent from us. Absence is popular in the Canadian imaginary, and it too is a spatial idea - it implies that the desired object is somewhere, just not here, like the girl's mother in *The Last Shot*, for she is off somewhere having her last shot at love, and the title character never appears. The narrative I have described is punctuated by a sense of absence from a centre. This too is a mark of colonial history which needs to be understood in relation to colonial discourse as a whole. The colonies gave rise to 'countless self-aggrandizing and self-centred narratives of settlement, exploration, conquest and other kinds of imperial service'; as Gillian Whitlock suggests these were 'produced within discourses of exploration, law, administration, religion, and science'.[33] In her discussion of early Canadian 'life writing', Whitlock contrasts the 'structural instability' of women's writing to the assured ('white, male, heterosexual') writing of colonial administration. The narrative spaces of 'others' were 'most unlikely to enter the records as an imperial subject'.[34] Whitlock offers as evidence of this 'other' space the autobiographies of Mary Prince (the first Black British woman to escape from slavery and publish a record of her experiences) and Susannah Moodie, literary transcriber of Prince's account (1831) and later, having emigrated to Canada, author of the canonical autobiography *Roughing It in the Bush* (1852).

By the time Moodie wrote *Roughing It*, the role of gentlewoman elaborated for colonial wives by earlier writers was no longer available to her. Moodie's voice is fallible, self-doubting, satirical; her sketches 'have all the marks of colonial counter-discourse, where the unsuitability of received systems of meaning, subjectivity and value are openly found wanting. *Roughing It*, Whitlock concludes, is 'at one and the same time a site of containment, cooperation and resistance'.[35] Misao Dean also observes a 'pattern of self-effacement' in Moodie's narrative form and describes 'the narrator's continual denials of her authority to speak on almost any subject'.

33. Gillian Whitlock, 'Exiles from Tradition: Women's Life Writing', in Whitlock(ed), *Re-Sitting Queen's English: Text and Tradition in Post-Colonial Literatures*, Amsterdam and Atlanta, Rodopi, 1992, pp12-13.

34. Ibid., p15.

35. Ibid., pp12, 18.

36. Misao Dean, "Concealing Her Blue Stockings: Femininity and Self-Representation in Susanna Moodie's Autobiographical Works', in Whitlock (ed), op. cit., p33.

37. On the subject of irony in Canadian culture see: Linda Hutcheon, *Splitting Images: Contemporary Canadian Ironies*, Toronto and Oxford, Oxford University, 1991; Jody Berland, 'Writing on the Border', *CR: The New Centennial Review*, Vol. 1 No 2 (2001): 139-170 (full version in J. Berland, *North of Empire*, Duke University, 2006); W.H. New, *Grandchild of Empire*, Vancouver, Ronsdale Press, 2003.

38. Allan Gould, *Anne of Green Gables vs. GI Joe: Friendly Fire Between Canada and the US*, Toronto, ECW, 2003.

39. W.H. New, op. cit., p18.

For Dean, 'This retreat into the stereotype of feminine self-effacement allows the narrator to implement the strategies of subversive communication developed by women to circumvent limitations of femininity'.[36]

The tactic of building subversive communicative strategies to communicate to others occupying parallel 'non-space' appears again and again in Canadian writing and performance. Literary theorists commonly point to irony as the dominant mode for conveying Canadian experience.[37] But the continuing transmission of the very un-ironic 'Anne' story can be usefully revisited as a contemporary strategy of 'containment, cooperation and resistance' central to the commodification of local cultures in a global market. Like Moodie, Anne resists the class snobbery and misogyny of her neighbours. But Anne also goes to college, falls in love and succeeds on the basis of her will and talent. Her domestication of subversion, together with the shrinking of wilderness and empire to the pastoral confines of Prince Edward Island, allows the Anne story to be embraced across the modern world as a parable of entrepreneurial femininity.

These texts participate in (if they also oppose) the space-gender imaginary that has for the last hundred and fifty years of popular imagery depicted the US as a severe Uncle Sam and Canada as a gushing or wily girl. Why is Canada always Anne, and the US always G.I. Joe, as the title of a recent best-selling book suggests?[38] How did this figure come to be such a firm convention? How much is it an outcome of narrative genealogy, how much a convention with enough familiarity and local colour to please arts councils and commercial publishers, how much a representation of lived experience? You will recognise this as Lefevbre's trilogy: perceived, conceived and lived space. Through a complex of creative, political, commercial and imaginative strategies, the feminine heroine is intractably embedded in the ways that readers inhabit the space called Canada.

Obviously narratives of hardy, independent, democratically minded women speak to the experience of some portion of the population. But this does not account for the lasting influence of the narrative identification between the female gender and the space of the nation. William New writes that 'The characterization of land as female, of Canada as the Empire's child, as wilderness as savage, of utility and domesticity as the only acceptable measures of the beautiful: such judgements, however questionable and in whatever measure repudiated, remain influential. These metaphors encode attitudes and expectations; they tell of what some people take to be true, whether they are or not, and hence they reveal the unstable ground of social norms.[39] Critics commonly explain that 'woman' is associated with 'land' as a way of rationalising the exploitation of both. But this projection of passivity (onto women, onto nature) sits uneasily with the narrative landscapes with which we are concerned.

R. Radhishkrinan argues that this metaphorical link between female gender and national identity replicates a perceived opposition of inside and outside - that is, an awareness of being outside the structures of ownership, kinship, and power - that defines the post-colonial experience.[40] Canada has always been marginal to and yet relatively intimate with the political and financial centres of power. It is not difficult to see parallels between that relationship and the simile of male and female. The woman dedicates herself to breaking down or circumventing established parameters of power and authority represented by men; by doing so she helps to inaugurate a more capacious, more equitable space for women, children, and foreigners, her natural allies. This triangulation of power, femininity, and foreignness, was, according to Ann Wilson, replicated in representations of the Charles-Diana-Dodi tragedy that so captured the world's imagination.[41] Diana figures as a compassionate outsider challenging aristocratic rules and conventions, a lover of foreigners, a people's princess whose empathic femininity transcended race and class. Her image communicates incontrovertible moral authority - more so in that she is not destined to survive. Her rebelliousness and compassion, according to Wilson, particularly endear Diana to Canadian fans. Diana's life mirrors the sense of exclusion from the corridors of power, whose rulers view Canada as spineless, indecisive, (almost) foreign, socialistic, and lacking in military prowess. Her character is preferred to the Other against whom it is encoded: the British Crown or the Oval Office. As with any discursive trope, there are limits to its horizons of possibility. Like a Victorian tragic heroine her moral uprightness may not serve her well in the end. With her morals and ideals she is a silly girl, and doesn't know what is best for her. How well the gender metaphor works at empowering us as national subjects depends, in part, on how successfully gender itself is challenged and re-valorised in our mapping strategies.[42]

I am interested in the continuity of themes and motifs in these narratives in the face of changes so widely described as inevitable. They evoke Regis Debray's important distinction between 'communication' and 'transmission'.[43] 'Transmission' resembles what Belton describes as an 'archive;' it is what happens when motifs, narratives, or ideas are transmitted over time, from one generation to another, rather than simply communicated through current media channels. It resonates with social experience and reinforces a shared understanding of subjects and space. The spatial imaginary 'transmitted' through these symbolic and discursive texts clearly maps Canada as a separate but marginal territory. Authors and readers continuously reinvest (even in their most critical commentaries) in the viability of a topography in which Canada provides a middle space between border and wilderness, autonomy and assimilation, capitalism and justice.

Drawing on Lefebvre, New suggests that such narratives have spatial as well as metaphoric effectivity; 'spatial metaphors - in particular, in the language of land - function in literature as part of the process of constructing, questioning, and confirming assumptions about social reality'.[44] This middle ground is depicted by a 'self-effacing' narrative subject whose location and voice confirm Slemon's depiction of narrative in the literature of the Second

40. R. Radhakrishnan, 'Nationalism, Gender and the Narrative of Identity' in Parker et al (eds), *Nationalisms and Sexualities*, New York, Routledge, 1992, pp77-95.

41. Ann Wilson, 'The Death of Princess Diana: Mourning a "Very British Girl"', in Lynne Van Luven and Priscilla L. Walton (eds), *Pop Can: Popular Culture in Canada*, Scarborough Prentice Hall Allyn and Bacon Canada, 1999, pp 159-66.

42. This theme is taken up again in J. Berland, *North of Empire* (forthcoming, Duke University Press).

43. Regis Debray, *Transmitting Culture*, Eric Rauth (trans), New York, Columbia University, 2000.

44. W.H. New, op. cit., p8.

World. The narrative space actualises a weak nation with a strong sense of internal plurality. Ian Angus makes the link explicit, suggesting that (English) Canadian national identity is weak enough to permit a coexistence between multiculturalism and nationalism. 'Respect is derived not from positive knowledge of all cultures ... But from a reflexive sense of one's own limitation. From this position, one can turn outward to encountering other cultures in a way that is genuinely expanding of one's horizon'.[45] Angus's encounter with others is not predicated on stereotyping, theorised so astutely by Chow and Jameson as a compacted representation mobilised when one group encounters, at a distance and on the surface, an ethnically distinct group of others. Rather, it arises through a kind of everyday abjection formed through routinised encounters between multiple *individual* others within specific socio-spatial and political contexts: kindergarten and school, dating and romance, work, commerce, street life, social services, politics, neighbours and friends, and with *collective* others gathered for religious events, street festivals, sports, music etc. This is not to exonerate Canada for its historical and contemporary racism, but to suggest that the everydayness of urban multiculturalism offers a different space for conceptualising self-other relationships. Neither a solution nor an obstacle to racism, multiculturalism is a contract and social space within which such work continuously occurs.

A PETITION

But there are other sites for the performance of Canada's spatial imaginary. Consider the mantra of place names. Canadians who were children in Canada might remember cold mornings when the car was warming up, listening to the radio announcer intoning temperatures from distant Canadian towns with exotic names: Sioux St Marie; Medicine Hat; Moose Jaw; Whitehorse; Tuktinuktuk; Kapuskasing; 'Thirty minutes later in Newfoundland'. Children's imagination of their compatriots is saturated with the names of strange places and the charismatic empathy of cold. Radio loves place names because radio production is discursively local.[46] Place names are discouraged in the lyrics of songs, whose producers seek a larger marketplace. Song-writers are expected to change 'Manitoba' to 'Montana' to enhance record sales, an interesting side effect of which is a suffused popular knowledge about the protective xenophobia of the continental music market. Using Canadian place names in their music, as the Tragically Hip did with their much beloved song 'Bobcaygeon', represents deliberate 'repatriation' and invites (if not intentionally) nationalist modes of fan appreciation.[47] When place names re-appear in sound they evoke not just the places but also the memories, the cold mornings and the ritual intoning of the radio. They reproduce the mediated legacy through which time and memory are attached to place.

This legacy lives on in the internet. In a recent electronic petition urging federal action on behalf of public health care - the largest electronic petition

45. Ian Angus, *A Border Within: National Identity, Cultural Plurality, and Wilderness,* Montreal, McGill-Queen's University, 1997.

46. J. Berland, 'Radio Space and Industrial Time: The Case of Music Formats'.

47. Cf. Minelle Mahtani and Scott Salmon, 'Site Reading? Globalization, Identity and the Consumption of Place in Popular Music', in A. Gedalof, J. Boulter, J. Faflak and C. McFarlane (eds), *Cultural Subjects: A Popular Culture Reader,* Toronto, Thomson Nelson, 2005.

ever to circulate across Canada - each signature is accompanied by a place name with appended commentary.[48] For many - including politicians during elections - it is universal access to health care that defines the Canadian body politic. In the petition defending this right against privatisation, place names constitute the status of citizenship, while the commentaries announce what this citizenship means. In this way the website functions as a kind of collective map of the country, a bit-based portrayal of what diverse Canadians think about the meaning of nationality. The petition explicitly aligns Canada with a compassionate, equitable social agenda. Some might deduce that the gendered inflection of nationhood as caring, compassionate and contained remains intact. More than 66 per cent of signatures were women's.

'Medicare is our national identity, please support it!' writes Frances Fry from Wabush, Newfoundland and Labrador (signature # 42,535). 'Our public health care system is a vital Canadian value. Please uphold what Canadians value so dearly!' writes Rev. Neil Elford from St Albert, Alberta (signature # 4,2247). 'Privatization of health care brings a lot of problems because all the good facilities will go to the people who CAN AFFORD THEM … is that really fair??' queries Mariam Adega of Saskatoon (signature # 42,560). 'Without at least health care we are just a more northerly US', warns Liam Rees Spear from Peterborough, Ontario (signature # 42,217). 'Save our medicare system, no to private for profit healthcare, this is Canada, not the US!' writes Timothy Kenny of Vancouver, B.C. (signature # 33,787). 'I couldn't agree more. Canadian healthcare is the one thing that truly separates us from our US neighbours, our identity' says Kenneth Graham of Smith Falls, Ontario (signature # 33,773). 'Thank you everyone that posted comments here. I needed a reminder as to why I MOVED TO THE US! I would love to move back home, just LOWER taxes and allow a two-tier system that includes PRIVATE, FOR PROFIT healthcare', says 'Moved to the US'. 'Privatization would mean the 'survival of the fittest and richest' - truly uncivilized in a modern society', argues Olubasayo Ekunboyejo of Scarborough, Ontario (signature # 42,487). 'Free public universal healthcare is the right of all Canadians. Let us all work together to improve our system not just for our sake but for the sake of future generations to come' writes Matthew Ng of Brampton, Ontario (signature # 43,263). 'Public medicare is our Sacred Trust', maintains Bill MacLellan of Glovertown, Newfoundland (signature # 10,161). 'Our public medicare system is what *binds us together* as a nation', writes Mary-Ruth MacLellan of Glace Bay, Nova Scotia (emphasis added).

The health-care petition mobilises Canada's narrative archive to restore the struggle for equality to the discourse of national citizenship. Is it just me that experiences a shiver of pleasurable complicity when I read those place names and commentaries? This petition asserts the power to draw boundaries by naming what is in them. Like the representational spaces described by Lefebvre, they show what is wished for. A popular representation of / intervention in space seeks to contest corporate strategies of neo-liberal

48. <http://www.petitiononline.com/mod_perl/signed.cgi?romanow>, last accessed July 2005.

economic expansion by means of a petition addressed to the Canadian state, while drawing on a popular tradition of debate that continues to interrogate the terms and terrain of the nation state.

(POST)NATIONAL SPACE

There is a space being delineated in these brief polemics. It is mobilised by a shared discourse in which the social dichotomies reinforced by private health care are elicited, emplaced, and denounced. These citizens oppose the neo-liberal agenda of global capital by evoking Canada as a nation state defined by a more just and compassionate relationship with its citizens. Insisting, like some political theorists, on the incompatibility of Canada and neoliberalism, they seek to mobilise the nation as a line of defence against globalisation and its spreading dissolution of public institutions and values. To be a Canadian, a noted historian remarks, 'is not a matter of birthplace, race, language, ethnicity, religious affiliation, genealogy, or some combination of these characteristics. To be a Canadian is to accept certain relations with others, to adopt a specific, historically moulded vocabulary ... to orient oneself to the past according to community choices made during the previous centuries ... to adjust to the inevitable contingency of the nation itself ... A matter of circumstances that have been summarized as "relational, cultural, historical, and contingent"'.[49]

These ideas are strongly enough fixed in the country's *topos* that they continue to matter in terms of social practice. But the nation state's attachment to social democratic and multicultural values is indeed relational and contingent. The Canadian government refused to go to Iraq and said 'no' to Bush's continental defence system, but this refusal apparently did not extend to technology and armaments contracts. Canada's peacekeeping forces counter the devastation of military interventions; peacekeeping supports military interventions. Canada stands for universalism and public good; but millions of urban children and First Nation communities live in unconscionable poverty. Canada is one with its cosmopolitan image; but the country is not what it pretends. Such is the ambiguous fate of the national imaginary in a political sphere that is increasingly global but absent of the rights of global citizenship.

The concept of the social is now linked irrevocably to the space in which it occurs. It has become commonplace to posit the end of place, and along with this the elimination of the social; like the binary structure that separates 'the West' from 'the Rest', this rhetoric simplifies the matter. One inhabits place and space, nation and globe simultaneously; the question is on what terms. For David Harvey, 'all socio-political projects are ecological projects and vice versa'.[50] In other words, social practices are implicated in environmental effects, and human communities participate in larger social and biological ecologies. The ecological paradigm also insists that transformations to one entity introduce larger alterations to the ecological

49. Gerald Friesen *Citizens and Nation: An Essay on History, Communication, and Canada*, Toronto, University of Toronto, pp224-5.

50. David Harvey, Justice, *Nature and the Geography of Difference*, Oxford, Blackwell, 1996, p174.

system. Thus communities can only partially be re-constituted throug memories, and re-remembering them encounters new contex obligations.

How effective are petitions, citizens, activists generally in contempo politics of the nation state? The answer is contingent. This one suppo the claim that the country's diverse inhabitants support Canadian 'values': tolerance over aggression, common welfare over private self-interest, multiplicity over identity.[51] The evocation of national space interacts with larger historical, political and ecological processes linked by interaction in their very being. What better illustrates this interaction than the term 'globalisation', which is 'in these terms a dream: more concretely we might qualify it as the name given to the 'reactionary utopia' - Samir Amin's term - which neo-liberal discourse is today inclined to project as an historical actuality.[52] The 'projection' of this imaginary global space helps to constitute and regulate social space through its pretence 'to *have resolved* what cannot in fact *be resolved* in terms of the market'. In this sense the spatial trajectory evoked by the term 'globalisation' functions as an alibi for its political effects, which are lived every day at a local and personal level.

Sustainable spaces can be constituted only by contesting this 'reactionary utopia' in appropriate terms. Through imagining an alternate *telos* defined by the articulation of culture and technology, space and time, citizenship and justice, Canada offers a challenging (post)national space for people struggling to define themselves as citizens, scholars, neighbours, and critical intellectuals.

Post-colonial literature and culture have been shown to offer an ambiguous relationship between resistance and complicity, yet such ambiguity continues to be displaced by the binarism and absolutism of First-World/Third-World theory. This is a strong argument on behalf of restoring Canadian cultural theory to the field of the post-colonial. There are many challenges to the sturdiness and flexibility of English Canada and its archive. Does Canada count? Can Canada survive? Does it matter? Regardless of the answer(s), the recognition that identities are not and need not be singular, that well being cannot be won for all independent of government, that states are not peoples, that diverse, mobile and loyal peoples are compatible with sovereign nations, and that place-specific narratives can be mobilised to progressive ends, are nonetheless crucial principles for progressive politics in the global era.

5. widen of values bei Canadians and Americans is presented in Michael Adams, *Fire and Ice: The United States, Canada and the Myth of Converging Values.* Toronto, London, Penguin, 2003.

52. Neil Lazarus, *Nationalism and Cultural Practice in the Postcolonial World,* Cambridge, Cambridge University, 1999, p44.

THE IDEA OF A CRITICAL LITERARY GEOGRAPHY

Andrew Thacker

PATHS TO GEOGRAPHY

The 'where' of literature has come to occupy a central place for many critics over recent years. As someone working in literary studies, especially upon early twentieth-century modernism, I have been concerned for some time with what literary criticism can learn from geography. I first consciously used such a terminology, and the concept of 'textual space', in a 1993 article on a group of modernist poets, the Imagists. The article examined how these poets represented the experience of the modern city, particularly a cluster of poems concerning movement and transport in the city. This work has continued up until the publication of a book, *Moving Through Modernity: Space and Geography in Modernism* in 2003.[1] In this work I was clearly (and thankfully) not alone, for over the last decade or so interest in the textuality of space and the spatiality of texts has come to form a recognisable strategy in certain areas of literary and cultural criticism. Here I trace a brief genealogy of this interpretative strategy and suggest some of the key issues for a critical literary geography (and some of its problems), and provide an example of this kind of approach. The direction of my focus is upon what literary and cultural critics can learn from a fuller engagement with theorists of space and geography, rather than the reverse. To say this is not to call for any policing of disciplinary borders between literary studies and geography, for the growth of a genuinely interdisciplinary field that studies the interface between texts and spaces is clearly an exciting prospect. But for reasons of disciplinary background and experience I am primarily interested here in how far, and in what ways, the analysis of literary texts can be enriched by the use of geographical ideas and practices.

Literary scholarship on modernism, for example, has long engaged with the pervasive influence of urban geography upon writers such as Virginia Woolf or James Joyce. London in *Mrs Dalloway* and Dublin in *Ulysses* were massive presences in these texts, instances where the insistent hum of the city intruded upon almost every page. Quite often, however, literary critics read these texts by subjugating their spatiality to that of an aesthetic theme or trope. For example, the depiction of London in T.S. Eliot's *The Waste Land* has been viewed as a metaphor for the spiritual decline of the twentieth century; the anomie of urban life, the brown fog and the commuters plodding over London Bridge into the city of London were incidental details that helped emphasize Eliot's central message in the poem about spiritual, social and cultural decline. That the spaces and places represented in this text might have been central to 'what the poem means', or that this urban

1. Andrew Thacker, *Moving Through Modernity: Space and Geography in Modernism*, Manchester, MUP, 2003.

spatiality could explain the strange forms and styles of Eliot's poem, was not really on the literary critical agenda.

Until, of course, 1989 when literary and cultural critics all read David Harvey's *The Condition of Postmodernity*. This is clearly not quite the whole story but certainly Harvey's book, along with Soja's *Postmodern Geographies* in the same year, signalled an emergent presence for questions of space and geography in many disciplines within the social sciences and humanities. One of the key figures in this rapprochement between the literary and the spatial was Fredric Jameson, whose 1984 article in *New Left Review* on postmodernism was perhaps the first time that a contemporary literary theorist consciously used a geographical methodology: crucially, Jameson's concept of 'cognitive mapping' was adapted from the work of urban geographer Kevin Lynch.[2] If the analysis of postmodernism was the occasion of this first flowering of a theory of textual spaces, it was not long before other periods and genres of literature began also to be viewed through a spatial lens. In the case of modernism this was partly because the appearance of postmodernism prompted a return to the scene of the modern; central to Jameson's very definition of the postmodern is its spatiality, a feature he contrasts with the supposed temporality dominant within modernism.[3]

Other moments in a genealogy of geographical criticism would have to include Tony Pinkney, in his provocative essays for the journal *News from Nowhere* along with his book on the novels of Raymond Williams. Pinkney was one of the earliest critics in Britain to explore what he called the 'accelerating spatialisation of cultural studies and literary theory'.[4] Pinkney's range of references started with Jameson, but rapidly moved through Bachelard, de Certeau, and Lefebvre, attempting to re-align a Marxist cultural materialism with a geographical and spatial agenda, following Soja's work in particular. Pinkney was also deeply indebted to Williams's own work, particularly that of *The Country and the City* (1973), and in the spatial trope of the 'border' that runs throughout Williams's work.

One final route into a spatial criticism came from the increasing status given to Walter Benjamin's myriad work upon the city, writings that influenced a now seminal text on urban modernity, Marshall Berman's *All That is Solid Melts into Air*. Benjamin's notion of the *flâneur* also prompted a series of responses from feminist critics such as Elizabeth Wilson and Janet Wolff, who demonstrated the complex ways in which urban experience was gendered.[5] Apart from the *Arcades Project*, with its focus upon the geography of Paris as the fulcrum for all that is modern, Benjamin wrote a number of fascinating essays on places - Moscow, Marseilles, Naples and Berlin - which again exhibit a highly spatialised imagination. Many of these are autobiographies written by means of specific relationships to places: in 'A Berlin Chronicle', for example, Benjamin declares that 'I have long, indeed for years, played with the idea of setting out the sphere of life - bios - graphically on a map'.[6]

Since the early 1990s, then, questions of space and geography have

2. See Kevin Lynch, *The Image of the City*, Cambridge, MA, MIT Press, 1960.

3. Fredric Jameson, *Postmodernism, or the Cultural Logic of Late Capitalism*, London, Verso, 1991, p16.

4. Tony Pinkney, 'Space: the Final Frontier', *News From Nowhere* no. 8 (Autumn 1990): p17. Also see his *Raymond Williams*, Brigend, Seren Books, 1991.

5. See, inter alia, Elizabeth Wilson, 'The invisible flâneur', *New Left Review*, 191 (Jan./Feb 1992): 90-110; Janet Wolff, 'The Invisible Flâneuse: Women and the Literature of Modernity', in her *Feminine Sentences: Essays on Women and Culture*, Oxford, Polity Press, 1990.

6. Walter Benjamin, *Reflections: Essays, Aphorisms, Autobiographical Writings*, ed. Peter Demetz, New York, Shocken Books, 1986, p5.

7. John Kerrigan, 'Countries of the Mind', *TLS*, 11/09/1998, p3.

8. Edward Said, *Culture and Imperialism*, London, Vintage, 1994, p6.

9. See Con Coroneos, *Space, Conrad, and Modernity*, Oxford, OUP, 2002; Chris GoGwilt, *The Invention of the West: Joseph Conrad and the Double-Mapping of Empire*, Stanford, CA, Stanford UP, 1995; Peter Brooker and Andrew Thacker (eds), *Geographies of Modernism: Literatures, Cultures, Spaces*, London, Routledge, 2005. A number of panels at the international Modernist Studies Association conference have addressed the topic of geographies of modernism.

10. See also the volume of *Early Modern Literary Studies* on 'Literature and Geography'; 4, 2 issue 3 (September 1998), <www.shu.ac.uk/emls/04-2/04-2toc.html>

11. John Barrell, *The Idea of Landscape and the Sense of Place 1730-1840: An Approach to the Poetry of John Clare*, Cambridge, CUP, 1972.

12. Ralph Pite, *Hardy's Geography: Wessex and the Regional Novel*, Basingstoke, Palgrave, 2002.

13. Clearly the link between writing and

become recognised as legitimate and important topics in many areas of literary and cultural studies, and setting out the sphere of literature, if not life, by some form of map a more familiar hermeneutic strategy. In a review from 1998 of several books addressing spatial themes, John Kerrigan noted 'how valuable the findings of a new literary geography could be'.[7] Such an approach was, arguably, fundamental to the rise of postcolonial studies: Edward Said, for example, describes his project in *Culture and Imperialism* (1994) as 'a kind of geographical inquiry into historical experience', and that his book showed how geographical conflicts crucially infused the cultural forms of imperial power.[8] Though the rise of postcolonial criticism has emphasised the significance of geography as a paradigm for understanding culture and power, it is important not to identify a critical literary geography with a version of postcolonial studies. Quite often a postcolonial reading strategy shades into a geographical approach to texts, and the imbrications between the two can probably not easily be disentangled. However, it is essential to note that questions of space and geography can be brought to bear upon texts without necessarily operating within the ambit of postcolonialism.

Much work in the field of modernist studies, for example, has grappled with space and geography, often impelled by a critique of Jameson's too-easy assumption that modernism equates to the temporal. Not surprisingly Conrad has been one favoured target for such work, showing the porosity of the links between a critical literary geography and postcolonial approaches: books by Coroneos and GoGwilt, and a number of essays in *Geographies of Modernism* concern the spatial texts of Conrad.[9] Critics working on other periods and areas have also begun to consider literary texts through the prism of space: John Gillies covers the early modern period in his *Shakespeare and the Geography of Difference* (1994);[10] Brian Jarvis in *Postmodern Cartographies* (1998) addresses the 'geographical imagination' in contemporary American writing, while Gerry Smyth considers contemporary Irish writing in his *Space and the Irish Cultural Imagination* (2001). The eighteenth and nineteenth centuries have also received attention from critics informed by a sense of space and place: a much earlier work by John Barrell on landscape in John Clare is a classic account of the role of the politics of place in poetry.[11] Ralph Pite's recent work on one of literature's most enduring geographical entities, 'Hardy's Wessex', shows a clear focus upon issues of place and location in Hardy's novels.[12] It is difficult to summarise such a diverse field of work, or to suggest that they all share common methodologies such as that of postcolonialism, but two initial observations seem pertinent.

First, though this work seems starkly new, there is an older genealogy to the idea of a literary geography, particular in the early part of the twentieth century.[13] Virginia Woolf's first review for the *Times Literary Supplement* in 1905 was of two books upon 'Literary Geography': the books, on Thackeray and Dickens, offered illustrated guides to the places represented in their texts. William Sharp, who also wrote under the name 'Fiona MacLeod', published a volume called *Literary Geography* in 1904 devoted to 'the distinctive features of the actual or delineated country of certain famous writers'.[14] Sharp's text considers the 'countries' of writers such as R.L. Stevenson, George Eliot, Thackeray, the Brontës, as well as how an assortment of writers have depicted regions such as the Thames or East Anglia. It consists of an interesting mixture of travel sketches and critical attempts to explore the influence of place and memory upon the psychology of the writer. Similar approaches can be noted in contemporary works by Vernon Lee and Arthur Symons.[15] Writing about London was also prominent in this period, with books such as *Literary Landmarks of London* and *A Literary Topography of Old London* capturing the cultural landmarks of the city as depicted by writers. As Andrea Zemgulys notes, the aim of these volumes of literary geography was to construct London as a literary and historical city, and was linked with other heritage projects promoted by the London County Council in the first decades of the twentieth century.[16] These texts indicate how the changes we associate with literary and cultural modernism, such as trying to represent fundamental alterations in time and space in the period, were also being registered by other writers, and that this earlier literary geography also endeavoured to understand the 'time-space compression' of modernity and modernization that David Harvey detects in the cultural modernism in the early twentieth century.[17] This form of literary geography continues up to the present-day with popular and heritage-based accounts of literature and landscape, such as the National Trust's book *Literary Trails: Writers in Their Landscapes* or a book combining literature, strenuous activity and epicurean delights: *Pub Walks in Hardy's Wessex*.[18]

The second point about recent versions of literary geography is that, in distinction to the earlier writers, this is a more self-reflexively theorised criticism revolving around a triumvirate of materiality, history, and power.[19] Con Coroneos, for example, notes how materialism 'is often the starting point for thoughts on the spatial turn', referring to the impact on literary and cultural studies of the Marxist conception of space as productive process found in Harvey and Henri Lefebvre.[20] Such a critical literary geography brings texts, in a variety of fashions, back to the materiality of socially produced spaces: the 'where' of texts is variously located in the brute matter of social space.[21] Such a spatial materialism fits other trends within the humanities, such as the reappearance of history as a dominant paradigm within much research within literary studies, a development out of the New Historicist challenge to post-structuralism in the 1990s. Some of the impetus for this spatial history can be traced back to Michel Foucault who as far back as 1977 proclaimed: 'A whole history remains to be written of spaces - which would at the same time be a history of powers'.[22] Foucault's insistence on the historical nature of various forms of material social life - for instance, the body or the prison - has had a major influence upon a new critical literary geography.[23] Equally, Foucault's conception of the productivity of

place is much older; witness the *genius loci* tradition or, to turn to the Irish context, the *dinnshenchas* tradition of medieval literature where stories are often used to explain toponyms.

14. William Sharp, *Literary Geography*, London, Pall Mall Press, 1904, foreword, <http://www.sundown.pair.com/Sharp/WSVol_4/bibliography>

15. See, inter alia, Vernon Lee, *Genuis Loci: Essays on Places* (1899) and *Ariadne in Mantua* (1903); Arthur Symons, *Cities and Sea Coasts and Islands* (1908).

16. See Andrea P. Zemgulys, '"Night and Day is Dead": Virginia Woolf in London "Literary and Historic"', *Twentieth Century Literature*, 46, 1 (Spring 2000): 56-77.

17. David Harvey, *The Condition of Postmodernity*, Oxford, Blackwell, 1989, pp260-283.

18. Christina Hardyment, *Literary Trails: Writers in their Landscapes*, London, National Trust, 2000; M. Powers, *Pub Walks in Hardy's Wessex*, Dorchester, Power Publications, 1997.

19. The type of work I describe here should also be distinguished from other approaches to the geography of literature which seem more indebted to the earlier tradition of literary geography. I am

thinking here of a book like Jane Brown, *Spirits of Place: Five Famous Lives in their English Landscape*, London, Penguin, 2001. Malcolm Bradbury's expansive, *The Atlas of Literature*, London, De Agostini, 1996, sits somewhere between Brown's approach and a more critical mode of inquiry.

20. Coroneos, op. cit., p4.

21. For a succinct statement of this view see Julian Murphet, 'Literary Theory and the New Geography', in Martin McQuillan et al (eds), *Post-Theory: New Directions in Criticism*, Edinburgh, EUP, 1999.

22. Michel Foucault, 'The Eye of Power', *Power/Knowledge: Selected Interviews and Other Writings 1972-77*, Colin Gordon (ed), London, Harvester Wheatsheaf, 1980, p149. For a comprehensive account of Foucault's relevance for the discipline of geography see C. Philo, 'Foucault's geography' *Environment and Planning D: Society and Space* 10 (1992): 137-61.

23. For Coroneos Foucault is 'perhaps the single most important figure in the spatial turn', op. cit., p17.

24. Derek Gregory, *Geographical Imaginations*, Oxford, Blackwell, 1994, p140.

power, rather than just power as domination, is important for thinking how subjects are located and produced within, and respond and react to, specific spaces. To think geographically about literary and cultural texts means to understand them in material locations, locations that can and should be examined historically and with an awareness of how diverse spaces can reflect, produce or resist forms of power.

This then explains my references to a *critical* literary geography: to stress the distance from an effortless mapping of represented landscapes in literary texts, and to raise more complex questions about space and power, and how space and geography affect literary forms and styles. It is a strategy that self-consciously works in an interdisciplinary fashion, adapting ideas and approaches from geography, and elsewhere, such as conceptions of the contrast between space and place; critical cartography (from Harley and Cosgrove); rhythmanalysis and representational spaces (from Lefebvre); thirdspace (Soja); heterotopia (Foucault); and time-space compression (Harvey).

CONCEPTUALISING A CRITICAL LITERARY GEOGRAPHY

Derek Gregory has noted the predominance of a 'textualization of landscape' in new models of cultural geography, commenting upon the attempts by critics to 'read space (...) as a text'.[24] My work commences from the other end of this nexus - I have been attempting to read *texts spatially*, to consider how such an approach can be articulated, and to draw out the implications for literary and cultural studies of a spatial turn. This process of reading and interpreting literary texts by reference to geographical concepts such as space and place, social space, time-space compression, and spatial history, is what I mean by a critical literary geography.

What would such a 'critical literary geography' look like in practice? Would it be a critical practice based on cartography?[25] One of the most theoretically elaborated accounts of such an approach is that of Franco Moretti's *Atlas of the European Novel* (1998) in which he argues that geography is an active force shaping the development of the nineteenth-century novel. Moretti's stimulating book reads literary texts spatially through a series of maps depicting various locations germane to the novels. His methodology attempts to demonstrate how 'geography shapes the narrative structure' of the novel.[26] This has a dual focus: firstly, upon *space in literature*, that is how certain spaces are represented in fictional texts; and secondly, upon *literature in space*, a study of where novels in Europe were read, an approach which considers features such as circulating libraries in provincial cities. I do not have the room here to consider Moretti's fascinating work in the detail it deserves, but I would note four problems with his belief in cartography as a guide to literary interpretation. First, Moretti puts a lot of faith in the 'objectivity' of maps, and pays little attention to critiques such as that of J.B. Harley of cartography's imbrication with power.[27] Maps should be regarded, argues Derek Gregory, like all 'practices of representation', as 'situated, embodied, partial',[28] with different meanings being signified as a result of features such as choice of cartographic projection, type of coloration or employment of scale. Second, sometimes you may draw a map of a novel, following Moretti's model, and then see nothing of note - does this invalidate a spatial reading of the text, or simply suggest a less cartographic approach to the space of the text? Third, can his method, which focuses upon narrative, also work for poetry or drama, where the link between narrative movements and positions on a map cannot so easily be made? Finally, the link between his two methods, literature in space and space in literature, seems rather underdeveloped, although a stronger critical literary geography would undoubtedly wish to see connections between the two. Despite these caveats, *Atlas of the European Novel* is undoubtedly a key work in the development of a new literary geography and requires much further debate.

Moretti uses maps as what he calls 'analytical tools' for studying texts.[29] Many contemporary critics seem to have taken a more metaphorical route for maps, perhaps taking a lead from Jameson's use of 'cognitive mapping' as a master-trope for interpreting contemporary culture. As Melba Cuddy-Keane notes, 'we are witnessing a conjunction between the charting of space and the charting of knowledge', shown in the ever-increasing number of titles that include the word 'mapping'.[30] For example, a recent excellent work on cultural modernism by Ann Ardis has an introduction entitled, 'Rethinking modernism, remapping the turn of the twentieth century'. Ardis's aim is to revise our conception of literary modernism by focussing on social and political agendas that were discredited by the canonical, and mostly male, modernist writers. She discusses, therefore, writers such as Beatrice Potter Webb and Netta Syrett who are not normally thought of in relation to modernism. Ardis also embeds the emergence of British literary modernism within debates such as those around Fabian and Guild Socialism, early twentieth-century ethnography, and the rise of the professions. What we conventionally describe today as literary modernism - Joyce, Pound, Eliot - is only a selective tradition of a group of writers who, at the start of the twentieth century, were engaged in quarrels with other competing groups for the ownership and definition of a modern aesthetic. This, then, is what Ardis means by 'remapping', a revising of what the term modernism means by reference to other historical formations within the period; it should produce, she writes, 'a much more detailed and nuanced topographical mapping of the period'.[31] Earlier in her introduction Ardis provides the following justification for her use of mapping:

The influence of contemporary cultural geographers extends far beyond the boundaries of geography as a discipline. 'Mapping' is this [that is to say, Ardis's project's central conceit because it so usefully glosses not only the social constructedness of literary history but also the extent to which a reading of literary history, like that of a landscape, employs vertical, horizontal, and temporal scales and comparisons.[32]

25. For an excellent consideration of the proliferation of 'mapping' as a strategy in the humanities and social sciences see Melba Cuddy-Keane, 'Imaging/Imagining Globalization: Maps and Models', <www.chass.utoronto.ca/ ~mcuddy/ mapping.htm>

26. Franco Moretti, *Atlas of the European Novel 1800-1900*, London, Verso, 1998, p8.

27. See, for example, J.B. Harley, *The New Nature of Maps: Essays in the History of Cartography*, Paul Laxton (ed), Baltimore/London, John Hopkins University Press, 2001 and the range of essays on the complexities of cartographic practice in Denis Cosgrove (ed) *Mappings*, London, Reaktion, 1999.

28. Derek Gregory, op. cit., p7.

29. Moretti, op. cit., p3.

30. See Cuddy-Keane, op. cit., p1.

31. Ann L. Ardis, *Modernism and Cultural Conflict 1880-1922*, Cambridge, CUP, 2002, p4.

32. Ibid., p4.

For Ardis, then, mapping is a metaphor, or 'conceit', since an analysis of literary history is 'like' a 'reading' of a landscape in its use of multiple scales. Overall, I have much sympathy with Ardis's interpretations of modernism, but I have reservations over how she employs concepts such as 'mapping' and 'scale'. My puzzle stems not only from the use of mapping as metaphor, but also from a lack of elaboration of scaling and mapping as hermeneutic terms. Literary histories clearly employ vertical and horizontal axes: vertically, or diachronically, we talk of the influence of a writer upon a later writer, or of the development of a style of writing over time (for example, we sometimes talk of early, high and late modernism); horizontally, we synchronically situate writers in groups or relationships to each other (so the Bloomsbury group consists of a certain range of figures whose influence upon each other can be traced or 'mapped'). Scale, for Ardis, seems to be used as a metaphor for judgements around *value*: Joyce is a more significant modernist writer than Ford Madox Ford, for example. But this does not really get us very far, as the key question here is *which scale* is being used, or rather, how is value being measured? What is the scale by which we judge a writer to be more modernist (or more influential) than another? For every literary Mercator projection, we might say, there is a competing Peters projection to contest judgements of literary value.

Ardis's claim shows some of the difficulties with using geographical tropes without closer consideration of the implications of such terms. In the rest of this article, I want to indicate four issues associated with using geographical ideas in literary interpretation, before presenting an example of a critical literary geography in practice.[33]

TEXTUAL SPACES

The first problem concerns the metaphorical nature of the spaces being discussed in literary and cultural studies. Neil Smith has argued that the use of spatial metaphors - such as mapping, margins/centre, deterritorialisation, or location - in a theoretical discourse such as postcolonialism operate at the expense of analysing the material spaces of, for example, the city. For Smith, spatial metaphors have the tendency to view actual spaces as dead or empty containers in which all objects or events can be located. Spatial metaphors in criticism are not to be rejected (if such a thing were ever possible), but Smith suggests that we seek to understand how metaphorical and material spaces are 'mutually implicated', and to view space not as a neutral canvas but as 'social space', produced according to social aims and objectives, and which then, in turn, shapes social life.[34] Here then is another reinforcement of the materialist and historicist emphasis of the new literary geography. If, as Crang and Thrift argue, neither theories nor social processes 'exists without geographical extent and historical duration', then tracking how a literary work is also to be located geographically is now a major challenge for literary and cultural studies.[35]

33. For a fuller consideration of the issues discussed in this next section see Thacker, *Moving Through Modernity*, pp1-45.

34. Neil Smith, 'Homeless/global: scaling places' in Jon Bird, Barry Curtis, Tim Putnam, George Robertson, and Lisa Tickner (eds), *Mapping the Futures: Local Cultures, Global Change*, London, Routledge, 1993, pp98-99. See also Smith and Cindi Katz, 'Grounding Metaphor: Towards a Spatialized Politics', in *Place and the Politics of Identity*, Michael Keith and Steve Pile (eds), London, Routledge, 1993.

35. See Mike Crang and Nigel Thrift (eds), *Thinking Space*, London, Routledge, 2000.

The second question for a critical literary geography concerns the representation of space in cultural texts. Here Henri Lefebvre's distinction between the *representation of space* and *representational spaces* is helpful: broadly, while the former refers to official organizations of space, the latter refers to unofficial, often aesthetic conceptions of space.[36] Lefebvre's sense of social space is very diverse: both internal and external, the space of the psyche, the body, the city, the house, or the room. By using Lefebvre and other cultural geographers we can analyse in more detail, for example, the spatial histories of specific cities depicted in literary and cultural texts: the Paris of the surrealists, or New York after 9/11.[37] Not only these cities in a general sense, however, but specific places within them become our concern when the scale of our geographical focus is upon smaller spatialities. Now, perhaps drawing upon Benjamin's model of analysing spaces of consumption such as arcades, we might consider how specific streets, stations, cafes, monuments or shops are represented in texts, and how such places offer an endorsement or contestation of official representations of space. Moving to a larger scale, another key dimension of urban representation is that of the transnational links between various global cities, opened up by the experience of the colonial migrant or artist in exile.[38]

The third issue considers the implications of such representations for the formal properties of literary and cultural texts. We should reconnect the representational spaces in literary texts not only to the material spaces they depict, but also reverse the movement, and understand how social spaces dialogically help fashion the literary *forms* of texts. Here we might recall Joseph Frank's old concept of spatial form as an intrinsic theoretical approach indebted to New Criticism; space is here conceived as the spread of text upon paper and page, or the narrative pattern of a text read through time.[39] A critical literary geography would trace how social space intrudes upon the internal construction of spatial forms. *Literary texts represent social spaces, but social space shapes literary forms*. The term *textual space* could then refer to this interaction between spatial forms and social space in the written text. Emphasis should be devoted to spatial features of literature such as typography and layout on the page; the space of metaphor and the shifting between different senses of space within a text; or the very shape of narrative forms, found in open-ended fictions or novels that utilise circular patterns for stories. Discussion of how the formal features of literature are influenced by social or historical circumstances is always fraught with difficulty; the links here between space, geography and literary forms are no less tentative. Despite this it is important not only to discuss space and geography thematically, but also to address them as questions with a profound impact upon how literary and cultural texts are formally assembled. To investigate a novel as a spatial text must amount to more than simply considering how that text represents an interesting location.

The fourth question returns to the debate around the impact of cartography on criticism. If metaphorical mapping is a problematic avenue

36. Henri Lefebvre, *The Production of Space*, Donald Nicholson-Smith (trans), Oxford, Blackwell, 1991, pp38-46.

37. See Peter Brooker, 'Terrorism and Counternarratives: Don DeLillo and the New York Imaginary', this issue.

38. For a consideration of transnational issues in relation to modernism see Andreas Huyssen, 'Geographies of Modernism in a Globalizing World' in Brooker and Thacker, *Geographies of Modernism*.

39. Joseph Frank, *The Widening Gyre: Crisis and Mastery in Modern Literature*, Bloomington, Indiana University Press, 1968.

to explore, then perhaps we should employ actual maps, as Moretti does, in order to accentuate a more materialist understanding of the spatiality of texts. As suggested above, there are problems attached to this cartographic critical approach, and another line of investigation for a critical literary geography might be to analyse the occurrence of maps and mapping in specific texts, analysing how cartography functions as an instance of visual culture in such texts. Perhaps as one response to globalisation maps are slipping more and more into literary texts, both in critical and creative works.[40] The obvious examples of these spatial texts are those of travel writing, within which there is a long tradition of maps as frontispieces or illustrations. Richard Phillips has drawn attention to an earlier use of maps in the adventure story genre of imperial writing, referring to texts as historically diverse as *Robinson Crusoe* and *Treasure Island*.[41] But also recent editions of many classic twentieth-century works, for example, employ maps: the Oxford University Press edition of Joyce's *Ulysses* contains a contemporaneous (1904) map of Dublin; the recent Penguin edition of Woolf's novels possess simple maps of the London locations referred to in *Mrs Dalloway* and *The Years*. The great Italian modernist, and friend of Joyce, Italo Svevo's *La coscienza di Zeno* (*Zeno's Conscience*) (1923) was recently published in a new translation in English, complete with a highly stylised map of early twentieth-century Trieste.[42] Moving away from the early twentieth century, a number of highly successful contemporary thrillers and detective novels employ maps as frontispieces: Peter Høeg's *Miss Smilla's Feeling for Snow* (1993) contains a map of Copenhagen; novels by Donna Leon and Michael Dibdin have maps of Venice.[43] Location, these maps imply, is another character in these works, and help create additional interest in a genre which is sometimes accused of treading an overly familiar narrative direction. Such texts, with their cartographic prompts, also construct particular places in the mind of the reader; we now see the material space through the lens of the textualised space, hence Dublin is Joyce's Dublin, and fans of Donna Leon see Venice as Commissario Brunetti's Venice. Here metaphorical space guides our engagement with material spaces.

What then is the epistemological status of such pictorial maps that accompany writing, seemingly peripheral textual features to the central narrative? Rather than only treating 'mapping' as a metaphor it seems important to return to the map as a set of material signs, and to understand what is at issue when a text employs an actual map as a component of the narrative. Informative examples are often found in instances of travel writing, and I have discussed one such case in a reading of Graham Greene's 1936 account of a journey to Liberia, *Journey Without Maps*.[44] A map, such as the one at the start of Greene's book, implies a marginal position in relation to the written text; but it is also an image that acts as a kind of guide to the journey taken by the author and retraced by the reader. The presence of maps in travel narratives often points to the fact that travel writers must *produce* space as an undiscovered entity before the narrative commences, in

40. See Cuddy Keane, op. cit.

41. Richard Phillips, *Mapping Men and Empire: A Geography of Adventure*, London, Routledge, 1997.

42. Italo Svevo, *Zeno's Conscience*, William Weaver (trans), London, Penguin, 2002.

43. Peter Høeg's *Miss Smilla's Feeling for Snow*, London, Flamingo, 1994; Donna Leon, *Doctored Evidence*, London, Heinemann, 2004; Michael Dibdin, *Dead Lagoon*, London, Faber, 1994.

44. See Thacker, 'Journey with Maps: Travel Theory, Geography and the Syntax of Space' in Charles Burdett and Derek Duncan (eds) *Cultural Encounters: European Travel Writing in the 1930s*, NY/Oxford, Berghahn, 2002.

order to justify their journey.[45] It is fascinating to see how a map functions as a representation of space, in Lefebvre's sense, altering how we read written texts, conveying meaning about the spaces travelled through, but also for the interaction between these visual and verbal signifiers. Harley notes that decorative features of maps should not be regarded as 'inconsequential marginalia' but rather 'the emblems in cartouches and decorative title-pages can be regarded as *basic* to the way they convey their cultural meaning'.[46] Connecting such cartographic signifying elements to the written meanings of the text provides another new focus for a critical literary geography.

Texts that contain maps should, then, be more closely correlated with an understanding of specific historical geographies, and of debates within cultural geography surrounding space and place. Textual maps often demonstrate, as Richard Phillips suggests, the ability of all maps 'to circumscribe geography, by enclosing, defining, coding, orienting, structuring and controlling space'.[47] There is also a significant interaction between these textual maps and the spatial form of the cultural text: in Greene's narrative in *Journey Without Maps* the cartographic image functions as a place-discourse against which Greene's narrative can construct a discourse of spatial movement. Interpreting such maps as forms of representation rather than naturalised images of 'fact' demonstrates how the discourses of space and place are not to be taken for granted, but must be understood as forms of Lefebvrean social space. In understanding the textual space of a book like *Journey Without Maps* equal attention must be paid to the textuality, visual and verbal, of the spaces represented, and to the spatialities of the text itself.

STREET NAMES

James Joyce once suggested he was more interested in Dublin street names than in the riddle of the universe and his interest in the interactive relation between words and worlds informs the whole of his geographical imagination.[48] In this attention to toponyms Joyce also recalls another urban visionary, Walter Benjamin. In one section of the *Arcades Project* Benjamin dwells upon the Place du Maroc, in Belleville, Paris. That 'desolate heap of stones with its rows of tenements became for me ... not only a Moroccan desert but also, and at the same time, a monument of colonial imperialism; topographic vision was entwined with allegorical meaning in this square'.[49] Benjamin compares this experience of the spatial history of a site, embodied in its name, to the power of intoxication: 'street names are like intoxicating substances that make our perceptions more stratified and richer in spaces. One could call the energy by which they transport us into such a state their *vertu évocatrice*, their evocative power - but that is saying too little; for what is decisive here is not the association but the interpenetration of images'.[50] For Benjamin, street names perhaps opened up the riddle of the universe, for in such signifiers, he wrote, 'the city is a linguistic cosmos'.[51] The evocative

45. I owe this point to Debbie Lisle.

46. Harley, op. cit., p160.

47. Richard Phillips, op. cit., p14.

48. See Cyril Connolly, *Previous Convictions*, London, Hamish Hamilton, 1963, p271. For further discussion of Joyce and geography see Gerry Kearns's essay in this issue and my *Moving Through Modernity*, ch.4.

49. Walter Benjamin, *The Arcades Project*, Cambridge, Mass., Harvard University Press, 1999, p518.

50. Ibid.

51. Ibid., p522.

power of street names, and the tangled textual spaces they represent, has often preoccupied writers. Making sense of this intoxicating discourse requires a detailed spatial history of the streets being named, and an assessment of how these social spaces inform textual space.

To illustrate this aspect of a critical literary geography I want to explore the topographic and toponymic qualities of Jean Rhys via one final literary map. Rhys is a writer much concerned with urban space. Her novels of the 1920s and 30s are overwhelmingly concerned with Paris and London. *After Leaving Mr Mackenzie* (1930) is typical. It concerns a solitary female heroine, Julia Martin, who drifts between cheap accommodation in London and Paris, and has a number of unsuccessful relationships with men and a rather more successful relationship with alcohol. Rhys's depiction of these cities is often quite precise; for example, five of the chapter titles in *After Leaving Mr Mackenzie* are toponyms.[52] However, the topography of Paris is worth a closer look, in order to ascertain how her writings engage with the geographies of this key modernist city.[53] The 'representational space' of Paris can be understood in two ways: first, in terms of how Rhys represents certain spaces and the meanings attached to particular locations; and second, how certain formal features of her text - such as narrative form and literary style - are influenced by a geographical encounter with these cities. Combining these two aspects helps offer an understanding of the textual space of Rhys's work.

In the past Jean Rhys has often seemed to fall off the metaphoric map of modernism. Peculiarly, she also drifts away from the revisionist map of modernist women writers discussed in Shari Benstock's influential guide, *Women of the Left Bank* (Fig 1) This is a fact that Benstock is aware of, arguing that like 'the women of her fiction, Jean Rhys did not find a place for herself on the literary Left Bank; she was an outsider among outsiders'.[54] To begin we can note that the geographical marginality of Rhys's heroines is not quite as clear-cut as Benstock makes out. True, Benstock does mostly discuss the novel *Good Morning Midnight*, but it does seem that a number of the key locations for Julia Martin in *After Leaving Mr Mackenzie* offer rather more complex relations to the literary Left Bank of the 1920s. For example, the two hotels in which Julia stays, shabby as they might be, are located on the Quai des Grand Augustins (number 1 on map) overlooking the Seine, and an unnamed hotel (possibly the Hotel Henri IV in the place Dauphine) situated on the Île de la Cité (number 2 on map). Neither site is perhaps exactly within the Latin Quarter or St Germain; but they are certainly not in the 'mean and uninteresting streets' of the more distant 13th arrondissement to which Benstock assigns Rhys's heroines.[55] We also learn that Julia pays sixteen francs for her room in the Hotel St Raphael on the Quai. It is described as a cheap, 'lowdown sort of place', but Julia likes the room as somewhere in which to hide, locking the door to feel safe. (All of Rhys's novels of the '20s and '30s pay great attention to the decoration and internal space of the hotel rooms.) The novel is set c.1925[56] and Baedeker's

52. Jean Rhys, *After Leaving Mr Mackenzie*, Harmondsworth, Penguin, 1971. Further references are in the main text.

53. For reasons of space I have discussed only Paris in this article.

54. Shari Benstock, *Women of the Left Bank: Paris, 1900-1940*, London, Virago, 1987, p448. Benstock's work shows a significant engagement with the issues of space and geography without explicitly demonstrating the focus of a critical literary geography upon form, power and spatial representation.

55. Ibid., p449.

56. I base this on the fact that the café le Select is mentioned, an establishment only opened in 1925; see Arlen J. Hansen, *Expatriate Paris: A Cultural and Literary Guide to Paris of the 1920s*, New York: Arcade, 1990, p121.

Fig 1: adapted from Shari Benstock, Women of the Left Bank, *1900-1940, London, Virago, 1987*

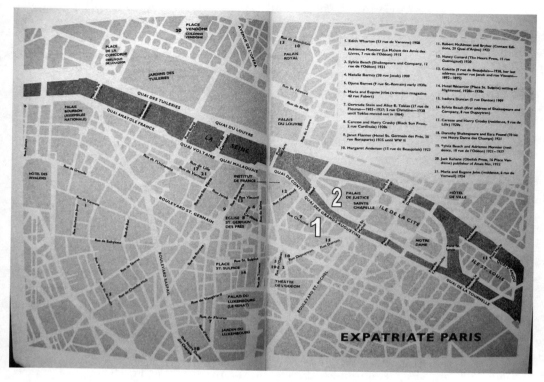

guide to *Paris et ses environs* of 1924 indicates that a 16 franc hotel room is certainly not at the luxury end of the market - rooms at the Ritz start at 50 francs. But neither is it the cheapest that the conservative Baedeker recommends for this area (or other *quartiers*). The Hotel de Quai-Voltaire, just westward along the left bank of the Seine from Julia's hotel, is said to have rooms for 10 francs; some *maisons de famille* establishments offer rooms for 6 francs.[57]

I am not disputing the social marginality of Julia in the novel, but suggesting that attention to the geographical history of Paris reveals a more intricate picture of Rhys's representational space. In an excellent account of 'Shifting Cultural Centres in Twentieth-century Paris', Nicholas Hewitt has shown how necessary it is to be careful when tracing those urban districts that became areas of important cultural production. Understanding the significance of the Parisian Left Bank for the geography of modernism requires a sensitive delimitation of how, for example, specific cafés and restaurants became important meeting points for writers, artists and intellectuals. Hewitt suggests that twentieth-century Left Bank culture is divided between two significant traditions: an intellectual and academic circle linked to the institutions of higher education and publishing houses; and a second bohemian tradition. While the first tradition remains relatively

57. Karl Baedeker, *Paris et ses environs: manuel du voyageur,* Leipzig, Baedeker, 1924, pp9-10.

58. Nicholas Hewitt, 'Shifting Cultural Centres in Twentieth-century Paris', in *Parisian Fields*, Michael Sheringham (ed), London, Reaktion, 1996, p31.

59. Here I am paraphrasing Hewitt, op. cit., pp31-43.

60. Francis Carco, *De Montmartre au Quartier Latin* (Paris, 1927), cited in Hewitt, op. cit., p40.

61. Hewitt, op. cit., p31.

62. Ibid.

63. Ernest Hemingway, *A Moveable Feast*, London, 1964, p72.

stable in its geography, the second shifts across the city, and is linked to factors such as changing patterns of migration, centres of entertainment and pleasure, areas around railway stations, the availability of cheap accommodation, and what he terms 'the indispensable frontier between the bourgeois city and the *classes dangereuses* that constitute the marginal space in which bohemian activity takes place'.[58] This bohemian tradition became established around Montmartre by 1900, continued here up till the outbreak of war, and was then re-established around Montparnasse after 1918. Montparnasse however was eclipsed after 1929, and the cultural centre of the 1930s shifted back to the Latin Quarter and the academic and publishing institutions of St Germain.[59]

For one contemporary in 1927 the post-war move from Montmartre to Montparnasse was principally due to the poet Apollinaire:

Montparnasse was created by Apollinaire ... His presence in this district, where the mixture of races provokes disquieting undercurrents, created a kind of 'union sacrée' of the arts ... As a neighbour of his cousin Paul Fort, whose domaine comprised the Boul'Mich', Bullier, the Luxembourg Gardens and the Closerie des Lilas, he traced the limits of his fief and, from the café of the Deux-Magots ... extended it along the rue de Rennes and the boulevard Raspail until it crossed the boulevard du Montparnasse.[60]

Aside from the movements of prominent artists, the popularity of the 'disquieting undercurrents' of Montparnasse in the 1920s can be traced back to the spatial history of Paris as a whole. Hewitt shows how the creation in 1784 of the so-called 'tax-collectors wall' (*Mur des Fermiers Généraux*) around the entire city split Paris into two areas: one within the wall of high taxes on such items as alcohol, the other outside the wall that ran along the outer boulevards such as the Boulevard du Montparnasse. Because of this difference the areas around the entries to the inner city, the *barrières* or customs posts, became zones of pleasure, populated by dance halls (the Bal Bullier) and places to drink and eat (the Closerie des Lilas).[61] As Hewitt notes, the 'geography of pleasure in the nineteenth- and twentieth-century city is closely allied to the Wall'.[62]

Julia Martin's relationship to the pleasurable pastures of Montparnasse is complicated. Her hotel on the quai overlooking the Seine is certainly away from the centre of Montparnasse life, if we define it, as Hemingway did in *A Moveable Feast* as 'the cafés at the corner of the boulevard Montparnasse and the boulevard Raspail'.[63] Again, if we look at where Julia eats and drinks we notice that she has an ambiguous relationship to certain areas. In the first section of the novel she lunches in a German restaurant in Rue Huchette, centrally in the Latin Quarter. After receiving a final sum of money from her former lover Mr Mackenzie she tries to find him by walking along the Boulevard St Michel to his flat; she then spies him walking into the Restaurant Albert on Boulevard Montparnasse. Julia thus moves through the 'right' area, but has a tendency to be found, unlike the men in the novel, in unnamed streets and cafés. For example, a young Englishman, George Horsfield, notices Julia's altercation with Mackenzie in the Restaurant Albert and then decides to befriend Julia. After finishing his meal Horsfield walks past the Dôme and the Rotonde and goes into the Sélect Bar for a drink. These are all famous Montparnasse venues, associated in this period with writers such as Joyce and Hemingway; Hart Crane was famously arrested in the Dôme in 1929.[64] The journalist Harold Stearns described the Sélect as 'a seething madhouse of drunks, semi-drunks, quarter-drunks and the sober maniacs'.[65] But Julia Martin - never one to avoid a drink or three - eschews these glittery locations and Horsfield only finds her in some nearby but anonymous bar (28-9).

Since Rhys is always so particular about the names of streets, cafés, and restaurants, when Julia enters an anonymous location it is somehow all the more striking. Her preference for such places is perhaps linked to her own deracinated status: early on we learn that her life has 'rubbed most of the hall-marks off her, so that is was not easy to guess at her age, her nationality, or the social background to which she properly belonged' (11). None of the cafés or restaurants that Julia enters alone are named in the book; this contrasts strongly with those encountered in Rhys's earlier novel, *Quartet*, based on her affair with Ford Madox Ford in 1923-4. In this earlier novel, many famous left bank venues are mentioned and visited: such as the Café Lavenue, the Rotonde, the Bal du Printemps, the Sélect, the Dôme, and the Closerie des Lilas. Julia thus exists within the same cultural geography as these sites of expatriate artistic rendezvous, but seeks out places for other reasons. Even in *Quartet*, the heroine of this novel, Marya, is said to dislike the 'glaring cafés' of Boulevard St Michel for the 'softer, more dimly lit' location of Boulevard Montparnasse.[66] The latter cannot really be said to be the more 'marginal' location, but it does possess a different psychic value for Rhys's heroines. Unlike the writers and artists encountered in *Quartet*, it seems that Julia Martin does not belong to such circles and thus does not feel comfortable in the more famous cafes inhabited by such people. Julia goes for a walk everyday after lunch, but 'was so anxious not to meet anybody she knew that she always kept to the back streets as much as possible' and when she 'passed the café terraces her face would assume a hard forbidding expression' (13).

The final section of the novel finds Julia back in Paris after a sojourn in London and, again, her location is not marginal, but significant in terms of the novel's literary geography. Her hotel is on the Île de la Cité, set between the left and right banks of the Seine. This island is an in-beween space, a geographical microcosm of Julia's own position in the text, shuttling between Paris and London, and between the two male lovers, Mackenzie and Horsfield. Julia decides to go to Montparnasse after dinner, a plan that is soon abandoned (after two more brandies in a unnamed café). Now she decides that she 'only wanted to walk somewhere straight ahead' (135) and

64. See Hansen, op. cit., pp121-4 for details.

65. Cited in William Wiser, *The Crazy Years: Paris in the Twenties*, London, Thames and Hudson, 1983, p207.

66. Jean Rhys, *Quartet*, Harmondsworth, Penguin, 1973, p54.

crosses from the Place St Michel on the Left Bank over the river to the Place du Châtelet. But Châtelet is a 'nightmare' and she turns left and walks 'into a part of the city which was unknown to her', somewhere near the back of the Halles market, she thinks (136). Julia stops, thinking 'I've gone too far', and sits at another café terrace, for yet another brandy.

There is a sense in which these chapters, where Julia wanders from the island to the Left Bank and then tries to go 'straight ahead', are geographical metaphors for her own life in the novel. For she ends where she began, meeting Mackenzie in a café, asking him for money, and saying that she has now left the Île de la Cité hotel for the Quai des Grands Augustins hotel mentioned at the start of the novel. This novel, like other Rhys novels, employs a circular narrative structure; Julia is unable to go 'straight ahead' and her attempt to escape from the Left Bank into some unknown part of the city fails. As a *flâneuse* we might say, Julia is a bit of a failure, echoing what Rachel Bowlby terms the 'negative *flâneuse*' of Sasha Jensen in Rhys's later novel, *Good Morning, Midnight*. Rhys's protagonists, notes Bowlby, tread the streets to fill in empty time rather than to take pleasurable strolls through London as exhibited in, say, Woolf's *Mrs Dalloway*.[67]

67. Rachel Bowlby, '"The impasse": Jean Rhys's *Good Morning, Midnight*', in *Still Crazy After All These Years: Women, Writing and Psychoanalysis*, London, Routledge, 1992, p53.

Another way to read the significance of the Île de la Cité location is in terms of Rhys's own island home in the Caribbean, Dominica. Historically the island had been divided between the colonial powers of Britain and France, and Rhys's life after she left Dominica seemed to repeat some of this separation between different nationalities. *After Leaving Mr Mackenzie* enacts this national division at the level of its narrative shape, with Julia shuffling between Paris and London, and also between the two languages, another important division replicated in Dominica's official English and the French-based Creole spoken by most islanders.

Towards the end of the novel Julia notes of her visit to London, that it had been 'a disconnected episode to be placed with all the other disconnected episodes which made up her life' (129). Her narrative life is indeed disconnected and the novel figures this in a geographical fashion by the shifts between London and Paris, and her location (living seems somehow too strong a word here) at four addresses within a few weeks. The conclusion to the previous chapter sees Mr Horsfield return to his house in London's affluent Holland Park, finally having decided not to help Julia again. As he shuts the door he realises that he has also 'shut out the thought of Julia', while his own home 'enveloped him' in a 'familiar world'. This sense of inner domestic space as comforting and familiar is not available to Julia and she is destined never to be enveloped in such a *place*; rather she is always ready to move on to another *space*, as in the next chapter's journey to Paris. Indeed the image of a journey between different locations is perhaps the dominant one in Rhys's fiction, shown in the manner in which her protagonists shift from one grubby lodging house to the next.

The novel's title suggests a story of the *time after* leaving a man; but the action often appears to revolve around the spaces moved through; *leaving* becomes not just a description of her emotional state after the relationship with Mackenzie, but of the various journeys in the novel. As the narrator comments of Julia, 'It was always places that she thought of, not people' (9). But just as her relationships to men are perpetually doomed, so her relationships to places are always subject to eventual disconnection. Disconnection, however, is a term that can be applied not only to Julia Martin's relationship to place, but also to the spatial style of the novel. Perhaps the most noticeable spatial feature of Rhys's texts is their peculiarly fragmented and discrete appearance on the page. Visually, the pages of Rhys's novels seem full of blank space, an effect reinforced by her tendency to use numerous single sentence paragraphs and multiple sections to chapters. Another spatial style is her use of line spaces or gaps between passages of prose. The effect of this heterotopic writing is thus to render her texts as disconnected mosaics, containing piecemeal images of her characters' lives that parallel the disjointed experience of different material geographies. One striking instance of how geography inscribes itself within the spatiality of the text is the image on the first page of the novel, a card for the Hotel St Raphael (Fig 2). This rectangle of type represents the interior space of the hotel room Julia takes, and perhaps a sense of enclosure, and hence temporary safety, in the room; it is also another little island, adrift on a page of type.

In this sense, I think, Rhys's fiction demonstrates a central point about social space made by Lefebvre: no space is ever singular: 'Social spaces

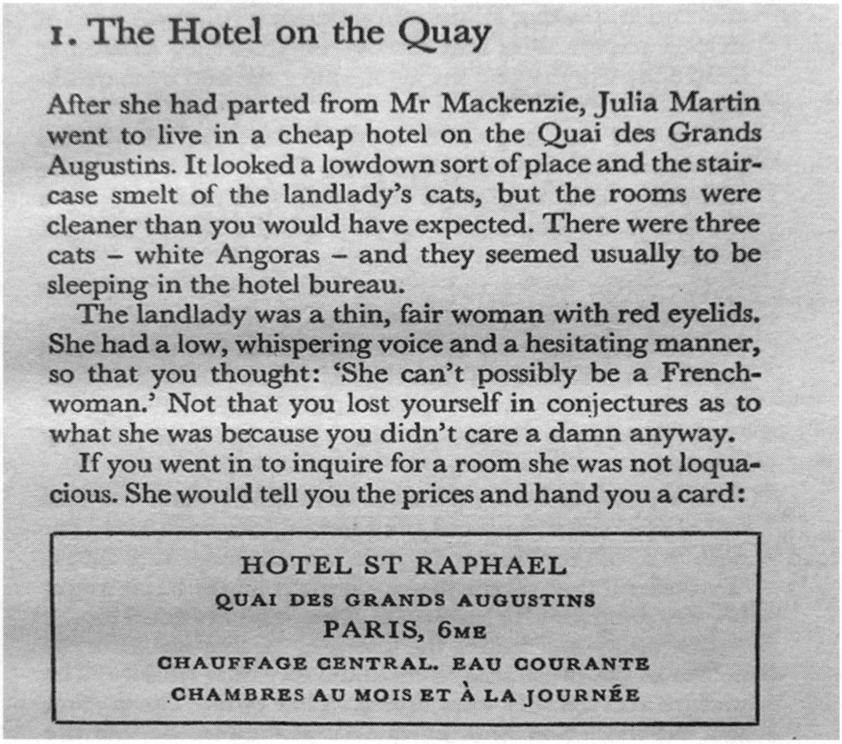

1. The Hotel on the Quay

After she had parted from Mr Mackenzie, Julia Martin went to live in a cheap hotel on the Quai des Grands Augustins. It looked a lowdown sort of place and the staircase smelt of the landlady's cats, but the rooms were cleaner than you would have expected. There were three cats – white Angoras – and they seemed usually to be sleeping in the hotel bureau.

The landlady was a thin, fair woman with red eyelids. She had a low, whispering voice and a hesitating manner, so that you thought: 'She can't possibly be a Frenchwoman.' Not that you lost yourself in conjectures as to what she was because you didn't care a damn anyway.

If you went in to inquire for a room she was not loquacious. She would tell you the prices and hand you a card:

> **HOTEL ST RAPHAEL**
> **QUAI DES GRANDS AUGUSTINS**
> **PARIS, 6ME**
> **CHAUFFAGE CENTRAL. EAU COURANTE**
> **CHAMBRES AU MOIS ET À LA JOURNÉE**

Fig 2: from Jean Rhys, After Leaving Mr Mackenzie, *Harmondsworth, Penguin, 1971*

68. Lefebvre, op. cit., p86-7.

interpenetrate one another and/or superimpose themselves upon one another'.[68] In Rhys the spatial style of her fiction bleeds into the hotel rooms of her characters, the sites of the city, and then into the wider national territories of her texts. Perhaps, then, it is this shifting between spaces that overlap that explains Rhys's absence from Benstock's map of the literary Left Bank; she inhabits no single space, just as her characters never quite dwell in Paris. But this only recapitulates a central point about the geography of the modernist city itself: that it is never a fixed entity, always a set of spaces with speculative histories to tell.

***

In a fascinating article in 1998, Chris GoGwilt offered an interpretation of three figures from the history of geography that stressed their relationship to ideas within literary and cultural modernism. His main focus is upon Halford Mackinder (over that of Friedrich Ratzel and Elisée Reclus) and the way in which his 'new geography' at the start of the twentieth century can be compared to certain modernist artists. GoGwilt summarises this argument when he writes that Mackinder's 'geography illustrates a formalist logic in the formation of geopolitics reminiscent of both the strategies of literary modernism and of

69. Chris GoGwilt, 'The Geopolitical Image: Imperialism, Anarchism, and the Hypothesis of Culture in the Formation of Geopolitics', Modernism/Modernity, 5, 3 (1998): p50.

the Freudian dreamwork'.[69] GoGwilt's argument is mainly concerned with the modernist and imperialist origins of the term 'geopolitics', and its relationship to the kind of 'logic of visualization' embodied in the geographical imagination of Mackinder. Here I just want to stress one element of what Mackinder termed the 'visualizing habit of mind', that is the way in which geographical spaces can be seen as textual spaces. GoGwilt quotes Mackinder from 1908 to illustrate this overlap between the two disciplines: 'A geography text should aim at literary form'.[70] What I have been discussing here, to an

70. Cited in Go Gwilt, ibid., p49, from Mackinder, The Development of Geographical Teaching Out of Nature-Study, 1908.

extent, reverses this focus: in discussing Rhys I have tried to explore the ways in which specific geographies shape literary texts. The *textual spaces* of their writings combine literary forms and social spaces in a manner similar to Soja's concept of 'Thirdspace', an idea that combines 'real and imagined places', or material spaces and imagined representations of space.[71] *After Leaving Mr Mackenzie* has thus been located within the cultural meanings of specific sites

71. See Edward W. Soja, Thirdspace: Journeys to Los Angeles and Other Real-and-Imagined Places Oxford, Blackwell, 1996, pp6-11.

within Paris. Interrogating these sites reveals interesting questions of gender and representation - particularly the contrast between the 'official' sites of bohemian Paris and the anonymous places sought by Julia Martin. And, in turn, these material spaces, via a consideration of Benstock's map, can illuminate aspects of the spatial style of Rhys's fiction. Such hermeneutic steps, considering the interlinking of material and metaphorical spaces, tracing issues of representation and power, the role of maps, and the impact upon spatial forms of particular geographies, are all crucial components of the practice of a critical literary geography. It is this attention to spatial forms, power and resistance, and to modes and histories of geographical representation that marks out a critical literary geography from one which is merely interested in how literature represents space.

Over the last century or so literary criticism has often been identified with forms of historical interpretation, whether in the guise of Marxism, New Historicism, or other practices of literary history. Criticism linking texts to social and political determinants has also been much in evidence - we can note feminism, gender and queer theory, postcolonial studies, and the re-emergence of the sociology of literature in the form of book history. We are now witnessing a spatial and geographical turn in diverse fields of literary criticism. One proponent of this turn is found in the feminist critic Susan Stanford Friedman's notion of 'geopolitical literacy', which she summarises as work which asks 'for an interrogation of how the geopolitical axis informs and inflects all cultural formations and identities, our own as well as that of others. It requires spatial, geographical thinking to complement temporal, historical analysis'.[72] Friedman's 'locational feminism' is thus 'a form of geographical imperative, requiring vigilant attention to the meanings of space as they intersect with the meanings of time in the formations of identity'.[73]

As Friedman notes, if we have a term for critiquing forms of ahistorical thought, then why don't 'we have a category of critique for the ageographical or the alocational?'[74] All texts are written, published and read *somewhere* - and it is these many 'somewheres' that now require further attention. Writers live, leave or travel through specific places that mark their perception of the world and many texts represent quite directly places, spaces, cities, nations and islands; thinking through the nature of the impact of these environments upon texts, in ways that can be added to existing social and historical modes of interpretation is clearly one way forward for a critical literary geography. I would not wish to be exclusionary and programmatic about what might constitute this practice, but I do think that there should be a more careful attention to the use of a geographically inflected terminology in literary studies. As I have shown when discussing Rhys, this critical literary geography is likely to be materialist in the sense that it analyses the spatial histories revealed in texts, and seeks to use this geographical knowledge to understand further the meanings of texts. Often those meanings relate to questions around space and power, as seen in Rhys's depiction of the gendered geography of the city. Or, as Edward Said once put it, just 'as none of us is outside or beyond geography, none of us is completely free from the struggle over geography'.[75] Fundamental to a critical literary geography, as to the engagement with representations of space and the impact of lived places upon writers, is the following question: how do all of these spatial dimensions affect what the texts means, and how we interpret it? If a critical literary geography can offer new and refreshing answers to this perennial problem for critical practice then it will be worth pursuing further.

72. Susan Stanford Friedman, *Mappings: Feminism and the Cultural Geographies of Encounter*, New Jersey, Princeton University Press, 1998, p130.

73. Ibid., p110.

74. Ibid.

75. Said, op. cit., p6.

Thanks to the other panellists at the IBG/RGS Conference session in 2003 for stimulating discussion on the day and to Richard Phillips for organising it. Thanks also to Moya Lloyd for helpful comments and suggestions on this paper.

1. Laura Chrisman, *Postcolonial Contraventions: Cultural readings of race, imperialism, and transnationalism*, Manchester, Manchester University Press, 2003, p120.

2. In 2003, Harcourt, Heinemann's owners, announced that no further new titles would be published in the *AWS*, effectively confirming the transformation of the *AWS* series into a backlist series.

3. See A.R. Yesufu, 'Mbari publications: a pioneer Anglophone African publishing house', *African Publishing Record*, 8, 2 (1982): 53-57; J. Rea, 'Aspects of African publishing, 1945-74', *African Publishing Record*, 1, 2 (1975): 145-149; P. Ripken, 'African Literature in the Literary Market Place outside Africa', *African Publishing Record*, 17, 4 (1991): 289-291. Also W. Griswold, *Bearing Witness: Readers, writers, and the novel in Nigeria*, Princeton, Princeton University Press, 2000; B. Lindfors, *Long drums and canons: Teaching and researching African literatures*, Trenton NJ, Africa World Press, 1995. For a re-consideration of African textualities during colonialism, see G. Desai, *Subject to Colonialism: African self-fashioning and the colonial library*, Durham, Duke University Press, 2001.

DISSEMINATING AFRICA:
BURDENS OF REPRESENTATION AND THE *AFRICAN WRITERS SERIES*

Clive Barnett

Laura Chrisman has recently argued that existing analyses of the circulation of postcolonial culture tend to presume the existence of a singular 'West' or 'First World'.[1] She suggests that the category of the West needs to be broken down into its 'national constituents' in order to better understand the transnational reception histories of postcolonial culture. While sympathetic to this argument, I want to focus on a case study that does not fit easily into the national frame that Chrisman suggests differentiate between contexts. The example is the well-known *African Writers Series* (*AWS*), launched by Heinemann Educational Books (HEB) in 1962 with publication of the paperback edition of Chinua Achebe's *Things Fall Apart*.[2]

The *AWS* is synonymous with the development of a canon of post-colonial African literary writing in English. It was not, as is sometimes supposed, the first such initiative. It had important precursors, in particular the example of Mbari publications in Nigeria. Furthermore, the *AWS* was only one of a number of metropolitan publishing initiatives that aimed to project a distinctively post-colonial African imagination into circuits of international public culture from the 1960s onwards. Longman emulated the *AWS* with its own highly successful *African Literature Series*. Penguin's *African Library* was a more explicitly political enterprise, publishing historical and contemporary analysis of African transformations. And in due course, the success of the *AWS* spurred the development of Heinemann's successful *Caribbean Writers Series*, as well as the less successful attempts at developing an *Arab Writers Series*. It is also important to underscore the existence of thriving popular literary publics in Africa, existing in tandem with local publishing sectors. The most famous of these is the so-called *Onitsha* market literature of Nigeria.[3]

The *AWS* was distinctive in mediating between the formation of the concept of African Literature and the growth of institutionalised literary pedagogy in post-colonial African states. As Kwame Anthony Appiah puts it, the *AWS* 'constitutes in the most concrete sense the pedagogical canon of Anglophone African writing'.[4] According to Appiah, the *AWS* belonged to a moment that 'has a profound political significance' because it provided a space in which Africans could write for and about themselves.

When it was first established, the *AWS* had a dual commitment. First, the Series aimed to establish itself as the publisher of record for modern African writing by re-publishing and keeping in print previously published

African texts. This included editions of classics such as *Equano's Travels* (*AWS* No. 10, 1967), Sol Plaatje's *Mhudi* (*AWS* No. 201, 1978), and Thomas Mofolo's *Shaka* (*AWS* No. 229, 1983), as well as collections of oral mythologies (for example, *The Origin of Life and Death: African Creation Myths*, U. Beier (ed), *AWS* 23, 1966). It also involved publishing extensive book-length collections of short stories, plays, poems, and later, innovative anthologies of women's writing (such as *Unwinding Threads: Writing by Women in Africa*, C. Bruner (ed), *AWS* No. 256, 1983).

Second, the Series pioneered the publication of original works in English by African writers. This included original works by novelists, including Achebe, Ngugi wa Thiong'o, Ayi Kwei Armah, Wole Soyinka, and Cyprian Ekwensi. In the 1970s, *AWS* was instrumental in publishing Bessie Head's work when no other British or US publisher would do so. The *AWS* also rapidly turned to translating works from other major languages into English, such as Ferdinand Oyono's *Houseboy* from French (*AWS* No. 29, 1966), and later Naguib Mahfouz's *Miramar* from Arabic (*AWS* No. 197, 1978). But publication of original work was not restricted to fiction. Right from the very start, the *AWS* also published writings by leading figures from the movements for African independence. No. 4 in the series, published in 1962, was Kenneth Kaunda's political biography, *Zambia Shall be Free*. Mandela's *No Easy Walk to Freedom*, first published by HEB in 1965, was reissued as No. 123 in the Series. Steve Biko's *I Write What I Like* (*AWS* No. 217, 1979), Ngugi's prison diary *Detained* (*AWS* No. 240, 1981), and Amilcar Cabral's collected writings on culture and politics (*Unity and Struggle*, *AWS* No. 198, 1980) all became staples of the *AWS*'s list.

There are two things worth noting about this range of titles. Firstly, the *AWS* was instrumental in making available a durable canon of African writing, that is, with keeping titles in print after their initial publication. Secondly, even from the above selection of titles, one gets a clear impression of just how catholic was the definition of 'Africa' that the *AWS* worked with. The *African Writers Series* list was not racially exclusive - its earliest works included writings by leading 'Coloured' South Africans like Alex La Guma, Richard Rive, and later Bessie Head, as well as translations from Arabic traditions. Nor was the Africaness of the Series defined solely by language or region. As the inclusion of political writings indicates, the *AWS* was strongly identified with a broad politico-cultural movement that asserted African political independence and cultural autonomy.

I examine the active role of publishers in laying the basis for more formal canon-formation through criticism and pedagogy. As already noted, Heinemann's *AWS* was critical in this respect because it made texts available and kept them available over time at affordable prices. Previously, books by African writers not only struggled to find publishers in the West, but even those which did get published often fell out of print very quickly. The story of *AWS*'s role in enabling subsequent processes of canon-formation is partly a story about commodification. But it is also a story about educational

4. K.A. Appiah, *In My Father's House: Africa in the Philosophy of Culture*, Oxford, Oxford University Press, 1992, p55.

5. See A. Hill, *In Pursuit of Publishing*, London, John Murray in association with Heinemann Educational Books, 1988; C. Achebe, *Home and Exile*, Edinburgh, Canongate, pp49-54; H. Chakava, 'Publishing Ngugi: The challenge, the risk, the reward', in C. Cantalupo (ed), *Ngugi wa Thiong'o: Texts and Contexts*, Trenton NJ., Africa World Press, 1995, pp13-28; H. Chakava, *Publishing in Africa: One man's perspective*, Bellagio Studies in Publishing, 1996; J. Currey, 'Interview', *African Book Publishing Record*, 5, 4 (1979): 237-239; J. Currey, 'African Writers Series – 21 years on', *African Book Publishing Record*, 11, 1 (1985): 11; A. Maja-Pearce, 'In pursuit of excellence: Thirty years of the Heinemann African Writers' Series', *Research in African Literatures*, 23, 4 (1992): 125-132; V. Unwin, and J. Currey, 'The African Writers Series celebrates 30 years', *Southern African Review of Books*, (March/April 1993), pp3-6.

6. Ngugi wa Thiong'o, *Moving the Centre*, London, James Currey, 1993.

7. G. Griffiths, 'Documentation and Communication in Post-colonial Societies: the Politics of Control', in A. Gurr (ed), *Year's Work in English Studies*, (1996): 21-37; G. Griffiths, 'Writing,

institutions, state-formation, and dispersed practices of cultural evaluation. Drawing on empirical materials from the editorial archives of the *AWS*, held at the University of Reading, I argue that publishing is best understood as a set of distinctively geographical practices that involve the *dissemination* of ideas and materials, and the articulation of texts with multiple contexts. By looking in particular at the interactions between publishing, commodification, and educational networks, I argue that the public spaces that the *AWS* helped constitute were never straightforwardly contained at a national scale, either actually or imaginatively.

REINTERPRETING THE AFRICAN WRITERS SERIES

Existing accounts of the *AWS* depend on a fairly limited evidential basis, primarily the first-hand biographical reflections of key players in the rise and development of the series.[5] Academic analysis of the Series is also characterised by a particular model of how cultural power is exercised and reproduced. It turns on a fairly simple understanding of the differential economic and ideological power between a 'core' region of Western Europe and North America and the 'periphery', the rest of the literary world. This dependency model is, of course, quite explicitly developed in the cultural theory of Ngugi wa Thiong'o, himself a key figure in the history of the *AWS*.[6] It also underlies Griffiths' discussion of patronage in the history of the *AWS*.[7] Griffiths interprets the role of publishers in shaping the styles of narrative that have come to represent Africa as a form of illegitimate control over what can be said. This implicit theory of cultural dependency also informs the self-consciously 'materialist' analysis of postcolonial publishing more broadly.[8] The general critical claim of these sorts of accounts is that publishing does a certain type of *ideological* work, always only ever reproducing a pre-existing set of relations of appropriation, dependence, and extraversion whose history stretches back to colonialism. Behind these analyses there lies an unstated notion that the integrity of writing, literature, and thought is compromised by its dependence on various intermediaries - publishers, printers, educationalists, reviewers and so on - who are always presented as agents for enforcing a zero-sum exchange of literary value from the periphery to the centre. In these accounts, the transnational circulation of postcolonial culture only ever reproduces neo-colonial relations of dependence.

Griffiths' account of the *AWS* identifies a continuity between colonial and post-independence relationships of patronage precisely because his focus is primarily on the relationship between authors and publishers. He suggests that the operations of publishers like Heinemann were 'as directive and invasive as that of missionary presses and the colonial publishing institutions'.[9] In contrast, I want to argue that the work of a series like the *AWS* is not primarily ideological at all, but rather more practical. It lies in the generation of new types of public space. Rather than thinking that commercialised postcolonial publishing simply reproduced the earlier role of mission presses, Karen Barber suggests that the shift from mission-based publishing to commercially published writing in the post-independence period institutes a fundamental break in the dimensions of African public cultures, by laying the basis for the creation of new forms of spatially and temporally extended public communication. The commercialisation of African writing, whether under the auspices of African or international publishers, is pivotal to this innovation, in so far as commercialised and commodified publishing made texts available through the market to anyone and everyone irrespective of identity, qualifications, institutional affiliation or status: 'it is the anonymity, the extensivity and the presumed equivalence of persons that makes an audience a public'.[10]

I want to trace the outlines of the publics summoned into existence by publishing initiatives like the *AWS*. By emphasising the internal relationship between commodification, textuality, and publicness, I argue that the determinate contexts through which postcolonial African writing has circulated are certainly not singular and undifferentiated, but nor have they ever been straightforwardly national either. Rather than simply presuming a map of distinct national contexts, the history of the formation and transformation of the *AWS* over forty years is better understood by reference to Paul Gilroy's intuition of the 'rhizomatic, fractal structure of the transcultural'.[11] Publishing will emerge as having been crucial in defining the horizons of expectation and interpretation through which the significance of African textualities are inscribed in geographically dispersed and socially fractured contexts of reception.

There are two features of the institutional and discursive complex of post-colonial African print cultures that distinguish them from the standard narrative of secularisation, democratisation, and seamless nationalism derived from an inward-looking interpretation of European modernity. The first of these is the legacy of ethnocentric conceptions of writing in Western thought.[12] There is a long history of assuming that writing is merely a visual substitute for speech, and in turn assuming that speech is the medium for self-conscious expression. During the colonial encounter, this understanding was instrumental in the denigration of African cultures, which were understood as standing outside of history on account of the projected absence of the means of historical memorialisation itself.[13] In fundamental respects, as Gates suggests, 'writing' is a racialised category in the self-understanding of the trajectory of the modern West. The deployment of the hierarchical opposition of oral and written culture in the denigration of African societies casts a long shadow over more contemporary practices of cultural expression. Not least, it has led to writing, and in particular literary writing, being identified as the privileged medium for the assertion of an African presence on the stage of international cultural exchange. It is this legacy that African writers consistently sought to overcome throughout the twentieth century. It is therefore no surprise that the most important and founding publishing

literacy and history in Africa', in M. H. Msiska and P. Hyland (eds), *Writing and Africa*, Harlow, London, 1997, pp139-158; G. Griffiths, *African Literatures in English: East and West*, Harlow, Longman, 2000.

8. G. Huggan, *The postcolonial exotic: marketing the margins*, London, Routledge, 2001.

9. G. Griffiths, 'Writing', op. cit., p153.

10. K. Barber, 'Audiences and the book in Africa', *Current Writing*, 13, 2 (2001): 16.

11. P. Gilroy, *The Black Atlantic*, London, Verso, 1993, p4.

12. See J. Derrida, *Of Grammatology*, Baltimore, Johns Hopkins University, 1976; R. Harris, *The Origins of Writing*, London, Duckworth, 1986.

13. C. Barnett, 'Impure and worldly geography: The Africanist discourse of the Royal Geographical Society', *Transactions of the Institute of British Geographers*, 23 (1998): 239-251; H.L. Gates Jr, 'Criticism in the jungle', in H.L. Gates Jr (ed), *Black Literature and Literary Theory*, London, Methuen, 1984; H.L. Gates Jr, *Figures in Black: Words, signs, and the 'racial' self*, Oxford, Oxford University Press,

1987; C. Miller,
*Blank Darkness:
Africanist Discourse in
French*, Chicago,
University of
Chicago Press, 1985;
V.Y. Mudimbe, *The
Idea of Africa*,
Bloomington,
Indiana University
Press, 1994.

14. V.Y. Mudimbe,
*The Surreptitious
Speech: Présence
Africaine and the
Politics of Otherness*,
1947-87, Chicago,
University of
Chicago Press, 1992.

15. M. Mamdami,
Citizen and Subject,
Princteon, Princeton
University Press,
1996.

16. C.R. Larson, *The
Ordeal of the African
Writer*, London, Zed
Books, 2001.

venture in African writing in the early part of the twentieth century was called *Présence Africaine*.[14]

If one legacy of colonialism for postcolonial African print cultures is this ideological one, then the second is more straightforwardly material, and follows from the distinctive sociology of literacy in modern Africa. As an instrument of colonial governmentality, print culture was not deployed as a medium of mass literacy, nor for the integration of whole populations into shared national imaginaries. In the case of British colonial Africa, print culture was deployed as a medium of differential, exclusionary colonial subject-formation restricted to a small proportion of the total population, consistent with a broader rationale of governmentality that distinguished between citizen and subject, urbanity and rurality.[15]

These twin legacies - of ethnocentric understandings of writing and representation, and of highly uneven and socially differentiated access to literacy - help to account for the precarious position of the African writer, whose position is defined by a double marginalisation: marginalised with respect to Western canons and publics by virtue of the legacy of racialised and ethnocentric constructs of writing, literature, and narrative; and marginalised with respect to African publics by virtue of the socio-economic-cultural privilege ascribed to and made accessible by print literacy and Western ideals of high culture.[16]

This, then, is the broad geo-historical context in which the *AWS* was initially conceived. The history of the *AWS* indicates that the received understanding of print culture and modernised nation building might require revision. The Series was specifically launched to develop original writing *by* Africans, thereby redefining the role of Western-based publishers, who had previously concentrated on publishing Western sourced writing for restricted African audiences. The explicit objective behind the Series was to develop and take advantage of two potential but as yet unrealised markets for published materials: on the one hand, to make writing by Africans available to Western markets on a more sustained basis; on the other hand, and crucial to the whole concept of the Series, to steal a march on other publishers by anticipating the emergence of new markets for African writing which would follow in the wake of independence, with curriculum reform leading to an imperative to supplement, if not replace, a canon of European and North American literature with African writing. In this second respect, the *AWS* served an important role in facilitating the development of a pan-African discourse of postcolonial cultural nationalism. This discourse was, nonetheless, an elite-led cultural movement, one that was (initially at least) dependent on the continued dominance of international publishing capital. This is to underscore the specific position of the AWS within a highly selective, elite complex of education, examination, and public debate largely restricted to specific strata of African post-colonial societies and states. As part of the project of post-independence nation building, the circulation of the *AWS* was largely contained within a pattern of social relations and institutional infrastructures in which literacy has continued to function as a key dimension of socio-economic differentiation.

The key point here is that, as an enterprise which explicitly aimed to project writing by Africans into the literary publics of the metropolitan Anglophone world as well as the educational publics of soon-to-be and newly independent African states, this effort at inscribing an African presence also necessarily involved a re-*inscription of difference*. This is not to do with the bad faith of publishers, or the lack of moral or political backbone of African writers. It is important to recognise this pattern of asserting presence and inscribing difference as a structural feature of the contexts in which the Series, as well as its imitators and competitors, have operated.

There are three axes around which this re-inscription of difference is hinged: the question of language; the question of genre; and the distinctive qualities of African reading publics. The first of these - the language question - is the dominant theme in African literary criticism. Ngugi wa Thiong'o's position is central to this debate. From the 1970s onwards, Ngugi chose to write his novels in his own language, Gikuyu, and then translate them into English, in line with his argument that African writers should use African languages to reach broader audiences and thereby ensure their wider relevance. Other writers and critics, including Achebe, Irele, and Soyinka, argue in favour of the Calibanistic strategy of appropriating the 'masters' tongue and 'writing-back'.

These debates often focus on the 'choice' of language by writers. Ngugi's position shifts attention to the broader structural determinants that often impose a choice upon writers, and this has the advantage of bringing into focus the important role of publishers in this set of debates. Nonetheless, it is in turn possible to overestimate this influence. As we have already seen, Griffiths interprets the relationships between writers and publishers in terms of patronage, arguing that the publishing imperative that lay behind the *AWS* was 'as strong in its controlling influence as any of the previous patronages of the colonial period'.[17] This claim is based on the assumption that Heinemann were concerned solely with publishing books in English. Griffiths asserts that there was an 'almost exclusive concentration on writing in the ex-colonial languages and seeming lack of interest in commissioning translations of works originally written in the indigenous languages'.[18]

In fact, the HEB archives show that the *AWS*'s editors were very active in pioneering the translation of works from Gikuyu, Kiswahili, Ndebele, Shona, Yoruba, Amharic. And furthermore, in the mid-1970s, they made significant efforts to develop a Series of Swahili translations of *AWS* originals. This initiative proved difficult to sustain, however, for reasons that indicate the extent to which the influence of publishers was significantly constrained by the *AWS*'s commercial dependence on educational prescriptions. HEB in London felt that publishing in vernacular African languages did not sell unless books were prescribed.[19] Thus, the proposed series in Swahili was 'a very risky market' because it was difficult to keep costs down in the absence

17. G. Griffiths, *African Literatures*, op. cit., p84.

18. G. Griffiths, 'Writing', op. cit., p153.

19. Letter, James Currey to Robert Markham, 9 March, 1972, University of Reading, Department of Archives and Manuscripts, HEB File NO. 6/8.

20. Letter, James Currey to D. Bolt, 14 August 1978, University of Reading, Department of Archives and Manuscripts, HEB File No. 6/6.

21. See C.L. Miller, *Nationalists and Nomads: Essays on Francophone African Literature and Culture*, Chicago, University of Chicago Press, pp120-121; A.O. Amoko, 'The problem of English literature: canonicity, citizenship, and the idea of Africa', *Research in African Literatures*, 32, 4 (2001): 19-43.

of a realistic expectation that books would be adopted on examination curricula.[20] These initiatives ran afoul of the reluctance of African states to use books in vernacular languages in their education systems, preferring to construct a version of nationalist education in which English (or other colonial languages) was privileged as the medium of instruction.[21]

The second area in which difference is re-inscribed in and through the mediums for making African writing present in the world is around the question of genre. As we have already seen, the *AWS* was explicitly set up as a series of African *writing*, not just literature. Titles in the Series included separate designs for novels (orange, famously copying Penguin's distinctive branding); for non-fiction (blue); and for poetry and plays (green). Nonetheless, it is for canonising the Anglophone African novel for which the *AWS* is most well known, and upon which its financial viability has largely depended (and in particular, Achebe's novels, followed by those of Ngugi). Since the 1980s, as the *AWS* shifted steadily away from publishing original titles to becoming a backlist series, almost all the new titles and in-print backlist have consisted of novels. This is significant because the novel is a distinctively European cultural form, in its origins at least. As with the question of language, and more so perhaps than with other non-European literatures, the politics of genre has also attracted much critical soul searching. The key question is whether the narrative rhythms, forms, and textures of what has come to be called 'orature' can be adequately transcribed into the rhythms, forms, and textures of the novel. More specifically, the *AWS* in particular has often been associated with the predominance of a particular style of novelistic discourse, one that is overwhelmingly realist in its aesthetic dispositions. The dominant aesthetic of the Series eschewed the styles of high literary modernism which constituted the taken for granted canon of 'Literature' in the West. This contributed to the reception of this tradition of writing as bearing a distinctively mimetic burden of representation that supposedly characterised Africa writing.

Moving away from the formal features of texts as such, the third dimension along which difference has been re-inscribed through the circulation of African writing in English relates to the broader question of reading publics and reading cultures. A recurring theme in commentaries on the dilemmas faced by both local and international publishers looking to extend markets in African contexts is the idea that, while reading publics certainly exist and even thrive, there is a tradition of 'serious' literature being *read for achievement*, as distinct from being *read for pleasure*.[22] There is, of course, an implicit evaluation contained in this analysis but it does nevertheless pinpoint one of the fundamental conditions for the establishment of reading publics for 'serious' English language writing in post-colonial African societies, namely the dependence on educational markets, directly connected to levels of state funding, curriculum design, and examination procedures. The *AWS* exemplifies this relationship, since it was launched and sustained for the first twenty years of its history as a

22. W. Griswold, *Bearing Witness*, op. cit., pp88-119.

series providing affordable and accessible paperback books for adoption in the reformed secondary and tertiary institutions of newly independent states such as Nigeria, Ghana, Kenya, and Uganda.

Here, then, we see the theme of contradictory conditions of possibility and limitation. The projection of a new tradition of Anglophone African literature was enabled by an alliance of Western publishing capital and state-funded educational reform in Africa. The *AWS* was, after all, an initiative of Heinemann Educational Books, a subsidiary of William Heinemann, and it remains, after successive takeovers in the 1980s and 1990s, embedded within an educational publishing conglomerate. Most of HEB's business when the *AWS* was first initiated and growing remained in educational textbooks, not in mainstream trade publishing for a general readership. The commercial significance of the *AWS* lay less in its being a source of high revenue or profits itself, but rather as an important 'loss-leader' for this broader educational publishing programme. Over the years, the *AWS* has become an important source of credibility for Heinemann: 'The *AWS* is a backlist led list. Chinua Achebe is perceived as the most important author on our list by the outside world. As publishers of this list we have entry to African educational markets and a kudos that other multinationals do not have'.[23] This status of the *AWS* served as one argument for continuing to publish new titles in the series in the 1990s, even as the margins on the series were increasingly squeezed:

> As the publisher of the African Writers Series we have entry into Ministries and a reputation and esteem in Africa which far exceeds our current market position. To stop publishing the series would have a huge negative effect and make entry into local publishing agreement much harder. We would be viewed as just another multinational but without the infrastructure and contacts that companies like Macmillan and Longman have.[24]

One consequence of the most important publisher of African literary writing being an educational publisher has been that this writing is constrained both positively and negatively to circulate through particular distribution networks of educational rather than general trade publishing, and this too has helped to reinforce a set of sedimented associations of African writing with didactic forms of storytelling and witness.

GEOGRAPHIES OF TEXTUALITY

The making present of writing in the world depends on the work of various intermediary devices that help to shape the horizons of meaning through which texts are made meaningful. The conventional interpretative vocabulary of 'text and context', whether used in literary studies, historiography, or historical geography, is shaped by a highly normative system of spatialised

23. Internal Memorandum on *AWS*, 1994, University of Reading, Department of Archives and Manuscripts, HEB File No. 56/6.

24. Memo, 'The African and Caribbean Writers Series Performance Analysis', 21 August 1996, University of Reading, Department of Archives and Manuscripts, HEB File No. 56/6.

25. See M. Curry,
The Work in the World,
Minneapolis,
University of
Minnesota Press,
1997.

26. C. Barnett,
'Deconstructing
context: Exposing
Derrida', *Transactions
of the Institute of
British Geographers*,
24 (1999): 277-293.

27. I. Hofmeyr, and
S. Nutall, with C.A.
Michael, 'The book
in Africa', *Current
Writing*, 13, 2 (2001):
7.

28. M. Warner,
*Publics and
counterpublics*, New
York, Zone Books,
2002.

29. G. Genette,
*Paratexts: thresholds of
interpretation*,
Cambridge,
Cambridge
University Press,
1997.

distinctions between insides and outsides.[25] One of the more peculiar things about this vocabulary of contextualisation is that it leads to the elision of perhaps the defining feature of modern print cultures, exemplified above all by the book, namely the portability of meaning.[26] The most important feature about the modern book is that it is extremely mobile. This connection between the concept of textuality, which emphasises movement and iteration, and the materiality of the book suggests a simple methodological principle: 'It is by following things in motion, exploring the conditions in which they circulate in space and time and according to different regimes of value, that we understand them to have a particular type of social potential'.[27]

It is by tracking the conditions of mobility of African writing that we can glean the ways in which the abstract potential of texts to convene publics is practically realised.[28] Publishing is a key mediating practice that links writers to markets and audiences, and helps to shape the formation of tastes and horizons of aesthetic expectation. In order to develop this argument, I want to focus on the role of a set of liminal devices (formal, material, and institutional) through which African writing was made available through the *AWS*. I develop this analysis of the dynamics of textual mobility by drawing on Gerard Genette's suggestive analysis of the 'conventions of the book', or what he calls *paratexts*.[29] By this, he means the whole set of devices through which 'texts', narrowly construed, are made available, or packaged. Genette's argument is that attention to these sorts of liminal devices - everything from titles to typeface and cover design, to reviews and criticism - thoroughly ruptures any lingering sense of there being a singular, idealised text that is differently packaged and differently interpreted according to different contexts. Rather, these devices and conventions are instrumental in making texts present in the world in the first place. Genette distinguishes between *peritexts* and *epitexts*. The former refers to those features that are proximate to the literary-textual object itself - illustrations, indexes, title pages, cover designs and so on. The latter refers to those more diffuse practices, such as reviewing, criticism, and pedagogy through which texts are inscribed into patterns of use. Genette's suggestion that these features help to cement a certain sort of contract between reader and text suggests that we should attend not so much to how texts are received in different contexts, but rather look at the *geographical constitution of reading-formations*. A reading-formation refers to:

30. T. Bennett,
'Texts in history: the
determinations of
readings and their
texts', in D. Attridge,
G. Bennington, and
R. Young (eds),
*Poststructuralism and
the Question of History*,
Cambridge,
Cambridge
University Press,
1987.

> a set of discursive and inter-textual determinations which organise and animate the practices of reading, connecting texts and readers in specific relations to one another in constituting readers as reading subjects of particular types and texts as objects-to-be-read in particular ways.[30]

I want to focus on the 'paratextual' practices of publishers in making texts available to different audiences through the manipulation of various rhetorical and material devices that facilitate the mobility of texts through multiple contexts. The 'peritextual' analysis that follows will show the importance of seemingly mundane devices such as cover design, glossaries, and illustrations in constituting and maintaining a particular type of publicness for the *AWS*. The 'epitextual' analysis looks not at the public world of reviews and criticism, but at the interactions between publishers and other organisational actors in negotiating the availability of African writing. In particular, it looks at the role that educational contexts have played in facilitating the growth of the *AWS*, both in Africa and in the West. The commercial viability of the *AWS* has depended on books being set, taught and examined in both secondary and tertiary institutions. We shall see that this relationship between commodification and education means that the institutions and conventions of legitimation that help shape the international publication of African writing are not, as might be supposed, solely located in the 'core' at all, but also include African elites, Ministries of Education, and publishers.

MAKING A DURABLE CANON

Genette's work on paratexts is just one example of a burgeoning field of book history that has focused attention on what D.F. McKenzie calls the 'expressive function of the material form of the book'.[31] McKenzie's focus is on typographic conventions; closer to our topic here, Laura Chrisman reads the back cover blurbs of South African novels to track the ways in which these works were framed for different audiences. It is this kind of attention to what one might call the phenomenology of the book - how the conventions of the book makes certain types of objects capable of appearing as bearers of meaning - that I want to bring to bear on aspects of the *AWS*.

The first thing to underscore is that the *AWS* was a paperback series. It reprinted previously published works and new titles, in both cases with the intention of providing texts in accessible forms - accessible in the basic sense of being in print, but also in terms of price. Historically, the paperback - portable and affordable - convenes a new sort of reading public. And in this respect, *AWS* was quite explicitly designed to emulate the example of Penguin Books.[32] The construction of the *AWS* as a *series* was crucial to establishing the long-term viability of the venture as a profitable publishing venture. This included colour-coding of the covers, and the numbering of each title in the series, as well as the inclusion of a full listing of all *AWS* titles on the inside covers of individual titles. From the outset, then, the Series was itself a hugely successful example of successful branding. The *AWS* became known simply as the 'Orange series', referring to the distinctive design of the fiction publications. In these ways, any given title was located within a broader frame, as part of a sequence of titles, and in the case of the *AWS*, as part of an explicitly programmatic publishing project - a project aimed at transforming the image of Africa held by Africans and non-Africans alike.

Another key feature of many *AWS* titles was the inclusion of illustrative

31. D.F. McKenzie, *Bibliography and the Sociology of Texts*, Cambridge, Cambridge University Press, 1999.

32. On Penguin, see S. Hare, (ed), *Penguin Portrait: Allen Lane and the Penguin Editors 1935-1970*, Harmondsworth, Penguin Books, 1995.

material in the text. Early titles had cover designs that were explicitly intended to illustrate the main topic or theme of the text. Many titles also included illustrations as front-pieces and between chapters. These illustrations tended to be distinctive line drawings or woodcut prints. Some books contained forewords and introductions; others contained glossaries explaining the meaning of phrases and words. *Things Fall Apart*, for example, contained a glossary when originally published. The latest *AWS* edition, published in 1996, also contains: an introductory essay on Igbo culture and history; an essay on Achebe's importance to African literature; maps; and suggested further reading. This clearly indicates the intended audience of schools and Universities. The presence of these sorts of supplementary devices in the *AWS* indicates the importance ascribed to making texts accessible to a wide readership. This is a constant concern of publishers and readers when assessing titles for the *AWS*. For example, commenting on a proposed collection of translated Swahili verse, one external reader recommended the inclusion of maps and tables in the book: 'Will readers in, say Lagos, Accra, Washington DC, be sufficiently familiar with location of Lamu, Mombasa, Tanga? Similarly, a table of the main historical events might also be useful as a point of reference for non-Swahili readers'.[33]

33. Memo, University of Reading, Department of Archives and Manuscripts, HEB File No. 15/3.

This sort of concern has two dimensions. On the one hand, it indicates the importance ascribed by publishers to ensuring that titles from one context would be readily accessible to audiences unfamiliar with those places. This was not simply a matter of making Western audiences familiar with African contexts. It was just as much about making texts from one part of Africa available to readers in other parts, a crucial concern given the overriding interest in having books set by Exam Boards. On the other hand, the use of this set of peritextual devices - illustrations, maps, glossaries, forewords and introductions - underscores the didactic intentionality inscribed into the very form of the *AWS* as a series of paperback books. This is not just a matter of providing context for the reader. It adds up to a set of conventions that helped to construct a horizon of expectations whereby one would read *AWS* books in order to *learn about other places*.

This was an important dimension of the marketing of the Series from the outset. In this respect, HEB received regular commendations from a range of organisations on the value of this way of using the books. For example, the Canadian University Service Overseas, responsible for the training and orientation of professional volunteers prior to their overseas assignments, regularly made large orders of *AWS* titles: 'We are most interested in new editions forthcoming which could be added to our library and individual copies sent to each of our perspective [sic] recruits destined for an assignments overseas'.[34] An Assistant US Secretary of State commended the series in these same terms: 'I frequently tell my colleagues and prospective travellers to African that there is no better way to know Africa today than to see it through the eyes of its contemporary authors'.[35]

34. Letter, 10 March 1969, University of Reading, Department of Archives and Manuscripts , HEB File No. 1/9.

35. Letter from R.M. Moore to James Currey, 31 January 1980, University of Reading, Department of Archives and Manuscripts, HEB File No. 24/12.

The *AWS* was produced, designed, and marketed according to a specifically didactic imperative, which meant that it was understood to bear a representative function in relation to African societies - speaking of them, certainly, but also claiming to speak *for* them too. This didactic/representative framing is sustained by a whole set of 'epitextual' and 'peritextual' practices that activated books as texts to be read in certain ways by readers with certain sorts of dispositions to learn about contemporary Africa. In this respect, the *AWS* also depended on the construction of a particular type of author-effect. In the original format of the series, each title contained on its back cover a picture of its author or editor, as well as a bibliographic portrait. The crucial signature is the country of origin of the author - a Nigerian, Ghanaian, Kenyan, and so on. These devices construct an author-effect that involves an ascription of the author as an authoritative witness to the traditions and transformations of the nation-states to which their works were attached. Importantly, this 'nationalising' effect is the condition of the construction of a pan-African canon of writing, in so far as the national form remained the dominant entry point into broader contemporary narratives of independence as the shared experience of postcolonial African societies. The importance of this feature - pinning authors down to particular places - has been reasserted more recently, as Heinemann refocused attention on the marketing value of the *AWS* as a *series* in the 1990s when redesigning the books:

> The back cover blurbs must mention the location of the novel and the nationality of the author. We have some back cover blurbs that never mention the location of the story or nationality of the author and yet we are supposed to be selling the African Writers Series. This does not help build the Series identity.[36]

The artifactual qualities of the *AWS* as a *series of books* both reflected and sustained the conditions through which this exercise in making Africa available was made possible - primarily in terms of a set of both formal and informal didactic or pedagogical objectives. They are examples of devices that open up texts to certain sorts of 'preferred readings' - as testimony, as representative, or as informative - inserting them into wider discourses in which the narrative forms of the novel in particular are attached to wider historical movements of anti-colonialism, national autonomy, and cultural self-consciousness.

The argument here is not that these devices - the peritexts that make 'texts' into 'books' - somehow determine the readings made of the text they surround. Rather, I would suggest that we can read them as *traces* of the institutional intentionalities that shape what is made publicly available, as well as of the practices of reading, judgement, and evaluation into which these objects were woven. So we need to consider the 'epitexts' of the *AWS* as well, the set of practices of interpretation that impinges upon 'the text' externally, at a distance, as it were. In this respect, there are two important

36. Memo on African and Caribbean Writers Series, 4 June 1992, University of Reading, Department of Archives and Manuscripts, HEB File No. 56/2.

37. C. Barnett, 'Constructions of apartheid in the international reception of the novels of J. M. Coetzee', *Journal of Southern African Studies*, 25 (1999): 287-301.

38. J. Guillory, *Cultural Capital: the problem of literary canon formation*, Chicago, University of Chicago Press, 1993.

39. A. Amoko, 'The problem of English literature', op. cit.

40. Letter from Keith Sambrook to Henry Chakava, 8 January 1981, University of Reading, Department of Archives and Manuscripts, HEB File No. 54/13.

41. Circular Letter No INS/80-35, Inspectorate, Ministry of Higher Education, Nairobi, 26 November 1980, University of Reading, Department of Archives and Manuscripts, HEB File No. 53/13.

dimensions to the shaping of the *AWS* as the medium for African writing in English. One might focus here on a metropolitan circuit of criticism and reviewing in literary reading publics located in Europe and North America.[37] But much more crucial to the history of the *AWS* is the role of educational public spheres, located in both Africa and in Europe and North America. As already noted, the original *raison d'etre* for the Series was to provide affordable paperbacks for a predominantly educational market in Africa with which Heinemann was already deeply involved. One of the determinate dimensions of the editorial process in the 1960s and 1970s was a set of calculations concerning whether titles were likely to be adopted as set texts by Examination Boards in African states.

The process of canonisation, in which Heinemann played a critical role through the construction of the *AWS* list, is not best thought of as a process of inclusion and exclusion, but more in terms of a process of selection by reference to explicit and implicit criteria.[38] In the case of the *AWS*, this selection process involved the ongoing negotiation of different, sometimes competing criteria adopted by those directly involved in the series, by HEB more broadly, as well as by educational actors and academics. But a critical point about the *AWS* is that the institutions of legitimation through which this canon of postcolonial writing was made present in Africa and worldwide were not located only in Western markets or institutions. A critical role was played by the ideologies of post-independence educational institutions in Africa, shaped by a firm commitment to shaping English literature programmes that reflected African writers, African idioms, and African realities, rather than slavishly following an inherited Western canon.[39] It was therefore crucial for HEB to keep track of the changing curricula and educational ethos in its key African markets. The *AWS* was originally established to take advantage of the increased demand for educational books that would follow from the expansion of secondary and tertiary school systems and the development of universal primary school programmes after independence. By the 1980s, the success of the *AWS* is illustrated by the predominance of *AWS* and HEB books on the set book list for the Kenya Certificate of Examination. These included setting at O Level: Ngugi''s *The River Between* (*AWS* No. 17, 1965); *Poems from East Africa* (*AWS* No. 96, 1971); Achebe's *No Longer at Ease* (*AWS* No. 3, 1963); Ngugi and Mugo's *The Trial of Dedan Kimathi* (*AWS* no. 191, 1976). While at A Level (alongside *Death of a Salesman* and *The Grapes of Wrath*) were set: Sembene Ousmane's *Gods Bits of Wood* (*AWS* No. 63, 1968); and Alex La Guma's *A Walk in the Night* (*AWS* NO. 35, 1968).[40]

This type of curriculum is indicative of a widespread policy of setting literature syllabuses that laid greater emphasis on African and Oral literature: 'This reflects the fundamental educational principle that education being a means of knowledge about ourselves, we must examine ourselves first and then radiate outwards and discover peoples and world's around us'.[41] The aim of syllabus design should, according to this approach, be to 'deepen the students' understanding and appreciation of Literature of the people of East Africa, Africa, the third world and the rest of the world in that order'.[42]

42. Ibid.

It was in this context that the *AWS* expanded in the 1960s, 1970s and early 1980s. It is worth noting that this ideology of Africanising literature syllabuses still depended on teaching through the medium of English. At the same time, it is also notable that in principle, and in the range of *AWS* books set (which included the Nigerian Achebe, the translation from French of Ousmane from Senegal, and the South African La Guma), the range of reference was not narrowly nationalistic or even regional, but covered the whole of sub-Saharan Africa. In this respect, the 'Africa' in the *African Writers Series* was never exclusive. Contrary to Phasanwe Mpe's argument,[43] race never wholly defined the *AWS* as a series of *Black* African writing, and the commitment to translation of originals ensured a broad coverage of writings from Francophone, Lusophone, and North African contexts as well.

43. P. Mpe, 'The role of the Heinemann African Writers Series in the development and promotion of African literature', *African Studies* 58, 1 (1999): 105-122.

A central criterion of selection for the *AWS* from the outset was, then, that books should have some chance of being prescribed by exam boards. This issue recurs when *AWS* editors considered whether to publish manuscripts. So, for example, the decision to translate and publish the Cameroonian novelist Oyono's *Houseboy*, written in local vernacular French, had to consider whether the language of the novel was 'too rough' and 'outspoken' for an educational book,[44] as well as the explicit treatment of sexual issues. These sorts of concerns recur all the way through into the 1990s. The consideration of whether to support the translation and publishing of Marlene van Niekerk's award-winning Afrikaans novel, *Triomf*, ran up against the concern that the 'presence of explicit sexuality in the text' would 'complicate its possibilities for classroom adoption'.[45] But it is important to acknowledge that these sorts of concerns were not hard and fast rules. The *African Writers Series* did publish *Houseboy*, and this in part reflected the fact that African Examinations Boards often turned out to be more tolerant of content than those in the UK. The important point is that the negotiation of educational criteria was a critical determinant of the editorial process shaping the development of the *AWS*'s list.

44. Letter from HEB to John Reed, University of Reading, Department of Archives and Manuscripts, HEB File No. 5/7.

45. Memo, HEB File No. 56/6.

Furthermore, HEB was not a passive actor in the process of the canonisation of its own headline series of African writing. From an early stage, HEB also developed a set of supporting publications designed to make the African writing knowable in specifically academic contexts. These included bibliographic guides, as well as a highly successful series of literary criticism. The aim was to help market the list. What developed as a result was a complimentary list of Heinemann critical editions, often written by African academics, about texts by African writers also often published by Heinemann. These supplementary publications contributed to making the *AWS teachable* in schools and Universities, providing a mechanism through which the presence of African texts in the marketplace could be translated, through the conventions of academic criticism and pedagogy, into an educational canon of African literature.

In short, it is impossible to underestimate the importance of educational reading-formations in the emergence of African writing as part of a canon of postcolonial literature. However, although the initial impetus behind the growth of the Series was African educational markets, from the late 1970s the focus of this educational context shifted fundamentally. An attempt to reframe the *AWS* as a general trade paperback list in the 1980s was not wholly successful, and in the 1990s the educational framing of the series was reasserted. Nonetheless, though African educational markets have continued to be important for the viability of the series, the last two decades have witnessed a discernible shift in the centre of gravity of the Series, both towards the United States and towards tertiary educational contexts. The next section explores the ways in which the publishers of the *AWS* negotiated this reorientation.

RELOCATING AFRICAN WRITING

For the first two decades of its existence, the AWS's primary market was in Africa. HEB practiced a dual pricing policy, according to which *AWS* titles were sold at lower prices in price-sensitive African educational markets compared to the UK and elsewhere. This policy depended on the ongoing vitality of education budgets in post-colonial African states. The cost structure of the *AWS* depended on the large bulk orders for African educational markets - a book being set by examinations boards was estimated to double the likely annual sales. Importantly, as we have already seen, the *AWS* was only one, relatively small, aspect of HEB's broader involvement as an educational publisher in African markets. HEB was, therefore, an exporting publisher, practicing a differential pricing policy for the *AWS* to sustain a market for schools, Universities and students. African countries increased the number of imported books in the 1960s and 1970s, with economies buoyed by vibrant commodity markets often supporting the expansion of education systems. By the late 1970s, however, this 'golden age' of educational publishing was under strain, as foreign exchange became increasingly expensive.[46] In the early 1980s following the devaluation of the Nigerian currency, the previously reliable African market for the *AWS* collapsed. The lack of foreign exchange meant that *AWS* books were more and more expensive, and domestic economic crisis meant that educational spending stalled or declined in HEB's established markets.

One effect of this period of market restructuring was the partial indigenisation of African literary publishing, as *AWS* increasingly entered into licensing agreements with African publishers - with David Philip in South Africa, for example, the Zimbabwe Publishing House, and Henry Chakava's East African Publishing House. These publishers licensed the rights of *AWS* books and printed and published them locally.[47] This tightening of the key African markets for the *AWS* also coincided with a succession of corporate takeovers that saw the ownership of Heinemann

46. John Watson to Keith Sambrook, 26 March 1980, University of Reading, Department of Archives and Manuscripts, HEB File No. 24/12.

47. This restructuring of markets and publishing sectors also helps account for the pattern found by Lindfors in his survey of literature syllabuses in African universities in the 1980s and 1990s. On the one hand, he found a predominance of *AWS* titles, but also found that this was a reflection of the dependence on old texts purchased a long time ago along with cheaper locally published books. Thus, the economics of publishing and book markets in Africa meant that an 'ideal syllabus' had given way to a 'practical syllabus' based on what books were available to be taught. The *AWS*, in this narrative at least, has become canonical by default. See B. Lindfors, 1995, pp45-60.

pass between four different companies in five years. During this period, James Currey, the main editorial force behind the growth of the series since the late 1960s, left Heinemann to establish his own eponymous imprint specialising in African history and social science. In the context of changing market conditions in Africa and a heightened imperative for the *AWS* to show its financial viability within an increasingly commercialised international publishing sector, the 1980s saw a shift in the geographical and institutional foci for the Series. With the relative decline of the African secondary and tertiary education market, Heinemann identified two new significant areas for potential growth: the general trade market in the UK, where it was felt that the *AWS* might be repositioned to take advantage of the growth of interest in 'Third World writing'; and in University markets in the United States in particular, where the growth of African-American Studies and Women's Studies programmes potentially provided an alternative public for the forms of African writing that the *AWS* had pioneered since the 1960s. The importance of the US market had been recognised from the 1970s onwards, where it was felt that the educational market provided an opportunity for HEB to market *AWS* titles for which it held the rights direct to this specialist market while avoiding competition with other editions of these titles held by US publishers. The diversification of the *AWS* list, to include new women writers like Bessie Head, for example, clearly supported this strategy.[48] From the 1980s onwards, this US College market became increasingly important in the positioning of the *AWS*.

A second issue that had been on the table since the 1970s, but which came to a head in the changed commercial situation of the 1980s, was the question of the design of *AWS* books. The African-based editors in Heinemann's offices in Ibadan and Nairobi held fast to the importance of retaining 'the Orange Series' as a marker of quality and as an instantly recognisable brand in African markets. The London based publishers, however, expressed concern over 'the message of the cover', worrying about the impression that the distinctive style of *AWS* books, primarily targeted at schools and universities in Africa, gave in UK trade publishing markets.[49] Following the incorporation of Heinemann in the mid-1980s into larger publishing conglomerates, a clear decision was taken to reposition the *AWS* in line with broader trends in general paperback markets in the UK and USA. This involved a shift to publishing the *AWS* in the larger 'B format', rather than the smaller 'A format' of the original list. In publishing and marketing terms, 'B-format' books are associated with prestige literary publishing. The idea was to make the books look like mainstream trade paperbacks, in order to capitalise on the *AWS*'s brand strength while also taking advantage of the revitalisation of paperback publishing being pioneered in the UK by Virago, Bloomsbury, Picador and others at this time. This repackaging of the *AWS* list was a response to a steady decline in sales, and was a clear expression of the sense that the future of the series depended on exploiting UK and US rights. The aim of the redesign was to

48. Letter from James Currey to Anna Cooper, 14 February 1978, University of Reading, Department of Archives and Manuscripts, HEB File No. 13/4.

49. Letter from James Currey, 8 October 1979, University of Reading, Department of Archives and Manuscripts, HEB File No. 24/12.

50. Letter from V. Unwin to Awoonor, 13 February 1986, University of Reading, Department of Archives and Manuscripts, HEB File No. 26/8.

51. Paper on the AWS/CWS, 21 November 1988, University of Reading, Department of Archives and Manuscripts, HEB File No. 56/2.

52. Ibid.

'revamp and repackage the series in a larger trade format with attractive four-colour covers and really try to make an impact on the UK/US markets'.[50]

The internal debate about the future of 'the Orange Series' was part of a reorientation towards new mainstream trade markets in the UK and US. This did not mean the abandonment of African markets, which have continued to be a central focus of *AWS* publishing. Indeed, in the new commercial circumstances of the 1980s, the *AWS* was recognised as an important asset that helped to maintain Heinemann's credibility as an educational publisher in Africa. This was a key reason to continue to publish the series: 'The *AWS* is the flagship of Heinemann International overseas. As major publishers of reading and literature the fame of the *AWS* is a great help in getting prescriptions [...] particularly in Africa'.[51] However, African educational markets were now primarily backlist markets, whereas in terms of selecting new titles, 'North America is the key influence in our choice of publishing'.[52]

The 1980s was, then, a period of considerable upheaval and uncertainty around the *AWS*, related to broader corporate and market shifts. An attempt was made to reposition the series as a mainstream trade list, but this was only partially successful. By the early 1990s, Heinemann's imperative was to refocus the *AWS* back on educational markets (along with the *Caribbean Writers Series* (*CWS*), now treated as one for publishing, distribution, and marketing terms):

> From 1986 we have been trying to establish a market presence that competes with Picador and Penguin B formats. The new covers and trade promotions have all supported this. This is good and we have definitely created a general trade presence but we need to compete on our terms, as specialists in our area, and not those set by the larger general paperback publishers. We now need to re-establish ourselves in the marketplace as specialists. We have the brand name and respect and we now need to concentrate on our core market.[53]

53. Memo on The African Writers Series, 1992, University of Reading, Department of Archives and Manuscripts, HEB File No. 56/6.

54. Memo on African and Caribbean Writers Series, 4 June 1992, University of Reading, Department of Archives and Manuscripts, HEB File No. 56/2.

55. Ibid.

This shift away from trade markets reflects a reassessment of *AWS*'s position as part of Heinemann's educational publishing strategy:

> As an African specialist publisher we have no competition, as mainstream international fiction publishers we fade into obscurity[54]

> we are niche publishers with a specialist product. We have lost many of our links with our core academic market chasing pipe dreams that each and every book that we publish, often by an unknown author, should be treated by the international literary world as if it were a new Chinua Achebe'.[55]

As this last statement suggests, one key aspect of the refocusing of the *AWS* was the recognition of the importance of its identity as a *series* to the successful publishing of new titles:

> We are not going to be successful publishing new unknown writers if they are introduced as individuals, they must carry the Series weight with them. The Series is a marketing tool and must always be seen as more important than its individual components.[56]

56. Ibid.

The early 1990s therefore sees further redesign of the Series as well as changes to the marketing strategy to re-establish the list with its core academic market, but this market is now increasingly located in the UK and especially the US University sector. This included a clear decision to focus the series on 'classics', by selectively pruning the backlist. This was an important shift in the rationality of the *AWS*. One of the original aims of the series was to act as the publisher of record for African writing, and this implied a strong commitment to maintaining backlist books in print even if sales dropped off. As early as 1980, a decision to put some titles out of print was made.[57]

57. *AWS* Policy, University of Reading, Department of Archives and Manuscripts, HEB File No. 39/1.

In the 1980s and 1990s, there was a two-step redefinition of the *AWS*'s publishing strategy. On the one hand, the *AWS*'s backlist is acknowledged as an important asset, but on the other hand, the continuing possibility of publishing new titles depended on streamlining the number of books on the backlist. Combined, these two factors see the *AWS* reoriented away from publishing original works, and towards publishing the canon of African writing. In the early 1990s, publication of new titles was limited to between four and six a year, and these had to stand a good chance of course adoption.[58] These should preferably be by new writers with a growing *academic* reputation, and it was also recognised that Heinemann should provide academic backup to new titles in the form of selections of critical essays. This in turn reflected a clear editorial decision to cultivate more direct feedback from academic networks:

58. Memo, 27 February 1992, University of Reading, Department of Archives and Manuscripts, HEB File No. 56/2.

> This feedback comes from the same people who are writing reports on our new books, organizing conferences which may pay to bring over our authors. They are the same people who are influencing student reading lists and writing academic critiques and generally contributing to the current body of thought on African literature.[59]

59. Memo on African and Caribbean Writers Series, 4 June 1992, University of Reading, Department of Archives and Manuscripts, HEB File No. 56/2.

These successive repositionings of the *AWS*, while clearly determined in 'the last instance', as it were, by the commercial considerations of Heinemann, were also overdetermined by the structural features of the list as a brand and as a 'loss-leading' asset in educational markets in Africa, the UK and Europe, and North America. In short, the commercial viability of publishing new titles, and of maintaining a backlist of classic titles, was in large part shaped by non-commercial, non-economic factors to do with curriculum design, canon-formation, and pedagogical trends.

This process of repositioning, redesigning, and repackaging the *AWS* involved different actors at Heinemann in the negotiation of different commercial and 'aesthetic' imperatives. And in turn, these different imperatives mapped onto the problem of reconciling the imperatives of geographically distinctive markets. So, for example, Heinemann's US operation, an increasingly powerful voice in shaping the *AWS* in the 1980s and 1990s, strongly favoured 'Americanising' the series, in terms of the selection of authors and advisors, sharing printing costs, and selecting titles that fit into a hybrid 'Trade + College' market. Heinemann UK favoured retaining the *AWS* as a UK-based list, on the grounds that the question of what would sell in African school markets remained a key to the success of the list, and it was the UK publisher that could take advantage of what was called its 'ex-colonial' profile and links with African and Caribbean markets.[60] Marketing of the fortieth anniversary of the series in 2002 reaffirmed the African market as core to the lists' future viability. There is, then, no once-and-for-all shift from an African-focused series to a UK and US based series, but rather a shift of emphasis in terms of editorial procedures. One key issue to underline is that the ongoing restructuring of the *AWS* list in the 1990s remains embedded in educational circuits of both economic and cultural capital. The refocusing on 'core' educational markets in the early 1990s after the experiment with trade publishing in the late 1980s clearly illustrates the key paradox of the success of the *AWS* in making African writing a 'presence in the world'. On the one hand, the success of this series over its first two decades depended on the combination of educational publishing expertise at Heinemann and educational expansion in African markets. This in turn established the brand value of the Series, and the asset value of the backlist rights, for Heinemann as it was restructured from the 1980s onwards. The flip-side of this success has been that the ongoing viability of the AWS has depended upon it being contained within institutionally specific circuits that constrict the circulation of titles to broader, non-specialist markets and publics (although, of course, *AWS* has also played an important part in establishing the possibility for non-*AWS* African authors and titles to enjoy success in these markets and publics).

If one of the costs of the success of the *AWS* has been this channelling within specialist educational publics, then a related aspect of this has been the reinforcement of the characteristic representative framing of the list. The refocusing on core educational markets has been associated with a clear definition of the strength of the list in this sector: 'Sell the pan-African appeal of the authors so that we can say we represent the continent'.[61] Marketing books to new audiences in US colleges and universities has, therefore, reaffirmed the representative framing for *AWS* (and *CWS*) titles: 'The books must be clearly definable as African or Caribbean and fit in with the experiences of the country'.[62] The criteria for publication in the *AWS* and *CWS* defined in the 1990s emphasised the idea that books should be representative of an area, and that while novels need not be set in Africa, nor necessarily authors be African, they

60. Agenda for the IAH Literature meeting, 7 September 1995, University of Reading, Department of Archives and Manuscripts, HEB File No. 56/6.

61. Memo on The African Writers Series, 1992, University of Reading, Department of Archives and Manuscripts, HEB File NO. 56/6.

62. The African and Caribbean Writers Performance Analysis, 21 August 1996, University of Reading, Department of Archives and Manuscripts, HEB File No. 56/6.

did need to convey a clear 'African perspective' and be based on a strong experience of African situations. Diasporic forms, in turn, were to be considered the exception.[63] Above all, this reflects not only the criterion that books should be suitable for secondary or tertiary education adoption, but the acknowledgement that the market value of *AWS* books continued to depend on them being constructed in strongly representative terms. The books

> must be able to be marketed as college texts, e.g. for Women's Studies, Post colonial studies, Commonwealth Literature, Anthropology, History, Religion, Politics, Afro American studies. They must not be too long. They must not be too expensive.[64]

What is most significant about such criteria is the clear recognition that the market for *AWS* and *CWS* lists extends well beyond Literature programmes, into both identity-based pedagogical programmes (Women's Studies, African-American Studies) and into History, Anthropology and other social sciences. And in the case of both of these markets, it is the framing of *AWS* books as *representative* - speaking of Africa, speaking for Africa, and speaking as African - that is the source of their entwined cultural and economic value.

BURDENS OF REPRESENTATION

The publishing history of the *AWS* can serve as a prism for exploring theoretical questions concerning relationships between markets, distribution, reading publics, state-formation, and cultural politics. Tracking the changing fortunes of the *AWS* scrambles any clear divide between the autonomy of aesthetic form and the instrumentality of the commodity form that defines 'the double discourse of value' of modern cultural criticism.[65] In this case, literature is clearly understood to have a set of instrumental uses that derive from a distinctively realist aesthetic, while the realisation of this value in commercial terms depends on a clear appreciation and manipulation of the aesthetic qualities of books as material artifacts.

One lesson of the *AWS* case study is that African writing is not naturally 'realistic' or 'representative' at all. Not only did the *AWS* bring to attention writing that is stylistically innovative - the work of Bessie Head, or of Dambudzo Marechera, for example - but more broadly, we have seen that the 'representative' qualities of this canon of writing are as much a construct of the 'paratexts' of the series - the design of books, and the imperatives of markets and institutions - as they are some integral quality of the texts themselves. The 'burden of representation' through which the *AWS* has been framed, marketed, read, adopted, taught and examined is the outcome of a deeper imperative that sees writing as a medium for asserting the presence of African culture in the West, as well as acting as a medium of self-representation for domestic educational and reading publics.

The representative qualities of the *AWS* have never been unproblematic,

63. Memo, 1996, University of Reading, Department of Archives and Manuscripts, HEB File No. 56/2.

64. The African and Caribbean Writers Series Performance Analysis, 21 August 1996, University of Reading, Department of Archives and Manuscripts, HEB File No. 56/6.

65. B. Hernstein-Smith, *Contingencies of Value*, Cambridge MA, Harvard University Press, 1991.

precisely because the territorialisation upon which representation classically depends is undone from the start by the distinctive geography of the *AWS*. Heinemann provided continent-wide distribution for writing in English, and helped construct a shared sense of African public culture which was geographically extensive, without perhaps ever being deeply embedded in African societies. In its early history, the *AWS* was instrumental in the institutionalisation of systems of national literary education which differentiated rather than integrated the subjects of newly independent national education systems in Africa; while subsequently, its continued survival has depended in no small part on being embedded in networks of multicultural post-nationalist secondary and tertiary education in the USA and Britain.

The *AWS* is, then, certainly a transnational cultural formation, but looking at the role of publishers brings to light the extent to which the conferral of cultural authority upon African writing in this case was never merely reserved for Western actors, but depended on the interactions of geographically dispersed institutional networks. Publishers, as embodiments of a rather peculiar form of multinational capital, were never all-powerful in shaping the forms of African representation circulating in the Continent or farther afield. The *AWS* is embedded in the wider history of nation-building projects that depended on extra-national institutional networks but also addressed only a limited section of national populations, yet stretched beyond national boundaries to constitute a de-territorialised discourse of African identity. The *AWS* was never a straightforwardly 'nationalised' project. Its predominant commitment was to pan-Africanism, and as time passed, many of the writers it helped support lived in exile. Its placement within education systems in African states meant that it was part of programmes whose effects are culturally differentiating rather than integrative. And its more recent dependence on UK and US Tertiary Education Markets is part of a broader movement of post-national multiculturalism.

The lack of congruence between language, identity, economy and territory is a dominant trope of postcolonial theories of culture and politics. From them, we have learnt that the assumption that culture and identity is or should be contained within the spatial boundaries of territorialised national cultures is a contingent product of the historical sedimentation of European traditions of reading, education, and publishing which underlies a whole critical apparatus of comparative analysis. The case of the *AWS* indicates not only that this model is not relevant to all contexts, but more than this, it sunders the assumed normativity of the national frame for analysing postcolonial cultural politics whether in the 'Western' core or the periphery of the 'Global South'.

This paper draws on research supported by a British Academy Research Grant, (Award No. 32829), entitled Recontextualising post-colonial African literature: reading formations, markets and the editorial process. *I would like to acknowledge the help of James Currey, Becky Clarke, and Andrew Gurr in helping me understand the contexts of African literary publishing. Thanks also to the staff at the University of Reading Library for their assistance in negotiating the Heinemann archive.*

Geographical Immediations: Locating *The English Patient*

Richard Cavell

That literary scholars are now meeting with geographers to consider questions about space (as at the conference where this paper was first given) is a sign of the increasing (though not unproblematical) confluence of space and text in theoretical discourse. The spatiality of literary texts is a relatively uncomplicated notion, in that spacing is the basis of linguistic signification. On the macrotextual level, the 'cultural logic'[1] of space has become a critical category within postmodernism and its questioning of master narratives. However, the textuality of space is more problematical. Historically, space can be said to have become textualised with the invention of the alphabet. More broadly, as David Summers has noted:

> [e]ven those parts of the world relatively untouched by modernization, or those parts of the world altogether uninhabited, have been subjected by us to planar order in being mapped and measured. All parts of the world now have their populations tabulated, their flora and fauna classified, their natural resources assessed, the structures of their languages, myths and social arrangements charted and diagrammed. The rectilinear borders of the modern political order, especially in the New World colonized by Europeans after the late fifteenth century, pre-supposed modern cartographic projections gridding the earth's whole surface.[2]

These tendencies - the alphabetical and the cartographic - are already shown to be in tension by the early seventeenth century in Michael Drayton's *Poly-Olbion* (1613), as they are in the opening scene of *King Lear* (1608; 1623), the *locus classicus* of McLuhan's examination in *The Gutenberg Galaxy*[3] of the changing spatial relations arising from the shift from orality to literacy.[4] The argument of that book suggested that these spatial relations were being further inflected by the increasing hegemony of electronic mediation.

If we are turning our attention at this point to the *language* of space in literary and cultural studies, it is not because literary works have suddenly become more spatial; Joseph Frank's groundbreaking essay on spatial form in modern literature appeared at the end of WWII,[5] and his avatars of the form were modernists such as Joyce and Flaubert. Rather, it is post-structuralist theory that has increasingly turned to the category of space as its prime arena of critique, under the influence of the language-based paradigm that grew out of Saussurean notions of synchrony. Post-Marxist

1. Fredric Jameson, *Postmodernism, or, The Cultural Logic of Late Capitalism*, Durham, Duke UP, 1991.

2. David Summers, *Real Spaces: World Art History and the Rise of Western Modernism*, London, Phaidon, 2003, p343.

3. Marshall McLuhan, *The Gutenberg Galaxy: the Making of Typographic Man*, Toronto, U Toronto P, 1962.

4. See Richard Cavell, *McLuhan in Space: A Cultural Geography*, Toronto, U Toronto P, 2002.

5. Joseph Frank, 'Spatial Form in Modern Literature', reprinted in *The Avant-Garde Tradition in Literature*, R. Kostelanetz (ed), Buffalo, Prometheus Books, [1945], 1982, pp42-37.

6. Jeff Derksen, "'The Obvious Analogy is with [Architecture]'": Megastructural *My Life*', in M.E. Diaz Sanchez and C. Douglas Dworkin (eds), *Architectures of Poetry*, Amsterdam, Rodopi, 2004, p117.

7. Irit Rogoff, *Terra Infirma: Geography's Visual Culture*, London, Routledge, 2000, back cover. Rogoff's comment is echoed by geographers such as Marcus Doel, who have commented that 'most of geography has become (un)stuck'. See 'Un-Glunking Geography; Spatial Science after Dr Seuss and Gilles Deleuze', in *Thinking Space*, M. Crang and N. Thrift (eds), London, Routledge, 2000, p119.

8. Ibid., p1.

9. K. Ludwig Pfeiffer, 'The Materiality of Communication', in H. Ulrich Gumbrecht and K. Pfeiffer (eds), *Materialities of Communication*, Stanford, Stanford University Press, 1994, p6.

10. Julian Murphet, 'Grounding Theory: Literary Theory and the New Geography', in M. McQuillan, G. MacDonald, R. Purves and S. Thomson (eds), *Post-Theory: New Directions in Criticism*, Edinburgh, Edinburgh University Press, 1999, p200.

critique has likewise turned toward space as a defining notion within cultural economies. Relatedly, the analytical category of space has been perceived by literary scholars as a way of engaging more directly with the lived dimension of the socius.

The common recurrence of notions of textuality as a way of interrogating such spaces is problematical, however, raising questions about the linguistic paradigm and about mediation more generally. Arguing in a related context, Jeff Derksen remarks that the 'grammar of architecture as narrative ... ultimately deflects a reading of architecture itself, as architecture must be textualised - rendered into *something else* - in order to be read. Once textualised, it cannot be text and architecture in the same moment. And once its constituent parts are reduced to grammar with programmatic uses, architecture takes on, once again, a static or even monumental appearance. Textualisation, following the textual turn, does not necessarily escape the crisis within literary studies'.[6] A similar problematic is attributed to geography by art historian Irit Rogoff, who has argued that '[g]eography is a language in crisis, unable to represent the immense changes that have taken place in a post-colonial, post-communist, post-migratory world',[7] and in particular 'the dislocation of subjects, the disruption of collective narratives and of languages of signification in the field of vision.[8] What emerges from this comment is the notion that textual space fails to capture the dynamic qualities of diasporic space (a dynamic which, Rogoff argues, visual art is able to address acutely). A similar problematic has been addressed in literary studies through a shift toward performativity; accordingly, '[c]ommunication is envisaged less as an exchange of meanings ... and more as performance propelled into movement by variously materialized signifiers'.[9]

Julian Murphet has traced the trajectory of this problematic to a post-1968 dissatisfaction with the inability of 'the mantras of Theory' to engage with questions such as 'How do cultural forms engage with social ones?'[10] Subtending these concerns was the sense that the linguistic paradigm had exhausted itself. It was at this point, suggests Murphet, that Marxist and Hegelian thought reconfigured itself within the discipline of geography:

What if production today no longer referred simply to the production of 'things' (goods, commodities, products) but to the total horizon of social space itself? To our cities, our interlinked spatial networks of production, distribution and consumption, our states, our very planet and its ecological limits? If this is correct, if we are now in a historical period defined by the *production of space*, then a new possibility for dialectical thought has arisen: the possibility of a unitary critical theory dedicated to this problematic of space. The principal theoretician of this reinvention of dialectical thought, Henri Lefebvre, once asked us to imagine that the dialectic '*is no longer attached to temporality*', but to space and spatiality. This lateral leap suddenly exonerates the dialectic from all the tedious charges that have accumulated around both Hegel's and Marx's successive-stage-models of social systems, and their supposed ideology of 'progress' and perfection. Instead, we are obliged to think the dialectic 'horizontally', in already familiar terms of centre and periphery, body and city, the simultaneously non-simultaneous, everyday life and state control, place and space, and to see these all interanimating in a total dialectical process of spatial production, consumption, control and appropriation, according to one, abiding economic logic (201).

Murphet suggests that these theoretical insights might be extended to the domain of literary theory through a particular consideration of the '*local-global dialectic*, an insistence upon the contradictory claims of global economic space and the intimate spaces of locality and identity' (203). This is to propose something more than the 'metaphorism of space' (203) that has come to characterise much literary theory; rather, it is to suggest an engagement with 'everyday life' and 'lived experience' (204). In Lefebvrian terms, this configures itself as an opposition between the abstractions of 'representations of space' and the lived materialities of 'representational spaces' (204), such that literary study would concern itself with their contradictions, producing a 'cognitive map' (206) of a space that fluctuates between repression and freedom.

***

There are a number of spaces in conflict in Michael Ondaatje's 1992 novel *The English Patient*,[11] making it a useful text through which to examine the notion that the 'language of space has assumed an important place in literary and cultural studies'.[12] The novel begins with an epigraph from the minutes of a Geographical Society meeting at Kensington Gore[13] in which the speaker laments 'the tragic circumstances of the death of Geoffrey Clifton at Gilf Kebir, followed later by the disappearance of his wife, Katharine Clifton'. Those events constitute the core of the story told by the English patient, whose identity remains in flux through the course of the novel - he is perhaps not English at all but a spy (possibly) named Almasy. The patient tells of his love for Katharine; Clifton discovers this through a British spy (the year is 1939 and Clifton is himself spying) and plots a double suicide/murder, hoping to crash his plane in which Katharine is a passenger by aiming it at Alamsy. The attempt kills Clifton and leaves Katharine fatally injured; the patient is burned beyond human recognition in his attempt to fly her out of the desert. 'Within two weeks even the idea of a city never entered his mind. It was as if he had walked under the millimetre of haze just above the inked fibres of a map, that pure zone between land and chart between distances and legend between nature and storyteller. Sandford called it geomorphology' (246). This orientalist geography of romance is shown to overlap with colonial space through the character Kirpal Singh (Kip), a

11. Michael Ondaatje, *The English Patient*, Toronto, McClelland & Stewart, 1992. Hereafter *EP*.

12. The proposition of the conference seminar at which this paper was first given: 'Textual Spaces/ Spatial Texts', Conference of the Royal Geographical Society (with the Institute of British Geographers), September 2003.

13. Where the Conference *likewise* took place.

bomb sapper. As a sapper, he becomes a servo-mechanism of the space in which he works, wired into it; this notion is underscored by his habit of listening to music through earphones when he defuses bombs, emphasising thus that this space is a feedback loop. Similarly, the English patient is 'wired' through the use of a hearing aid, his unrecognisable human form giving him the appearance of a primitive cyborg. And the Italian villa, used now as a hospice, in which most of the novel is set, has been wired with bombs by the retreating Germans.

Other spaces come into play through the story the patient tells; he is an expert, for example, on desert winds, commenting that, '[i]n the desert it is easy to lose a sense of demarcation'. These winds are nonetheless material for all that they are invisible: 'There is a whirlwind in southern Morocco, the *aajej*, against which the fellahin defend themselves with knives. There is the *africo*, which has at times reached into the city of Rome. The *alm*, a fall wind out of Yugoslavia. The *arifi*, also christened *aref* or *rifi*, which scorches with numerous tongues' (16). The war turns this geography into co-ordinates of battle: 'What did most of us know of such parts of Africa? The armies of the Nile moved back and forth - a battlefield eight hundred miles deep into the desert. Whippet tanks, Blenheim medium-range bombers. Gladiator biplane fighters' (19). For Kip, these details form a different kind of invisible geography: 'the rogue gaze could see the buried wire under the surface, how a knot might weave when out of sight' (111). Kip learns bomb disposal from Miss Morden and from Lord Suffolk. 'In spite of being Lord Suffolk he lived in Devon, and until war broke out his passion was the study of *Lorna Doone* and how authentic the novel was historically and geographically' (185); both Lord Suffolk and Miss Morden die defusing a bomb. In a number of ways, the various explosions in the novel signal the collision of its various spaces. Perhaps most powerfully, the geography of decolonisation collides with the Eurocentric geography of romance - geography *as* romance. For the English patient, Katharine Clifton finally *becomes* the desert in one of the more venerable tropes of colonisation: 'There was a time when mapmakers named the places they travelled through with the names of lovers rather than their own' (140). The patient's friendship with Kip (who has likewise romanced the British upper classes) comes to an end when Kip learns on his 'wireless' that atomic bombs have been dropped on Hiroshima and Nagasaki. 'If he closes his eyes he sees the streets of Asia full of fire. It rolls across cities like a burst map, the hurricane of heat withering bodies as it meets them, the shadow of humans suddenly in the air. This tremor of Western wisdom' (284).

The conflict of these spaces is not resolved, but that lack of resolution is significant. The novel undermines the romantic trope it set up with the patient's story by producing a counter-narrative in the romance of Kip and Hana (the patient's Canadian nurse). The last three pages of the novel take place after the war, although the time and place are not directly recorded. 'Now where does he sit as he thinks of her?' (299), asks the narrator, and it

14. See especially Stephen Henighan, 'Free Trade Fiction', in *When Words Deny the World: The Reshaping of Canadian Writing*, Erin Ontario, Porcupine's Quill, 2002, pp133-156.

15. Henri Lefebvre, *The Production of Space*, Donald

is significant that this simultaneous space is not available to the novel's narration. Kip is now a doctor in India, married, with children; Hana is in a Canada defined for him by memory and imagination. 'Now there are these urges to talk with her during a meal and return to that stage they were most intimate at in the tent or in the English patient's room, both of which contained the turbulent river of space between them' (301). The space that embodies Kip and Hana - at once here and there, local and global, material and abstract, *uncontained* - is unrepresentable in narrative terms and, as such, asserts the spatial problematic around which the entire novel turns. 'I wish for all this to be marked on my body when I am dead' says the patient. 'I believe in such cartography - to be marked by nature, not just to label ourselves on a map like the names of rich men and women on buildings. We are communal histories, communal books. We are not owned or monogamous in our taste or experience. All I desired was to walk upon such an earth that had no maps' (261).

Ondaatje's novel represents a local/global dynamic in a number of ways, including its representation of Canada as geographically displaced, given that the story that it relates largely takes place in Europe, with brief scenes in North America and Asia, though all these spaces are conflated in various ways. This dynamic returned to haunt the novel's reception, when it was critiqued for writing to a global audience[14] in order to be eligible for international awards (one of which, the Booker Prize, it was the first Canadian novel to win), and for movie adaptation. (It was, in fact, brought to the screen by Anthony Minghella, in a film that won nine Academy Awards). This sense of displacement surfaces most crucially in the novel's concluding section (where the postwar Kip in India seeks to imagine Hana in Canada). The scene poses a significant problem on a number of levels - spatial, textual, literary. If, as Henri Lefbvre has remarked, 'Representational space is alive: it speaks',[15] then it would appear from this scene that the local/global dialectic must speak dialogically - that is, as part of a dialogue but also out of a sense of more than one logic. It is here, I think, that the crises alluded to by Rogoff et al have their source. Indeed, the local/global dialectic is *unrepresentable* in univocal terms, since it seeks to map a space that is both here and not here at the same time, a space of de-territorialisation, of diaspora, of terror and trauma.[16] It is also an *invisible* space, the space of an increasingly networked planet, and yet a space that also constitutes part of our everyday lived experience.

Murphet addresses these issues in their literary context, arguing that the reader who approaches the literary text through an awareness of the production of space is more sensitive to the embodiment of such spaces (in that they are socially produced). Such a reader is particularly sensitive to affect, which opens the text to spatial practices other than the visual (such as the acoustic and the tactile). This recurrence to affect represents a major attempt in theoretical discourse to move beyond the linguistic paradigm, as a host of recent works suggest,[17] through explorations of performativity

Nicholson-Smith (trans), Oxford, Blackwell, 1991, p42.

16. The notion that the events of 11 September 2001 remain beyond comprehension partly because of their spatial complexity recurs in the conversations that Giovanna Borradori has with Jürgen Habermas and Jacques Derrida in *Philosophy in a Time of Terror: Dialogues with Jürgen Habermas and Jacques Derrida*, Chicago, University of Chicago Press, 2003.

17. See, for example, Eve Kosofsky Sedgwick and Adam Frank (eds), *Shame and Her Sisters: A Silvan Tomkins Reader*, Durham, Duke UP, 1995; Brian Massumi, *Parables for the Virtual: Movement, Affect, Sensation*, Durham, Duke UP, 2002; Jackie Stacey and Sara Ahmed (eds), *Thinking Through the Skin*, London, Routledge, 2001; Rei Terada, *Feeling in Theory: Emotion after the 'Death of the Subject'*, Cambridge, Mass., Harvard UP, 2001; Sianne Ngai, *Ugly Feelings*, Cambridge, Mass., Harvard UP, 2005; and Teresa Brennan, *The Transmission of Affect*, Ithaca, Cornell UP, 2004. Brennan most clearly explores affect within the context of communication; Tomkins set the stage through his use of the Shannon-Weaver model of communication.

18. I am thinking particularly of the discussion of aporia by Richard Beardsworth in *Derrida and the Political*, London: Routledge, 1996, pp114-118.

19. This is to accept Baudrillard's argument that any recursion to the 'real' is itself a form of fetishisation of that which one seeks to critique. Reality is an effect and thus mediated, and any critique must consider those mediations. See the discussion by Bradley Butterfield in 'The Baudrillardian Symbolic, 9/11, and the War of Good and Evil', *Postmodern Culture*, 13,1 (2002): 1-17, especially 2-3.

20. Gayatri Chakravorty Spivak, 'Cultural Talks in the Hot Peace: Revisiting the "Global Village"', in *Cosmopolitics: Thinking and Feeling Beyond the Nation*, P. Cheah and B. Robbins (eds), Minneapolis, University of Minnesota Press, 1998, p329.

21. As McKenzie Wark writes in *A Hacker Manifesto*, Cambridge, Mass., Harvard UP, 2004, 'A double spooks the world, the double of abstraction. The fortunes of states and armies, companies and communities, depends on it' (para. 001); abstraction is double because of the spectral nature of mediation, 'the transformation of

and material embodiment that have profound epistemological and ontological implications, as well as raising important questions about where one positions oneself critically in these increasingly infolding spaces. Electronic media, as modes of knowledge production and as bio-technologies, exacerbate these issues, given that they occupy non-linear, non-Euclidean spaces which, like the layered spaces of hypertext, are aporetic,[18] such that one space opens onto another processually,[19] at once connected to and disconnected from other spaces. That these spaces, finally, belong to the realm of *invisibilia*, while remaining material, is what Kip encounters every time he defuses a bomb, each one of which becomes an extension of himself - paradoxically, his life depends on this, as might his death.

The local/global dialectic poses particular problems of representation for the visual domain. Gayatri Spivak has argued that the

> 'globe' is counterintuitive. You walk from one end of the earth to the other and it remains flat. It is a scientific abstraction inaccessible to experience. No one lives in the *global* village. The only relationship accessible to the globe so far is that of the gaze.[20]

Yet our experience is increasingly of such abstractions - millions live within the electronic gaze of satellite technology, of CCTV, of the camera eye. As Spivak goes on to argue:

> In the contemporary context, when the world is broadly divided simply into North and South, the World Bank and other international agencies can divide the world into maps that make visible the irreducibly abstract quality of geography. One of the guiding principles of geography - 'nation' - being inextricably tangled with the mysterious phenomena of language ... and birth ... both discloses and effaces this abstract character (337-8).

The difficulty of mapping the global village is that it represents a dynamic relationship; this relationship becomes a major focus of the literary critic in Murphet's model, which involves '"mapping" the contradictory space of the mode of production *onto* the subject' (205). One such contradictory space is narrative itself, which 'exists, in part, to normalize spatial habits that are in reality in a constant state of flux' (205), suggesting one reason why Ondaatje self-consciously fails to represent the concluding scene in his novel.

It is precisely the abstract[21] - which is not to say unsituated or immaterial - nature of global communications networks that has allowed a concept such as cyberspace to move freely between social, literary, cultural and geographical discourses. This collapse of the material and the abstract has occasioned the crisis of positionality which Rogoff and others have written about: how can I be situated as a critic, how can the geography I seek to theorise be located, if I acknowledge that both I and it occupy a mediatised domain which is at once local and global and in which I am at once here and there as well? As Rogoff puts it:

> we realize that it [geography] has always been a form of positioned spectatorship; that such categories as 'the Middle East' or 'the Far East' or 'the Sub-Saharan' are viewed from positions (in this instance centres of colonial power) which name and locate and identify places in relation to themselves as the centre of the world. Like spectatorship in the filmic arena, geographical naming of this kind equally reflects certain desires for power and dominance and certain fantasies of distance and proximity and transgression which come into expression in the act of geographical naming (11).

At the end of Ondaatje's novel, this Eurocentric positioning has been radically disrupted as the narrator tries to imagine a postcolonial space that simultaneously includes Canada and India.

***

The inquiry into conjunctions of text and space is an *effect* of the current epistemic crisis occasioned by the shift from rigid notions of territoriality, especially as embodied in nationalist/imperialist discourses inherited from print culture (as Benedict Anderson[22] and others have argued), to an electronic culture that contests this territoriality at every point. As Jonathan Boyarin has commented, 'our reified notions of objective and separate space and time are peculiarly linked to the modern identification of a nation with a sharply bounded, continuously occupied space controlled by a single sovereign state, comprising a set of autonomous yet essentially identical individuals'.[23] It is precisely through this concept of territory that text and space coincide. The collapse of these territorial certainties (including those of 'inside' and 'outside') brings us back to globalisation and its critical crux: how precisely can the critic of spatialisation analyse a phenomenon in which s/he is immersed? Here Barthes' 1971 essay, 'From Work to Text', is useful, in that it ties the notion of text at once to '*social* space' and to 'the destruction of metalanguage'.[24] The one is a function of the other: if we understand ourselves as 'worldly' (as opposed to universal) then we understand ourselves as becoming, as in process. This understanding, however, deprives us of any Archimedean positionality outside this flux: we are all immersed in this flux - critics have no special dispensation - and thus we must articulate our critiques from within. This is precisely the crisis of positionality identified by Rogoff. It need not, however, be understood as the ultimate act of complicity, because, as a processual model, it identifies a dynamic, what Barthes in the same essay calls a '*practice* of writing' (164, my emphasis) and

the landscape of everyday life toward its vectoral form' (note to para. 228).

22. Benedict Anderson, *Imagined Communities: Reflections on the Origin and Spread of Nationalism*, London, Verso, 1991.

23. Jonathan Boyarin, 'Space, Time, and the Politics of Memory', in J. Boyarin (ed), *Remapping Memory: The Politics of TimeSpace*, Minneapolis, University of Minnesota Press, 1994, p2.

24. Roland Barthes, 'From Work to Text', in *Image Music Text*, London, Fontana, 1971, p164.

that word 'practice' has precisely the same force that 'production' has in Lefebvre's famous account of spatial dynamics, a place no longer of writing, but of reading, of performativity. This particular sense of space is the one that has now come increasingly to enter into discourses of literary studies and geography alike - the sense of a processual, relational *production* of space.

Barthes in fact identifies the text as a 'network', which is a crucial shift in his terminology, allying the notion of 'text' with a more processual concept than that enabled by its traditional association with aspects of the book. Clive Barnett's argument that the implications of textuality extend to a critique of 'universalist epistemologies'[25] through the 'linguistic indeterminacy' (280) provided by the notion of text thus needs qualifying and extending. In a move similar to Spivak's, Barnett elides the technological domain, yet it is this domain which coincides with the indeterminacy he seeks to theorise. It is *electronic* texts that cannot be bound; in fact, they are characterised by their ability to escape borderlines and to contest ontological certainties. They are neither texts nor spaces in the traditional sense; rather, they are processes, and as such they tend to resist in numerous ways the regime of the visible that underpins our sense of text and space alike. To Barnett's question, 'Is it not possible to imagine the space of language differently?' (282) from the traditional, bounded one, I would answer 'yes', as he does, but would argue that the 'writing' that constitutes this *différance* has more in common with the *texting* whose object is the message that we produce on our mobiles than with the 'book' whose deconstruction was Derrida's prime object.

This electronic *écriture*, a 'writing' that is outside the bounded model of print, shades inevitably into a form of speech retrieved from the very depths of print culture; it is thus affective and performative. The unboundedness of the space of this 'writing' becomes the basis for a re-articulation of the material of our critique, not, however, from a position outside a space conceived of as fixed, but from within, such that the production of space is not 'just' another metaphor but a critical imperative - we must perforce locate ourselves critically (even if that means nomadically) in these hyper-tectonic spaces because we live in them[26] in ways that the notion of text cannot begin to acknowledge. Mark Wigley puts this compellingly:

Nowhere escapes the net. A map of all the webs passing through any particular space would be impossibly dense. Invisible networks seemingly threaten visible means of defining space, dissolving the walls of buildings. The architecture of borders, walls, doors, and locks gives way to that of passwords, firewalls, public key encryption, and security certificates. Indeed, the idea of a space occupied by networks or superimposed by them has been replaced by that of overlapping networks within which physical space only appears as a fragile artefact or effect. Space itself can only be seen when caught in the net'.[27]

25. Clive Barnett, 'Deconstructing Context: Exposing Derrida', *Transactions of the Institute of British Geographers*, 24 (1999): 279.

26. '*The* issue of culture [is] not simply the fact of the existence of the new technologies of mass information and communication, but the reshaping of the everyday lives and struggles of subaltern classes and peoples by those new forms', Michael Denning, *Culture in the Age of Three Worlds*, London, Verso, 2004, p5.

27. Mark Wigley, 'Network Fever', *Grey Room*, 4 (Summer 2001): 83.

If the incursion of the notion of 'text' into spatial discourse signals the move, philosophically and theoretically, from one sort of space - bounded, Euclidean - to another - open, processual, dynamic - then the space described by Wigley suggests that we have gone beyond the domain of 'text' as Barthes theorised it and have entered into a space more akin to hypertext, whose spaces deploy aporetically. If, as Barnett argues, '"text" is repositioned [in this process] as *the very medium* [my emphasis] across which the division [between inside and outside] is established and traversed' (284), and if '[t]ext is just one figure for an understanding of mediation cut loose from an origin or a teleological end', then this is to suggest that the medium is the message, where 'medium' is at once episteme and vector of power, operating through a 'network of interruptions' as Barnett puts it, which is precisely the process of electrical communication, its prosthetic off/on a series of articulations and disarticulations, connections and disconnections.[28] This *différance*, as Barnett reminds us, is dialogistic (in the sense I have previously used that term) and has reference to space 'in the sense of difference as apartness and separation, and dispersal; and to temporality, in the sense of deferring, delay and postponement' (p287). It is, in short, a spacetime located in a 'para-site', which is to say, like the global village, it is 'proximate *and* distant, similar *and* different, inside a domestic economy but not [exclusively] of it' (p289).

28. See Barnett, op. cit., p288.

***

This writing that is not only written but also spoken, and not only spoken but also texted, constitutes in the broadest sense the space that we are increasingly encountering in cultural contexts, to the extent that it is now a new epistemic paradigm, but it is a paradigm not of text or of writing as we have come to know them but of a form of mediation we are only beginning to learn how to describe. Hence Ondaatje's impasse at the end of his novel; unable to narrate this scene (as it is not one that exists in the dimension of time), he presents it in terms of (spatial) images. It is precisely through the spatial turn that literary and cultural studies are encountering this realm of mediation, Derrida's *writing* functioning more as an electronic hypertext (a series of images without any necessary narrative connection between/among them) than as a printed text - we should recall that it was as a review of a book on bio-technology that *Of Grammatology* began its life.[29] This electronic writing has much more in common with speech, especially speech as an embodied phenomenon, and hence the deconstructive move to appropriate speech for writing. Electric speech constitutes the ultimate displacement of the visual regime. In the global village, sites are always between, spaces of resonance, mediate and immediate. The term 'text' bears with it its legacy of print, which cannot accommodate the dynamism that characterises the geographical spaces identified by Rogoff as having placed the *language* of

29. As Derrida remarks in the footnote to the preface of that book, the first part of the *Grammatology* began life as a review of three books, one of which was André Leroi-Gourhan's, *Le geste et la parole* (1965), which bears 'a strong commitment to technology as *the* point of access for understanding human cultures' according to Randall White in his introduction to the English translation, *Gesture and Speech*, Anna Bostock Berger (trans), Cambridge, Mass., MIT Press, 1993.

geography - or, I would say, a certain spatial discourse - in crisis, and in that use of the word language she identifies the source of the crisis. At the same time, Rogoff's argument that the deficiencies of the *language* of geography can be addressed through visual art recognises, indirectly, that image (or iconicity) has taken over the role of text in the mediation of experience.[30] As Wlad Godzich puts it, '[w]e are living in the midst of a prelogical affirmation of the world, in the sense that it takes place before the fact of *logos*, and it threatens us with an alienation that modern thinkers could barely conceive'.[31] Reality thus takes on the guise of being 'immediate' (as Godzich states), that is, coinciding with its own mediation, becoming 'the very expression of the imaginary' (369).[32] Hence the *shock* of the new, as Robert Hughes put it in his classic history of modern art, art in which we recognise neither ourselves nor the visual spaces that we have come to naturalise.[33]

It is in these ways that the notion of text as elaborated within deconstruction and principally by Derrida is inadequate to the nature of our contemporary experience of geographical (and textual) space. As Mark Hansen argues,

[o]n Derrida's account, technology is functionally subordinated to the movement of *différance*, to which it owes its existence ... For Derrida, technology is thus derivative in two senses. Functionally, technology is limited to the role of material support for the 'possibilities of the trace'; like writing in the restricted sense, it is merely the means by which *différance* exteriorizes or expresses itself. And ontologically, technology remains radically dependent on the quasi-vitalist movement of *différance*; again like writing in the restricted sense, it is the product of the primordial 'arche-writing' that conditions its very emergence ... Unlike those critics ... who seek to employ the cybernetic theory of communication as a model for thinking about the interrelationship of various autonomous spheres, Derrida seizes on the notion of the cybernetic program precisely because it allows him to restrict technology to this doubly derivative status and consequently to support the totalizing grasp of his ontology of *différance*. ... What Derrida does not say is that this grammatological dissolution of metaphysical opposition generates an enabling opposition of its own, since it owes its possibility to a subordination of technology to the genetic or quasi-vitalist principle of *différance* ... So long as it functions 'in the service of language', technology remains thoroughly mechanical and can readily be assimilated to the figure of the machine ... [T]he reduction Derrida imposes on technology reflects ... his decision to consider technology exclusively as part of an ontogenetic, language-centred program and to use the generative text-machine as a model for encompassing technology as such.[34]

Hansen argues that 'technologies *underlie* and *inform* our basic "ways of

30. The crucial distinction here is between the perspectival space of the visual regime and the iconic *hyper*space of the electronic one.

31. Wlad Godzich, 'Language, Images, and the Postmodern Predicament', in Gumbrecht and Pfeiffer (eds), op. cit., pp368-9.

32. Jameson allies this notion of 'immediation' with globalisation itself, writing that it 'seems to concern politics and economics in immediate ways, but just as immediately culture and sociology, not to speak of information and the media, or ecology, or consumerism and daily life': See 'Preface' to Jameson and M. Miyoshi (eds), *The Cultures of Globalization*, Durham, Duke UP, 1998, pxi.

33. Robert Hughes, *The Shock of the New*, London, Thames and Hudson, 1991.

34. Mark Hansen, *Embodying Technesis: Technology Beyond Writing*, Ann Arbor, University of Michigan Press, 2000, pp84-5.

seeing" the world and thus cannot be thematised as "objects" that are constituted by such paradigmatic holistic perspectives' (2-3); indeed, technologies mediate our experience of space and time, as he goes on to argue (221), taking over the role played by the alphabet in the previous cultural epoch. Thus, '[g]iven the extensive role that technology's indirect and amorphous impact has on our basic modes of perception and experience, we can easily make sense of the common imperative guiding recent cultural investigations of technology - the imperative to secure technology's impact within some delimited, theorisable "space"' (3-4). In this context, technology comes to represent alterity (as it does for Spivak), always thus 'subordinate to a more central overriding theoretical purpose' (5). It is counter-productive, in these terms, to theorise an 'illimitable' *textual* space, since that space is precisely limited by its exclusion of the technological and its concomitant subservience to the linguistic. The 'homology ... between textual structures and thought' ultimately divorces thought from phenomenality, at which point 'it simply loses its jurisdiction over the experiential domain' (13). As Thomas G. Pavel puts it, '[w]hen, at the end of the 1960s, Derrida attempted a synthesis between the phenomenology of language and Saussurian semiology, he was not so much offering semiology a supplement of meaning as imposing the reign of the sign'.[35] Further, 'The enigmatic transcendental space from which the Kantian Idea had withdrawn will thus be conceded to writing understood as a mixture of deferral and dissonance that gauges the performance of the thinking subject. Consequently, at the junction of the two forces - deferral and disharmony - the temptation will become irresistible to postulate a kind of hyperspace of dissonant subjectivity for whose epiphany no classical philosophy has prepared us, since in the past all philosophies of paradox and disorder preferred to look for them in the subject itself' (p66).

If we understand technological spaces as not representational of something else (as the iPod might be said to represent *écriture*, for example) then we begin to understand how they 'structure our lifeworlds and influence our embodied lives at a level ... below the "threshold" of representation itself' (4), as Hansen states, in this way 'mediat[ing] the material rhythms of embodied life' (94). Language, in this understanding, is no longer the exclusive domain of experience. Here, one would want to critique Murphet both for his assumption that the metaphoricity of space is limited to what Hansen calls 'technesis' - the putting of technology into discourse - and for his invocation of 'cognitive mapping' as if it were something other than a metaphor of the real (thus implying that technology has no direct impact on the real[36]). There is, in other words, a 'materiality outside the space governed by textuality'.[37]

If we bring this discussion back to *The English Patient*, a number of congruencies emerge; and while there is a danger in reading literary texts as allegories of critical ones, the critical self-reflexiveness of Ondaatje's novel invites such a reading. I have already remarked on the series of displacements

35. Thomas G. Pavel, *The Feud of Language: A History of Structuralist Thought*, L. Jordan and T. G. Pavel (trans), Cambridge, Basil Blackwell, 1989, p43.

36. See Hansen, op. cit., p19

37. Ibid., p125

38. See Glen Lowry, 'Between *The English Patients:* Race and the Politics of Adapting CanLit', *Essays on Canadian Writing*, 76 (2002): 216-46, as well as Josef Pesch, 'Dropping the Bomb? On Critical and Cinematic Responses to Michael Ondaatje's *The English Patient*', in J.-M. Lacroix and M. Ondaatje (eds), *Re-Constructing the Fragments of Michael Ondaatje's Work*, Paris, Presses de la Sorbonne, 1999, pp229-46; Gillian Roberts, 'Sins of Omission: *The English Patient*, *THE ENGLISH PATIENT*, and the Critics', *Essays on Canadian Writing* 76 (2002): 195-215; Raymond Aaron Younis, 'Nationhood and Decolonization in *The English Patient*', *Literature / Film Quarterly*, 26, 1 (1998): 2-9; D. Mark Simpson, 'Minefield Readings: The Postcolonial *English Patient*', *Essays on Canadian Writing*, 53 (1994): 216-37.

39. Denning op. cit., relates the story of asking students in a seminar on globalization to help him create a list of 'the most representative or valuable cultural texts since 1945' (p29). What surprises him is their insistence on including 'networks like the Internet (which is like saying that one of the key cultural texts of the American Renaissance was the telegraph network - surely true, but it rarely appears on the same list as Emerson, Melville, Douglass, and Stowe') (p29).

(or aporia) around which the novel is structured and how displacement raises issues of representation in the novel. Ondaatje extends this concern to the technological through one of the bravura pieces of writing in the novel, which describes Kip's dismantling of a bomb. What is significant in this description is the way in which Kip himself must be 'wired' in order to effectively work on the bomb - he has developed the habit of wearing earphones and listening to music on his wireless as a way of enhancing his concentration; this emphasises that he is himself an extension of the bomb - if it goes off, he goes off. Indeed, at the end of the novel, when Kip learns (over that same wireless) of the use of the atomic bombs in Japan, he does 'explode', wielding his gun at his companions as he rails at them for having betrayed the 'brown races' (*EP* 286) who helped them win the war. While this scene was read by a number of critics as lacking psychological realism, it is consistent with the novel's treatment of technology as materially embodied. Not only is the English patient himself wired through his use of an earphone to enhance his hearing, but in another crucial scene, Hana must hold a trip wire for Kip as he defuses a bomb in the villa, thus 'wiring' herself to him in a way that is proleptic of their subsequent relationship (and thus the reverse, in this sense, of the patient's relationship with Katharine). Again, it is important to note that the space produced in this scene of two individuals who are wired together is a space of displacement.

The fact that these scenes have attracted no attention in the intervening decade or so of the novel's critical study[38] suggests that technesis, as defined by Hansen, is at work not only at the theoretical level but also at the 'applied' level of literary and critical studies, and that the concept of text may have outlived its usefulness in reading the spatial deployments of fiction. 'Text' remains useful for our understanding of a fundamentally mediatised space only to the extent that it can be understood as having superseded the regime of writing, as in Barthes' suggestion that texts are networks. One advantage of understanding a text as a network is that it allows us to understand technology *within* the context of literary and cultural studies,[39] and, indeed, as fundamental to our lived, material existence. Ondaatje gestures toward this moment when he questions the possibility of narrating the local/global space evoked at the end of his novel. Moving into the present tense, he brings his readers with him in the urgency to locate themselves in that space and to encounter it critically.

The Spatial Poetics of James Joyce

Gerry Kearns

Literary commentators are well used to studying narratives. The organisation of time within a work is part of the way meaning is conveyed.[1] Much less attention has been paid to questions of space. There are two ways this is changing. In the first place, geographers, touched by a cultural turn, have begun looking at the co-production of artefacts and contexts. Work on landscape design, on architecture, and on city forms has emphasised the way that physical space resonates to cultural politics.[2] There have also been studies of a sort of geography of creativity that has emphasised the relations between locality and the cultural forces that drive innovation, be it economic, or artistic.[3] Closer to the concerns of this paper are studies of Dublin as an inspirational locality for Joyce,[4] of the geography of Dublin as a project of the reproduction of social class,[5] and of the landscape of Dublin as shaken by contested schemes of political representation, British and Irish.[6] None of these concerns are exclusive to Geography and geographers have also been influenced in their work by the second major spatial trend and that is the way that postcolonial and postmodern theories have stressed spaces of simultaneous difference at the expense of teleologies of unfolding essences.[7] Noticeable certainly in Said's discussion of Yeats, is a concern to read an agonistic geography of imperialism in which the master narrative of the coloniser is never able to avoid or silence that of the subaltern.[8] Because so much of the force of the enlightenment discourses that marginalise colonised persons come from a particular way of reading the trajectory of modernity, it is not surprising that postcolonial critique is premised upon a 'radical revision of the social temporality in which emergent histories may be written'.[9] We may pit an alternative space of cultural difference and of incompatible chronologies against the singular time of modernity's unfolding. Again, with regard to the concerns of this paper, works such as those of Kiberd, Smyth and Graham take up these postcolonial themes within Irish Studies in very productive ways.[10]

For quite some time, however, Frederic Jameson stood at the head of a short column of space cadets among literary critics. Modernism, he suggested, turned to space from time.[11] For Jameson, as for David Harvey, it was the dramatic reshaping by capital of world economic geographies, what Harvey calls time-space compression, that induced a vertiginous turn to space in culture.[12] Industrial capitalism produced a world of global economic crises, of ever-denser and more rapid movements of ideas, people and goods, and of multiplying promiscuous interdependencies. By the late nineteenth century, citizens found that the here-and-now no longer anchored experience, nor could the here-and-then. A whirligig of there-and-to-be

1. Paul Ricoeur, *Time and Narrative, Volume I*, Chicago IL, University of Chicago Press, 1984 [1983]; Hayden White, *The Content of Form: Narrative Discourse and Historical Representation*, Baltimore MD, Johns Hopkins University Press, 1987.

2. See Stephen Daniels, *Fields of Vision: Landscape Imagery and National Identity in England and the United States*, Cambridge, Polity Press, 1993; Denis Cosgrove, *The Palladian Landscape: Geographical Change and its Cultural Representation in Sixteenth-Century Italy*, Leicester, Leicester University Press, 1993, James Duncan, *The City as Text: the Politics of Landscape Interpretation in the Kandyan Kingdom*, Cambridge, Cambridge University Press, 1990.

3. See Allen Scott, *Technopolis: High-Technology Industry and Regional Development in Southern California*, Berkeley CA, University of California Press, 1993; Alison Bain, 'Constructing contemporary artistic identities in Toronto neighbourhoods', *Canadian Geographer* 47, 3 (2003): 303-317.

4. Nuala Johnson, 'Fictional journeys: paper landscapes, tourist trails and Dublin's literary

texts', *Social and Cultural Geography* 5, 1 (2004): 91-107.

5. Ruth McManus, *Dublin, 1910-1940: Shaping the City and Suburbs*, Dublin, Four Courts, 2002.

6. Yvonne Whelan, *Reinventing Modern Dublin: Streetscape, Iconography and the Politics of Identity*, Dublin, University College Dublin Press, 2003.

7. Edward Soja, *Postmodern Geographies: the Reassertion of Space in Critical Social Theory*, London, Verso, 1989; Alison Blunt and Cheryl McEwan (eds), *Postcolonial Geographies*, London, Continuum, 2002.

8. Edward Said, *Culture and Imperialism*, London, Chatto and Windus, 1993.

9. Homi Bhabha, *The Location of Culture*, London, Routledge, 1994, p. 171. Thank you to one of the reviewers for this suggestion.

10. Declan Kiberd, *Inventing Ireland: The Literature of the Modern Nation*, London, Jonathan Cape, 1995; Gerry Smyth, *Space and the Irish Cultural Imagination*, London, Palgrave, 2001; Colin Graham, *Deconstructing Ireland: Identity, Theory, Culture*, Edinburgh, Edinburgh University Press, 2001. See the discussion in Gerry Kearns, 'Ireland after theory', *Bullán: an*

would shape the only, and provisional, here-and-now that could be made sense of. Space imploded as home came the empire, home came the bank or crop failures of distant places, home came echoes of drums with rumours of war. These interconnections put simultaneity on the cultural agenda. We emerged, not from a noble or a primitive past, but from a chaotic, spatially-distended future. This was a world always in the unmaking, in the words of the *Communist Manifesto*, a world in which '[a]ll that is solid melts into air'.[13] Marx and Engels believed that this new world freed workers from the fetishes of tradition and religion. Workers should now see themselves as victims of determinate property relations that could be changed, rather than as pawns of god or fate. Yet, the spatial kaleidoscope of world war, intercontinental migration, and global depression could itself become fetishised as a new geopolitical order, dictated by environment and derived cultures and beyond revolutionary challenge.[14]

This is certainly the moment of James Joyce's *Ulysses*. It was written in eight years from 1914 to 1921, against a background of revolution, war and currency instability. As a friend from those days recalled, '[n]o permanence was in the air'.[15] These matters were certainly on Joyce's mind. The Dublin of his youth was pounded by British artillery defeating the anti-colonial revolution of 1916. The First World War forced him out of Trieste and into neutral Zurich while his brother, Stanislaus, also living in Trieste, was interned by the Austrian authorities. Money was ever a problem and Joyce depended upon gifts from abroad. He was no stranger to the unstable geographies of money. There is, as Margot Norris notes, a good deal of materialism in Joyce's world-view, and his texts are replete with historical context.[16] This historical materialism means Joyce is no spatial fetishist. Joyce was sympathetic to socialism and saw representing change as intrinsic to contemporary art. He recognised that 'everything is inclined to flux and change nowadays and modern literature, to be valid, must express that flux'.[17] The Dublin of *Ulysses* was being transformed by 'the velocity of modern life'.[18] Joyce had a geographical imagination but while representing flux was important aesthetically, his ethics promoted other geographical themes. Joyce's spatial poetics are more about Irish identity than about the dynamics of capitalism and to read the first through the second, while plausible, would be to marginalise much that animated his work. British colonialism and its agonistic Irish nationalism were central concerns of James Joyce and his geographical imagination address the dilemma of making the second under the impress of the first.

In Trieste, writing *Dubliners*, Joyce longed for 'a map of Dublin and views and Gilbert's history' of the city.[19] He wanted, he said, 'a map of Dublin on my wall'.[20] His newspaper articles about Galway were both based around the discussion of maps.[21] When his son essayed a singing career, Joyce not only advised him on repertoire but also sent him a map of Ireland thinking 'it might be useful or instructive to locate any places mentioned in any Irish songs'.[22] Joyce used maps when writing *Ulysses*. Budgen described him with map, ruler and stopwatch plotting the action in the 'Wandering Rocks' episode,[23] and Joyce's notes for 'Penelope' feature a sketch map of Gibraltar.[24] His father said of him that '[i]f that fellow was dropped in the middle of the Sahara he'd sit, begod, and make a map of it'.[25] The topography of Dublin mattered. His father had worked for Thom's, the publisher of the street directory Joyce made such trusting use of in *Ulysses*, had tramped the city canvassing advertisements for the *Freeman's Journal*, and as a rate collector for the Corporation, had acquired an intimate knowledge of the houses, inhabitants and lore of many districts of the city. On 'long walks in the lovely surroundings of Dublin', their father passed on to Stanislaus and James an 'inexhaustible fund of Dublin small talk'.[26] Working on *Finnegans Wake*, Joyce wrote his father with questions about Dublin places and folk they knew. No reply came and he sent a stenographer to collect the information directly.[27]

Joyce used conventional maps but his art cannot be reduced to them.[28] The map promises an objective account of external reality and Joyce saw modern literature as concerned with the 'subjective', the 'subterranean complexities which dominate the average man and compose his life'.[29] Hegglund notes the tension between the closed logic of the map and the multiple and various logics of the individual itineraries described in *Ulysses*.[30] Both sides of the dialectic have their place in the novel and in its attendant critical works.[31] Joyce put a significant amount of topographical detail in the book, in part because he wanted to draw attention to the indeterminate but significant relations between routes and itineraries, between path and intent, between environment and perception, between names and meanings. Yet, Joyce's attention to Dublin and to its spaces is not only a matter of modernist aesthetics.

The home of his works is no etiolated metropolis. Urging Grant Richards to publish *Dubliners*, he pointed out that Dublin was comparable to European cities such as Venice and yet did not have a significant literature to call its own. He also claimed that to write a 'chapter of the moral history of my country', he had fallen upon Dublin.[32] This was 'the focal point of Ireland [...], its heart-beat you may say, and to ignore that would be affectation'.[33] His diagnosis, at least in *Dubliners*, was serious; the city was sclerotic, paralysed by religion, colonialism and romantic nationalism. His choice of Dublin as the locus for a discussion of the condition of Ireland question was a political choice, an ethical one that set his apart from the geographical imaginaries of the contemporary Literary Revival with its celebration of an originary Ireland out west.[34] Yeats spoke of a 'geographical conscience' in Shaw, and Black finds the same in Joyce.[35] Names can evoke places and James told his brother Stanislaus that he would take his copy of his first published volume, the poems of *Chamber Music*, 'and (so far as I can remember) at the top of each page I will put an address, or a street so that when I open the book I can revisit the places where I wrote the different songs'.[36] Similarly, whereas it has become common to name the episodes in *Ulysses* after the episodes in

Irish Studies Journal 6 (2002): 107-114.

11. Frederic Jameson, *Postmodernism or, the Cultural Logic of Late Capitalism*, London, Verso, 1991.

12. David Harvey, *The Condition of Postmodernity*, Oxford, Blackwell, 1989.

13. Karl Marx and Friedrich Engels, 'The manifesto of the Communist Party' [1848], in Marx, *Political Writings, Vol. 1. The Revolutions of 1848*, London, Penguin Books, 1992.

14. Neil Smith, *American Empire: Roosevelt's Geographer and the Prelude to Globalization*, Berkeley CA, University of California Press, 2003.

15. Frank Budgen, 'James Joyce and the making of *Ulysses*' [1934], in idem, *James Joyce and the Making of 'Ulysses' and Other Writings*, Oxford, Oxford University Press, 1989, pp1-320, p196.

16. Margot Norris, *Joyce's Web: the Social Unravelling of Modernism*, Austin TX, University of Texas Press, 1992.

17. Arthur Power, *Conversations with James Joyce*, London, Millington, 1974, p95.

18. Joyce, *Ulysses*, Hans Walter Gabler

(ed), London, The
Bodley Head, 1986
[1922], 17: 1773,
henceforth *Ulysses*.

19. Letter to
Stanislaus Joyce, 13
November 1906, in
Richard Ellmann
(ed), *Letters of James
Joyce. Volume II*, New
York, Viking Press,
1966, p194.

20. Letter to
Stanislaus Joyce, 6
November 1906, in
Letters II, p186.

21. Eric Bulson,
'Topics and
geographies', in
Jean-Michel Rabaté
(ed), *James Joyce
Studies*, London,
Palgrave Macmillan,
2004, pp52-72.

22. Letter to George
and Helen Joyce, 8
January 1935, in
Ellmann (ed), *Letters
of James Joyce. Volume
III*, New York, Viking
Press, 1966, p341.

23. Budgen, 'Joyce',
op. cit., p125.

24. Bulson, 'Topics',
2004, op. cit..

25. John Wyse
Jackson and Peter
Costello, *John
Stanislaus Joyce: the
Voluminous Life and
Genius of James Joyce's
Father*, London,
Fourth Estate, 1997,
p201.

26. Stanislaus Joyce,
*My Brother's Keeper:
James Joyce's Early
Years*, New York,
Viking Press, 1958,
p64.

27. Jackson and
Costello, *John
Stanislaus Joyce*, op.
cit., p392.

Homer's *Odyssey* they echo, between themselves, his brother Stanislaus referred to 'Oxen of the Sun' as the 'Holles street episode' and to 'Circe' as the 'Tyrone st. episode'.[37] Tymoczko sees this mnemonic use of place-names as characteristic of an Irish bardic tradition.[38] It is a tradition that preserves history through geography. For Tymoczko, 'Joyce acts like a *senchaid* of Irish tradition: he states directly that he wishes to preserve geographical knowledge and local history from extinction, and in this desire he is acting on behalf of the tribe'.[39] If this is a modernist agenda, it is a resolutely Irish one. The statements that literature made about the world should be responsible and Joyce spoke of 'an intellectual outlook which dissects life' and tries 'to get down to the residuum of truth'.[40] Literature has consequences and Joyce's complaint against Dadaism was its irresponsible nihilism while he was not slow to detect an intolerance of difference in the vaunted universalism of high modernists such as Eliot and Pound.

A full examination of the spatial poetics of James Joyce would have to consider the spatiality of his texts, not only the typography and layout,[41] but also the evocation of maps and flags on the cover of the first edition of *Ulysses* with its Greek colours and representation of islands of letters in a blue Mediterranean sea.[42] It would also be necessary to explore the varying conceptions of landscape and its passive or active elements in each of his works. There is also much to be said about the dialectic of space and time in their gendered opposition and contradictions, from the Newtonian geometry of *Dubliners* to the dialectical interpenetration of *Finnegans Wake*. Even within *Ulysses* there are a dozen ways a geographical imagination is made to convey meaning and in many cases the spatial poetics turn upon the contemplation of issues of Irish identity in a modern, if semi-colonial, world.[43] There is the general theme of conflation with the nesting and contested equivalence of scales. There are extended reflections upon the porosity of boundaries and what that means for originary identities. In the remainder of this paper, however, I will focus on only three spatial themes that, I believe, had a local political resonance for James Joyce. These are circulation, labyrinth and palimpsest.

These three spatial motifs provide a set of metaphors that allow Joyce to reflect critically upon Irish identities. Circulation is offered in part as a way of addressing the semi-paralysis of ways of being Irish that are so mired in anti-colonial assertion that they can see no value in any of the technological achievements of British civilisation. Joyce wants to draw attention to the need for Irish nationalists to take seriously the material needs of the people; they cannot live on shamrock alone. This is a more dynamic metaphor of interconnectedness than would be the alternative one of 'network', and, although I am emphasising the spatial dimension here, it is quite clear that these metaphors each produce a distinct conception of time alongside their spaces. In terms of emphasis we may choose to talk about the importance of space in *Ulysses*, but we must not forget that space and time are inevitably co-produced.[44] A labyrinth is a space of simultaneity. Joyce uses it to emphasise the importance of contingency. In terms of Irish identities, contingency and simultaneity are counterposed to necessity and hierarchy. It is the Church and the Crown that insist upon the last two. People are placed by both into subject positions whereas, in Joyce's vision of the city, the imperial and clerical gaze cannot comprehend the diversity of life nor address the egalitarian necessity of respecting each life equally. Finally, the palimpsest is the space of memory, of echoes of the past. It is, therefore, also a spatio-temporal concept but here the time produced is that of narrative history. This is the nightmare of a past that forever threatens to determine identities on the basis of past grievances. Living 'on another man's wound',[45] may, in Edward Thompson's resonant term, continually 'renew the raw nerve of outrage', but if that outrage prevents a clear understanding of present sources of discontent, then, living in the past lets present oppressors off the hook.

Before turning to the ways Joyce makes space produce meaning in his works, we need also to recall that he made space produce meaning in his life. Cixous is one of the many critics who have explored why exile was so important to Joyce.[46] Cixous understood that Joyce's removal of himself from Ireland was central to his sense of being able to address the ideological fetters that constrained artistic license in Ireland. She also understood that he needed to continually cultivate a sense of hurt over that very separation. Exile was a lived metaphor for the way Joyce thought Ireland treated its heroes. He saw himself as an artistic Parnell, a sexual outlaw in literature rather than in politics. The seriousness of his artistic purpose was in some way guaranteed by the need to seek exile. Artistic independence required the literary son to turn prodigal and forgiveness from the father, thought Joyce, was 'probably not the way of the world - certainly not in Ireland'.[47] In explaining why his play on the theme of vicarious and virtual adultery was called *Exiles*, Joyce noted that '[a] nation exacts a penance from those who dared to leave her payable on their return'.[48] In 1939, when he was working on what became *Finnegans Wake*, Joyce wrote of his reluctance to return to Ireland: '[h]aving a vivid memory of the incident at Castlecomer, when quicklime was thrown in the eyes of their dying leader, Parnell, by a chivalrous Irish mob, he did not wish a similar unfortunate occurrence to interfere with the composition of the book he was trying to write'.[49] Joyce's exile was necessary for personal and, relatedly, for artistic reasons. As Ellmann notes, Joyce's 'experiment in living [...] required that he experiment with living elsewhere'.[50] To live flagrantly with unmarried Nora, he had to leave Ireland. To combat puritanical literature, he had to defy puritanical morals and to do so in Ireland was too difficult for Joyce. He left Dublin in 1904 and returned but twice. On his last visit (1912), he paid a penance for his revolt. Cruel friends threw a serpent into his un-wedded bed with the claim that Nora had been unfaithful to Joyce during the earliest days of their courtship. This trauma provided the emotional core for the play, *Exiles*.

Many Irish writers left Dublin for the larger and richer public of London,[51]

28. Michael Begnal, 'Introduction', in Michael Begnal (ed), *Joyce and the City: the Significance of Place*, Syracuse NY, Syracuse University Press, 2002, ppxv-xx.

29. Power, *Conversations*, op. cit., p74.

30. Jon Hegglund, '*Ulysses* and the rhetoric of cartography', *Twentieth Century Literature* 49:2, 2003, pp164-182.

31. Clive Hart and Leo Knuth, *A Topographical Guide to James Joyce's Ulysses*, Colchester, A Wake Newslitter Press, 1975.

32. Letter to Grant Richards, 5 May 1906, *Letters II*, p125.

33. Power, *Conversations*, op. cit., p97.

34. Luke Gibbons, 'Synge, country and western: the myth of the West in Irish and American culture', in idem, *Transformations in Irish Culture*, Cork, Cork University Press, 1996, pp23-35.

35. Martha Fodeski Black, 'Joyce on location: place names in Joyce's fiction', in Begnal (ed), op. cit., pp18-34, p34.

36. Ellmann, *James Joyce*, second edition, Oxford, Oxford University Press, 1982 [1959], p232.

37. Letter from Stanislaus Joyce, 7

August 1924, *Letters III*, pp103-4.

38. Maria Tymoczko, *The Irish 'Ulysses'*, Berkeley CA, University of California Press, 1994, p 161.

39. Ibid., p158.

40. Power, *Conversations*, op. cit., p36.

41. Andrew Thacker, 'Toppling masonry and textual space: Nelson's pillar and spatial politics in Ulysses', *Irish Studies Review* 8:2 (2000): pp195-203.

42. Letter to Allessandro Franci Bruni, 7 June 1921, *Letters III*, 46.

43. Derek Attridge and Marjorie Howes, *Semicolonial Joyce*, Cambridge, Cambridge University Press, 2000.

44. Harvey, *Justice, Nature and the Geography of Difference*, Oxford, Blackwell, 1996; Doreen Massey, *For Space*, London, Sage, 2005.

45. Ernie O'Malley, *On Another Man's Wound*, London, Rich and Cowan, 1936.

46. Hélène Cixous, *The Exile of James Joyce*, New York, David Lewis, 1972 [1968].

47. Joyce, 'Entries in a notebook [on *Exiles*], now at Buffalo', in *idem*,

but Joyce's attempt to avoid the colonisation of his art by the English took him into European modernism and to multilingual cities such as Paris, Zurich and Trieste. There was also a need to establish distance from a changing Dublin in order the better to preserve his memory of a particular moment in the face of the inevitable erosion of that memory by the accumulating experience of a city in flux. For all his criticisms, Joyce was also nostalgic for the Dublin of his father's generation yet only in exile could he suspend anger long enough to be generous. Given that distance and separation were so important to his artistic life, it is perhaps less surprising that he should turn to these and many other geographical metaphors in rendering his artistic vision of the city of his birth.

FROM HEMIPLEGIA TO CIRCULATION

Dubliners announced its trio of themes, or symptoms, as the gnomon, simony, and paralysis. Each was used as a vehicle to think about Irish identity across the three dimensions, or leading causes, of language, colonialism and religion. Indeed, the themes of the stories could be explored through a consideration of the nine cells in a cross-tabulation of these symptoms and causes. In *A Portrait of the Artist as a Young Man*, the same three causes are figured as nets, or snares, set to entrap the soul of Stephen Dedalus, seeking to strike it with the hemiplegia that affects the rest of the Irish. To language, and the afflatus of Irish rhetoric, Stephen can offer his silence, to the bondage of colonialism, his voluntary exile, and to blandishments and threats of, in Stanislaus' resonant term, the 'religion of terrorism', his cunning.[52] In Weir's brilliant analysis, the gnomon is a form of mediation.[53] A geometric figure in which a parallelogram has a smaller but similar parallelogram removed from one corner, the gnomon figures absence, reduction and replication. English spoken in Ireland recalls the disappearance of Irish, its subsidiary relationship with the tongue of the master, and its reproduction of the literary culture of the conqueror. Colonial Ireland has no parliament of its own, is infantilised by its governors, and is always an inadequate mimicry of them. Likewise, Catholicism adverts to the Pope granting temporal sway in Ireland to an English monarch, to the obeisant politics that betrayed Parnell at the behest of the bishops, and to the Jesuitical education that passes subservience down to the rising generation.

Simony is the selling of sacred things. If the Irish language was a 'rich sea of words', that might have been the basis of a 'national letters',[54] then, its use by nationalists threatened to do no more than breed hatred of all things English. Joyce took Irish language classes with Patrick Pearse but 'dropped out in disgust and boredom at the continual ridicule aimed by the overenthusiastic lecturer at English: sound, sense, syntax and all'.[55] Even the literature written in English under an Irish sign 'surrendered to the popular will' and 'must now be considered the property of the rabblement of the most belated race in Europe'.[56] The apostolic church took the sacred life of the body with its natural desires and turned them against the soul as denial and guilt. In *Portrait*, under the tyranny of a religious retreat, the schoolboy Stephen wants to embrace a discipline that means mortifying his body, killing his natural life: '[I]nto the grave with it. Nail it down into a wooden box the corpse'.[57] Likewise, colonialism set up a moral economy where the sacred was profaned and the colon learned complicity. The British administration relied upon corrupting the Irish to get ears among the nationalists and to have them betray any leader with chance of success, and beyond the darkness of corruption there was the corona of suspicion. In *Dubliners*, 'Ivy Day in the Committee Room' is a case study of this corrosion. The best, and worst, that can be said of any politician was that he may be a hireling or not, '[t]here's no knowing'.[58] Trust turns toxic.

Dubliners and *Portrait* are *bildungsroman* of distinctive types. *Dubliners* documented the development of a conscience to show the near impossibility of honest, independent thought or action in Ireland. Corroded by Rome, London and an ersatz Connacht, marginalised by their eccentric geographies, the contemporaries of James Joyce were, in his view, almost literally shameless. The testimony of someone who had refused to serve this trinity might announce a new sentimental education, might give the people of Ireland 'one good look at themselves'.[59] Youth, adolescence, maturity and public life; over each of these the elements of the corrosive trinity cast their nets, but honesty might yet prove salve after the venom, might even inoculate. In *Portrait*, movement allows Stephen to explore the injunction to only mediate. First the streets of Dublin and then displacement to Paris teach with experiences outside the dreams of Jesuit philosophy. Paralysis could be physical, physiological and psychic. The competing claims of church, coloniser and country immobilise, and each challenges the inclinations of a natural life.

The spectre of syphilis haunts Joyce's Dublin. It is understood as a general paralysis of the insane, familiarly g.p.i.. It erupts all over the body politic. It has echoes in the request for a beer, a glass of plain porter: 'Here, Pat, give us a g.p., like a good fellow' (*Dubliners* p84). It is there in the gossip against Stephen: 'that fellow I was with in the Ship last night, said Buck Milligan, says you have g.p.i.' (*Ulysses* 1: 127-8). Yet in physiological terms, Joyce resists the moral implications of g.p.i., insisting that sexually transmitted infections are no more than 'venereal ill luck'.[60] Misfortune may deliver a good soul into a syphilitic place.

Gabriel Conroy, in 'The Dead', is paralysed by the competing claims of the trinity and even as his status is inflated by his own benediction, his self-assurance proves no protection against the inscrutability of a wife challenged on all three counts. She is inaccessible to him because he is a West Briton and she is a Galway girl. He resists the brogue that makes three syllables of his surname and patronises those who do not. He is easy with literary references that he imagines his fellow Irish dinner guests would be embarrassed to admit beyond them. He fancies his wife feels the same erotic

'Poems' and 'Exiles', J. C.C. May (ed), London, Penguin Books, 1992, pp342-54, p344.

48. Loc. cit..

49. Ellmann, *Joyce*, op. cit., p338.

50. Ibid., p110.

51. Fintan Cullen and R. F. Foster, 'Conquering England': Ireland in Victorian London, London, National Portrait Gallery, 2005.

52. Joyce, *My Brother's Keeper*, op. cit., p18.

53. David Weir, *James Joyce and the Art of Mediation*, Ann Arbor MI, University of Michigan Press, 1996.

54. Herbert Gorman, *James Joyce*, New York, Octagon Books, 1974 [1940], pp15-16.

55. Ibid., p60.

56. Joyce, 'The day of the rabblement' [1901], in Ellsworth Mason and Richard Ellmann (eds), *The Critical Writings of James Joyce*, New York, Viking Press, 1959, pp68-72, p70.

57. Joyce, *A Portrait of the Artist as a Young Man*, Boston MA, Bedford Books, 1993 [1916], p104, henceforth *PAAYM*.

58. Joyce, *Dubliners*, London, Penguin Books, 1992 [1914], p122, henceforth *Dubliners*.

59. Letter to Grant Richards, 23 June 1906, in Stuart Gilbert (ed.), *Letters of James Joyce. Volume I*, New York, Viking Press, 1966 [1957], p64.

60. Letter to Stanislaus Joyce, 4 October 1906, *Letters II*, p171.

flush as he at the prospect of an evening in a hotel whereas she is in a reverie about a lover from a Galway he has never known. With behaviour made pompous by class and genealogy, he is embarrassed too easily by the enthusiastic nationalist, Molly Ivors, because he would lose caste venturing with her upon a discourse of insecurity and indeterminacy. He finds it hard to be authentic and when he tries it, he is misunderstood. The only way he can put himself right in the eyes of those around him seems to be in the indulgent gaze following his death, 'his journey westward', that he may as well begin, to 'the descent of their last end' (*Dubliners* 225).

These themes of paralysis and syphilis recur in *Ulysses*. *Portrait* had finished with Stephen refusing to pay in his 'own life and person' for his Irish ancestors' betrayal of their language and independence (*PAAYM* 177). He would address the amorality of the Irish psyche by bearing witness to the miasma out of which it condensed. He would accumulate other experiences without the mire of Dublin. This is the revolt of the artist but *Ulysses* also offers other resources of hope, other prophylactics. Circulation is one of these.

Circulation is central to the 'Aeolus' episode. In Homer's *Odyssey*, Aeolus was the god of winds and in defiance of their master's instructions, the sailors travelling with Odysseus open the bag of winds and their boat is upended. Leerssen notes that Aeolus is also a pun on a Gaelic word for knowledge and learning.[61] The episode announces that the location is 'the heart of the Hibernian metropolis' (*Ulysses* 7: 1). We are at Nelson's column as trams arrive and leave. We are outside the General Post Office as the Royal Mail arrives and leaves. The dray of the Guinness Brewery is being loaded up to make a delivery. Bloom enters a newspaper office noting the placing of doors on opposite sides of it to allow the wind to come in one and out the other. Communications of all kinds are the theme with both the phone and the telegram in use. All this in the first two pages of the chapter.

61. Joep Leerssen, *Remembrance and Imagination: Patterns in the Historical and Literary Representation of Ireland in the Nineteenth Century*, Cork, Cork University Press, 1996, p84.

In a newspaper office, Simon Dedalus and others discuss a piece of high-flown nationalist rhetoric given the night before by Dan Dawson. Dimissed as 'Bladderbags' by one, they also note he gets money from an elderly relative on 'gale days', that is when the payment of overdue rent is demanded, and that when the old man dies, Dan will get a 'Windfall' (*Ulysses* 7: 260, 266). Metaphorical breezes gather with speculations about 'What's in the wind, ' worries about the dangers of gambling as 'reaping the whirlwind', reference to an opportunity as 'wind of a new opening', to inconstant journalists as 'Weathercocks' who 'veer' about selling their opinions to the highest bidder although the treason is soon forgotten for 'all blows over', dismissal of Dawson as an 'inflated windbag' (*Ulysses* 7: 292-3, 304, 309, 311, 315). When the discussion turns to the critique of English civilisation, the topic is again circulation. The English, it seems, are as famed for their sewers, their 'cloacal obsession', as the Jewish people are for their altars (*Ulysses* 7: 490). The treatment of Dublin, though, is of failed circulation. The tramcars are halted all over the city by a failure of electricity, 'becalmed in short circuit' (*Ulysses*

7: 1047). The nationalist rhetoric moves none of its auditors. The physical force nationalists, the Invincibles, are reported as promising to 'paralyse Europe', probably with dynamite (*Ulysses* 7: 628).

Yet Dublin needs circulation. Bloom is concerned with all kinds of circulation. He recalls, for example, marking a florin 'for circulation on the waters of civic finance, for possible, circuitous or direct, return' (*Ulysses* 17: 983-4). Physical circulation might ease congestion. The pragmatic Bloom has schemes in mind for the city. A tramline from the cattle market to the quays would avoid the city's streets being congested with beasts marching out of Ireland to slaughter in England (*Ulysses* 6: 400). The city needs sanitation. Germs circulate as in Bloom's contemplation of the common use of a drinking cup at a fountain: 'Rub off the microbes with your handkerchief. Next chap rubs on a new batch with his' (*Ulysses* 8: 712-3). Down at the beach, Stephen walks warily along the 'unwholesome sandflats' with their 'sewage breath' (*Ulysses* 3: 150-1). Bloom notes that the Dublin Bay oysters feed on sewage, (*Ulysses* 8: 865) and his scientific bent is pertinent for later on he recalls the O'Connor family who all died after eating mussels infected by sewage (*Ulysses* 13: 311). The sanitation of Dublin may be a rebuke to British administration, and as the vice-Regent passed by, the 'Poddle river hung out in fealty a tongue of liquid sewage' (*Ulysses* 10: 1196-7). However, these matters are under the direct control of the City Corporation, elected on a broad franchise and at this time under nationalist control. Bloom knows their failures well. The Corporation has not completed the main sewerage system nor does it provide a secure supply even of water, being forced to ration it during the summer (*Ulysses* 17: 175). Bloom, again, has a scheme. Ireland should convert its human sewage into agricultural fertiliser to reclaim its wastelands, the benefits were evident and the quantities available 'immense' (*Ulysses* 17: 1704). The tidal waters of Dublin Bay should be used to drive a 'hydroelectric plant' (*Ulysses* 17: 1712). Dublin needs practical measures to aid circulation not windy rhetoric that will yet leave the bark of state becalmed, short-circuited.

LABYRINTH

Barta has suggested that the modernist novel shows the city as a 'maze without a centre'.[62] The Dublin of *Ulysses* is a labyrinth wherein, as Kernan notes of Lord Edward Fitzgerald, a rebel might hide until someone, in this case a 'sham squire' gave them away (*Ulysses* 10: 789). There are hidden passages such as the 'secret door in the wall', through which, reputedly, Emmet's body was brought into Glasnevin cemetery for its midnight burial (*Ulysses* 10: 770-1). The city is a place of concealment so that by moving location one can place oneself beyond knowing eyes and follow furtively private actions in public places, like Bloom's 'bookhunt along Bedford row' (*Ulysses* 17: 2048-9), for pornographic novels for Molly, or Bloom serving himself by wandering in search of the erotic charge of the chance sighting

62. Peter Barta, *Bely, Joyce and Döblin: Peripatetics in the City Novel*, Gainesville FL, University Press of Florida, 1996, pxiv.

of a woman's petticoats or her stockings as she gets into a carriage. His aim is to look without being seen: 'Girl In Eustace street hallway Monday was it settling her garter. Her friend covering the display of. *Esprit de corps*. Well, what are you gaping at?'(*Ulysses* 18: 294-9) But Molly has seen enough to know him well: 'I saw him before he saw me however standing at the corner of the Harold's Cross Road with a new raincoat on him with the muffler in the Zingari colours to show off his complexion and the brown hat looking slyboots as usual what was he doing there where he'd no business they can go and get whatever they like from anything at all with a skirt on it and we're not to ask any questions but they want to know where were you where are you going' (*Ulysses* 18:294-9). Clearly, mobility is gendered, but Molly has the house during the day and she conducts a life rich in correspondence and visitors. She orchestrates her web of admirers through a strict control of time - Boylan, for example, is told to not turn up until 4pm.

The labyrinth is an image of mess and complexity. In *Portrait*, Joyce gave his alter-ego the name Dedalus. Dedalus was given in myth as an inventor, creating labyrinths and even wings. The artist then would weave a labyrinthine narrative and could contemplate soaring above the constrained lives of his fellow Dubliners, conveying complexity and objectivity, rather than simplicity and idealisation. Restuccia argues that *Ulysses* moves from a physical to a linguistic labyrinth.[63] *Ulysses* is not the novel that Dedalus could have written. It is not merely a view from above of the external lives of its characters. The physical and linguistic labyrinths interdigitate. Texts circulate in this city: the letters posted and read (Molly to Boylan, Bloom to Martha), the sandwich-board men weaving 'HELYS' through its streets, the bill advertising the arrival of a preacher ('Elijah is coming'), and the newspaper as the repository of the stories of the city. Kiberd proposes that '[t]he meaning of a newspaper is largely a do-it-yourself construction on the part of the reader-as-stroller. Likewise in *Ulysses*, the juxtaposition of elements is a deliberate denial of older hierarchies of value, in a sheer excess of detail much of which must be skimmed for the sake of the reader's sanity'.[64] The novel, like the newspaper, like the city, is a maze.

The city as 'living labyrinth' is a place of simultaneous but colliding lives.[65] Events realise but one of the set of contingent possibilities of a context: '[t]ime has branded them and, fettered, they are lodged in the room of the infinite possibilities they have ousted' (*Ulysses* 2: 49-51). But great events bequeath an aura of significance on all aspects of their context, refocusing attention on precedents that would otherwise be lost to the hazard of chance recall. *Ulysses* is set on 16 June 1904, the day of Nora Barnacle's first date with James Joyce. In honour of her earth-shattering 'yes', Joyce wanted to consecrate a whole context in its memory. Somewhere out in the labyrinth the contingent meeting of James and Nora took place. All manner of events might have supervened to prevent the promise of the encounter being kept. But they did not.

The labyrinth is most extensively developed in 'The Wandering Rocks'

63. Frances L. Restuccia, *Joyce and the Law of the Father*, Harvard CT, Yale University Press, 1989, p153.

64. Declan Kiberd, *Irish Classics*, London, Granta Books, 2000, p466.

65. Stuart Gilbert, *James Joyce's 'Ulysses'*, New York, Alfred A. Knopf, 1930, p216.

episode. In *The Odyssey*, the hero is warned of a sea passage bedevilled by wandering rocks that drift apart and together to crush a ship. Odysseus does not attempt the crossing but Bloom, bolstered by love as was Jason, the only successful navigator of the wandering rocks, sets out into a city of contemporaneous lives, contingent and often hostile collisions of citizens. A labyrinth fed by the venous and arterial systems of transport and rivers, the main bodies in motion are other Dubliners. Like every other chapter, this one focuses on one bodily organ as Joyce builds up his picture of the body of the city. This chapter is about the circulation of the blood. The chapter consists of nineteen sections which overlap and which are interrupted by the intrusion of comparable events tied in time and theme but distant in space. Father Conmee leaves home to go to a school for indigent children where he will press the case of one of the Dignam boys. Their father's funeral was earlier attended by Bloom. On his mission of mercy Conmee thinks about the ingratitude of monarch towards the clergy. He sees a crippled sailor for whom the Crown has no further use, although he himself keeps his own crown safely in his pocket in the face of the beggar's appeal. As he passes Mrs M'Guiness, elsewhere in the city Denis Maginni, a flamboyantly dressed dancing instructor, passes Lady Maxwell who has herself come from a meeting with Father Conmee. Conmee continues on his walk and passes the funeral parlour where Corny Kelleher is marking up his daybook of jobs completed. Conmee walks on and takes a tram. Then it's back to Kelleher as Conmee passed him. Keller arcs a stream of spit into the street just as, elsewhere in the city, Molly throws a coin arcing down to a passing invalided sailor. Then it is back to the sailor as he begins his walk along Eccles street towards the window from which Molly will disburse her gift. Meanwhile in another part of the city another down-at-heel supplicant is soliciting alms. J.J. O'Molloy has gone to see Ned Lambert for a favour. But back to the sailor: Conmee had already refused him, but Molly's coin lands at the feet of a street urchin who pops it into the sailor's hat. In these first three sections, then, we have chance encounters, generosity, reflections upon ingratitude. These are all part of the city's monologue as it tells its own tale of complexity and time-geographic simultaneity. And Joyce develops this across nineteen sections and numerous coincidental sparks of association or coincidence.

Budgen described Joyce plotting this chapter with map, ruler and stopwatch. He also says that at this time, Joyce 'bought a game called "Labyrinth," which he played every evening for a time with his daughter Lucia'.[66] Budgen notes that in this chapter the focus is not on the trio of Molly, Bloom and Stephen, which dominates the rest of the book, but instead the city itself takes centre-stage. It is rather civic society that is the focus. After the critical diagnosis of Dublin in *Dubliners*, Joyce confided to Stanislaus that he may have been harsh on his old home for he had not given the reader much sense of its 'ingenious insularity and hospitality'.[67] It is this quality of everyday courtesy and conviviality that Joyce celebrates. Social life is produced as contingent interactions. Community rests upon

66. Budgen, 'Joyce', p125.

67. Letter to Stanislaus Joyce, 25 September 1906, *Letters II*, 166.

68. Hegglund, 'Ulysses', p183.

69. Budgen, 'Joyce', p69.

70. Loc. cit.

71. Enda Duffy, 'Disappearing Dublin: *Ulysses*, postcoloniality and the politics of space', in Attridge and Howes, *Semicolonial Joyce*, pp37-57.

72. Budgen, 'Joyce', p69.

73. Ibid., p123.

74. David Spurr, 'Colonial spaces in Joyce's Dublin', *James Joyce Quarterly* 37, 1-2 (1999-2000): pp23-42, p34.

75. Kiberd, *Inventing Ireland*, op. cit., p330.

76. Paul Schwaber, *The Cast of Characters: a Reading of 'Ulysses'*, New Haven CT, Yale University Press, 1999, p5.

77. For clarification of many of the historical details in this section, I have relied upon Don Gifford, *'Ulysses' Annotated: Notes for James Joyce's 'Ulysses'*, second edition, Berkeley CA, University of California Press, 1988 [1974].

'coincidence rather than essence'.[68] The city has a 'personality that emerges out of the contacts of many people'.[69] Budgen follows this comment by recalling Joyce claiming that he wanted 'to give a picture of Dublin so complete that if the city one day suddenly disappeared from the earth it could be reconstructed out of my book'.[70] It is certainly true that the revolution of 1916 saw the destruction of some of the principal streets of the city and Duffy has suggested that this is behind Joyce's concern about preserving his city in his book.[71] The topographical detail in this chapter with, as Hegglund notes, over two hundred place-names, lends support to this claim but I think that it is at least as likely that the city Joyce really had in mind was of a social rather than a physical order for, even as he and Budgen took in a panoramic view of the city of Zurich, his panegyric continued: 'And what a city Dublin is! [...] I wonder if there is another like it. Every body has time to hail a friend and start a conversation about a third party'.[72]

By shifting the viewpoint, Joyce gives us a vertiginous vision of a whirling city without privileging the perspective of any one individual. This is not a disclosure narrative in which a traveller penetrates to the dark heart of a foreign land and learns its secrets. There is no single secret here. The chapter began with a representative of the Catholic Church moving northeast and ends with a representative of the Crown moving southeast but this X of the tenth chapter marks no spot with hidden treasure but rather frames the lives lived under its sign. Those lives, and Budgen used the phrase 'wandering anarchic individualism' to describe them, always exceed the reach of these authorities.[73] As the Viceregent moves across the city, people salute, ignore and insult him, even in ways that he either misses or misinterprets. Spurr notes in particular that Simon Dedalus, having just left a urinal, lowers his hat to cover the flies he has forgotten to re-button, which the Viceregent acknowledges as a mark of deep respect.[74] If *Dubliners* was about the impossibility of free will under colonialism, then, suggests Kiberd, *Ulysses* recovers the dignity of everyday life.[75] 'Wandering rocks', then, offers a 'democratic vista' because it endows a whole cast of city characters with complex internal lives most novelists reserve for their heroes alone.[76] The labyrinth is a democratic space with significance distributed evenly over its surface. It is also a form drawing attention to the art of the maze weaver, from Dedalus to Joyce.

PALIMPSEST

Standing in his warehouse Ned Lambert tells the tale of the building to a visiting vicar.[77] It, St Mary's Abbey (see Fig 1), was the oldest religious building in Dublin. Lambert points out its associations with Irish independence, used as a meeting place for the knights of Henry VIII, it was 'where Silken Thomas proclaimed himself a rebel in 1534' (*Ulysses* 10: 408-9). Lambert points out this too was the site of the old Bank of Ireland 'till the time of the Union' thereby reminding the priest that when Ireland's own parliament had been dissolved in 1800, the parliamentary building was converted to a bank so that it might never again be used for debates or assemblies (*Ulysses* 10: 411). Its historic use was interrupted. Lambert also reminds the vicar of the persecution of the Jews pointing out the site of 'the original Jews' temple' (*Ulysses* 10: 412). The Anglican clergyman was given a brief history lesson through Dublin's landscape. Here was the oldest abbey in Dublin, dissolved by the founder of the Anglican church. The stones of the city could be made to tongue the lesson of English religious and political oppression. If Lambert's is a Catholic litany of the landscape, his friend, Tom Kernan, has a Protestant tale he would make the city tell. Born a Protestant, Kernan converted to Catholicism in order to marry a Catholic but his sympathies remain Protestant. He still refers to O'Connell bridge by its former name 'Carlisle bridge' (*Ulysses* 10: 747). Carlisle was viceroy when, in 1791, the building of the bridge was begun but the bridge had been renamed after the Catholic Liberator in 1882. Gibson notes that with the accession of nationalists to power in the Dublin Corporation after 1884, there was a concerted campaign to re-label the city under more Irish signs.[78] Walking near the site of Robert Emmett's execution (a hanging followed by beheading on the steps of a church), Kernan recalls the Protestant gentlemen who defended the right of the Irish to their own parliament and who fought the English to keep it in 1798. Walking northwards down Watling street, he recalls the ambush planned there to entrap another of the men of '98, Lord Edward Fitzgerald. He thinks of these protestant gentlemen as dashing rakes, gambling and romantic. Emmett, he thinks, got into fights over cards, Fitzgerald evaded the English soldiers so that he could sneak back to his wife for evening trysts in the stables. 'Bad times those were', he reflects, the 'Times of the troubles' (*Ulysses* 10: 781). In those 'faroff days', swashbuckling Protestants found themselves, as he notes, 'on the wrong side' because they had promised to defend the Irish parliament (*Ulysses* 10: 790). Thus, exceptionally and uncomfortably, they wound up making common cause with their peasant and Catholic compatriots. Kernan's sympathies are resolutely Ascendancy. He rushes to catch a glimpse of the Lord Lieutenant as he passes along the quays at the foot of Watling Street. He is sure that 1798 was an aberration: 'over and done with' (10: 767). Lambert would have disagreed.

78. Andrew Gibson, *Joyce's Revenge: History, Politics, and Aesthetics in "Ulysses"*, Oxford, Oxford University Press, 2002, p95.

Joyce helps the reader feel history shouting at his Dubliners from all corners of their city. In a carriage with others, Bloom sets out from the Dignams' house in south-east Dublin to accompany the body of Paddy Dignam to its grave in Prospect Cemetery on the north-east of the city. As they pass diagonally across the city, Joyce tells of the statues they pass (see Fig 1). Philip Crampton, a famous surgeon with a commission to the British army, but unknown to Bloom who wonders 'who was he?' (*Ulysses* 6: 191) Others evoke more immediate resonances: William Smith O'Brien (*Ulysses* 6: 226), the leader of the 1848 rebellion; Daniel O'Connell (the 'hugecloaked

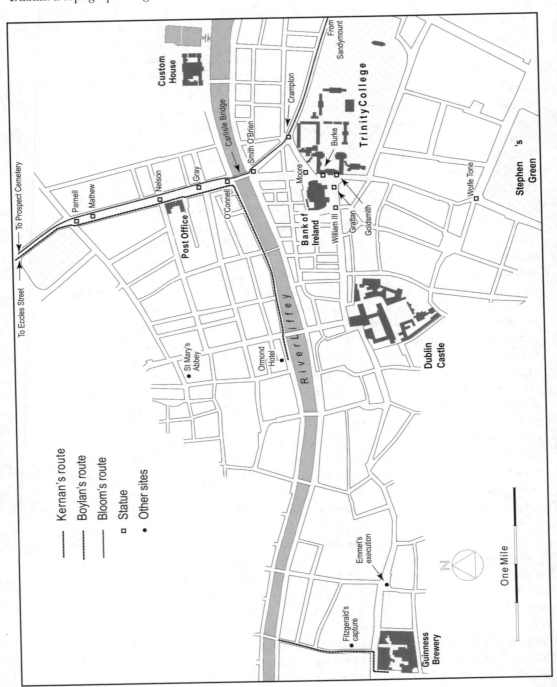

Fig 1, Dublin as palimpsest. I am very grateful to Paul Laxton for drawing the map. It is based on George W. Bacon (ed), New large-scale atlas of the British Isles from the Ordnance Survey with plans of towns ... (London, G.W. Bacon and Co., 1890) plate 71, and upon Ian Gunn and Clive Hart, James Joyce's Dublin: a topographical guide to the Dublin of 'Ulysses' (London, Thames and Hudson 2004).

Liberator's form') (*Ulysses* 6: 249) who secured Catholic emancipation; Sir John Gray ('Farrell's statue') (*Ulysses* 6: 228), the Protestant Irish patriot who brought Dublin its water supply and edited the journal on which Bloom now works; Horatio Nelson on his 'pillar' (*Ulysses* 6: 293) outside the General Post Office; Father Mathew, the temperance reformer who ensured good discipline at O'Connell's mass meetings (recalled in their conversation about Dignam being taken from them by the drink); Charles Parnell, the Home Rule advocate, for whose statue a 'foundation stone' (*Ulysses* 6: 320) stood ready at the top of Sackville street; and, as they enter the graveyard, the 'cardinal's mausolem' of Edward MacCabe, an archbishop (1879-85) antipathetic to independence (*Ulysses* 6: 534). All those Bloom recognises bear some relation to the cause of independence. Upon arriving in the graveyard, the mourners are beset by statues and commemoration. They note the O'Connell tower, and are pleased that he rests 'in the middle of his people' (*Ulysses* 6: 643). Although they also recall that his heart is buried in Rome which gives him an unstated kinship with their next port of call, Parnell of the broken heart and Episcopal betrayal. The nationalist, Joe Hynes, and the police detective, Jack Power, decide to take a turn by the grave of this man they both revere as the Chief. There, 'following their slow thoughts', they consider the rumour that Parnell is still alive but Power adds that 'Parnell will never come again' (*Ulysses* 6: 921, 926). While the carriage was passing Gray's statue, Power had been laughing at an anti-semitic joke and perhaps out of respect for Gray, he 'shaded his face from the window' (*Ulysses* 6: 257). Each character ossified in memorials recalls a complex of values still pertinent to Bloom and his companions - for or against independence, for or against violence, for or against the Catholic Church. As such, one's visits to and comportment about these stones spoke volumes. Murphy has suggested that in 'The Dead' Gabriel Conroy's ignoring of all the British and Ascendancy statues he passed, and his saluting alone the statue of Daniel O'Connell, shows a form of resistance both to British colonialism, but also to the charge that he is a West Briton, rather than properly Irish.[79] In *Ulysses*, there are clear references to the explicit as well as subliminal ways people respond to memorials. As the funeral cortege passed O'Brien's statue, Bloom had seen a bouquet there and guessed correctly that it must be 'his deathday' (*Ulysses* 6: 227). His own response to a statue of Thomas Moore was less respectful. Recalling Moore's poem, 'The meeting of the waters', he mused that '[t]hey did right to put him up over a urinal' (*Ulysses* 8: 414-5). In *Portrait*, Stephen had contemplated the same statue and had read it in more distinctly colonial terms, reviewing Moore's peddling of sorrowful nonsense about Ireland's past to entertain its colonial masters, but a different strain of irony rescues Moore for Stephen for as he looks at the statue, he thinks it 'seemed humbly conscious of its indignity' (*PAAYM* 158).[80]

Even empty space could speak volumes. The pedestal that had been awaiting a statue of Parnell underlines the poignancy of Bloom recalling

79. Michael Murphy, 'Political memorials in the city of "The Dead,"' in Begnal (ed), *Joyce and the City*, pp110-122.

80. Spurr, 'Colonial spaces', op. cit.

how he died: 'Breakdown. Heart' (*Ulysses* 6: 320). 1798, interpreted so divergently by Kernan and Lambert, was still contentious. The leader of a French-sponsored invasion, Theobald Wolfe Tone had a pedestal but nothing more, 'the slab where Wolfe Tone's statue was not' (*Ulysses* 10: 378). Robert Emmet, who led an assault on Dublin Castle in 1803, had no monument although this was his own wish for, as Bloom reads in his courtroom speech displayed in a shop window, Emmet requested no epitaph until '*my country takes her place among*', and here Bloom breaks off to break wind before the sentence concludes, the '*Nations of the earth*' (*Ulysses* 11: 1284-5, 1289). Dublin is the centre of an aborted nation and Ireland is not, in Joyce's terms, a 'logical and serious country' but instead an 'eternal caricature of the serious world' for 'even when the monuments are for the most popular men, whose character is most amenable to the will of the people, they rarely get beyond the laying of the foundation stone'.[81] Clearly, it cannot be a serious nation until it is able to use its public space to express the will of its people. Instead, its public spaces are given over to the ostensible displace of colonial power and to histories that retail competing grudges.

81. Joyce, 'James Clarence Mangan' [1907], in Mason and Ellmann, *The Critical Writings*, pp175-86, p176.

These statues, buildings and street names provide a historical and moral stage-set for Dublin's citizens. Once the lessons had been taught, the reading of the landscape became involuntary. Blazes Boylan, on his way to cuckold Bloom, passes many of the same statues and sites as had Bloom. His interior monologue is much less attentive to his surroundings, thinking only of the sexual conquest ahead. Yet, even he cannot exclude the city from his thoughts. Proceeding northwards from the river and up Sackville (now O'Connell) street, Bloom is aware of passing 'by monuments of sir John Gray, Horatio onehandled Nelson, reverend father Theobald Mathew' (*Ulysses* 11: 762-3). The associations are more moral than historical here. For Boylan, Gray is not a philanthropist, but the founder of the newspaper for which Bloom works, and Nelson is not a naval hero but, as elsewhere in the novel a 'onehandled adulterer' (*Ulysses* 7: 1072) (the phrase Boylan avoids completing), and Mathew is the disciple of abstinence. Immediately after Mathew, Boylan would have passed another famous adulterer, as his carriage went around the plinth raised for the statue to Parnell. Boylan makes no comment but at this point he urges his horse faster forward. Joyce highlighted the hypocritical contrast drawn by British politicians between Nelson, heroic, and Parnell, villainous adulterer, and his notes for the revisions of the 'Ithaca' and 'Penelope' reflect this.[82] Gogarty recalled that the medical students that Joyce mixed with in Dublin used to render Nelson's famous signal as: 'England expects every man to commit adultery'.[83]

82. Phillip F. Herring (ed), *Joyce's Notes and Early Drafts for 'Ulysses': selections from the Buffalo Collection*, Charlottesville VA, University Press of Virginia, 1977, p43.

83. Oliver St John Gogarty, *Tumbling in the Hay* [1939], Dublin, The O'Brien Press, 1996, p299.

Dublin as palimpsest is important to Joyce because it establishes the city as drenched in history. It is this history of rebellion, repression and resistance that is important to Joyce's Dubliners. The effective history of Irish identity was not the Celtic legends, the oral traditions of the peasant's fireside, it lay here in the capital, retold by Kernan, Lambert, Haynes, Power, and Bloom. But Joyce is worried about these retellings. When in Rome, Joyce found the multitude of monuments overbearing and Ellmann reports that his 'head was filled with a sense of the too successful encroachment of the dead upon the living city'.[84] Stephen, teaching in a school, looks with pity on his charges: 'For them too history was a tale like any other too often heard, their land a pawnshop' (*Ulysses* 2: 46-7). Recalling Shakespeare's history as a tale told by an idiot, Stephen is also implying that Ireland's present is in hock to its obsession with its past; because history too often heard keeps alive longstanding enmities. This is not quite the alibi that Haines claims for England when he said 'history is to blame' for England treating Ireland 'rather unfairly' (*Ulysses* 1: 649). When Crawford, the editor, speaks of a newspaper giving its readers 'the whole bloody history' (*Ulysses* 7: 676-7), Stephen recalls having told the headmaster at the school where he teaches that 'History [...] is a nightmare from which I am trying to awake' (*Ulysses* 2: 377). But the immediate context of his remarks was his contemplation of the history of Jewish people: 'their eyes knew their years of wandering and, patient, knew the dishonours of their flesh'. This history of persecution must produce its own vengeance on Christians for 'What if a nightmare gave you a back kick?' (*Ulysses* 2: 379) Two suggestions are ventured here: that the crimes of injustice may find a people out and that the cultivation of a memory of hatred may itself 'make a stone of the heart' in Yeats' words.[85] The phrase Stephen uses when referring to the shock revenge that history might exact is the same he uses to refer to the God's vengeance, 'a shout in the street' (*Ulysses* 2: 386). Stanislaus explains that Joyce 'means that the idea of God is something that startles you when you are hard at work, and makes you jump-up and look out the window'.[86] Out in the streets, religion and history interrupt and distract lives.

Bloom takes up the same theme in his argument with The Citizen. Bloom says he belongs to a race which has been 'Plundered. Insulted. Persecuted' (*Ulysses* 12: 1470). 'I'm talking about injustice, says Bloom' (*Ulysses* 12: 1474) and when John Wyse Nolan tells him he should stand up and fight injustice, Bloom's reply surprises his nationalist auditors: 'But it's no use, says he. Force, hatred, history, all that. That's not life for men and women, insult hatred' (*Ulysses* 12: 1481-2). Bloom tells them that life is about love. What chance had love in a city such as this where the very stones hollered injustice? The parallels between Irish and Jewish history are repeatedly sounded in *Ulysses*: 'their dispersal, persecution, survival and revival' (17: 755-6). The Citizen is given pure hateful prose of the purest John Mitchel water.[87] England has destroyed Irish manufactures, starved many Irish people and dispersed others: 'Where are our missing, twenty millions should be here instead of four, our lost tribes?' 'What do the yellowjohns of Anglia owe us for our ruined trade and our ruined hearths' (*Ulysses* 12: 1254-5). 'We'll put force against force, says the citizen. We have our greater Ireland beyond the sea. They were driven out of house and home in the black '47' (*Ulysses* 12: 1364-6). 'But those that came to the land of the free remember the land of bondage. And they will come again and with a vengeance' (*Ulysses* 12: 1372-

84. Ellmann, *Joyce*, op. cit., p244.

85. William Butler Yeats, 'Easter 1916', l. 58, in *The Collected Poems of William Butler Yeats*, New York, Simon and Schuster, 1996, p180.

86. Stanislaus Joyce, *My Brother's Keeper*, op. cit., p20.

87. Gerry Kearns, '"Educate that holy hatred": place, trauma and identity in the Irish nationalism of John Mitchel', *Political Geography*, 20 (2001): pp885-911.

4). This is the history that frightened Joyce and why he was so distrustful of the idealisation of Cathleen ní Houlihan. In the Circe episode Stephen has a vision of Ireland as the old hag, but not as one who could be rejuvenated by the blood of her young, but as 'Old Gummy Granny', with 'the deathflower of the potato blight on her breast' (*Ulysses* 15: 4578-80). Stephen hails her as 'The old sow that eats her farrow!' (*Ulysses* 15: 4581-2) The city as palimpsest educates a people to a pitch, not so much of 'bewildered love'[88] for the abstracted mother country, but to such a fever of hatred that their capacity for self-respect and humanity is defined by the Manichean, Cyclops vision of the Citizen. War, hatred and conflict are presented as a sort of falling into history.[89]

88. Yeats, 'Easter 1916, l. 73.

89. James Fairhall, *James Joyce and the Question of History*, Cambridge, Cambridge University Press, 1993, p215.

FROM SPATIAL POETICS TO LITERARY POLITICS

The critique of the Literary Revival that Joyce developed in *Dubliners* and *Portrait* seemed to propose other, better ways of examining Irish identities than in the peasant plays of the Abbey. A fully responsible Irish literary culture could serve not king, nor Caesar, nor Pope, nor Cathleen ní Houlihan. Yet the individualistic rebellion of Stephen Dedalus was in danger of producing an etiolated aesthetics. This, I think, is where Joyce's historical materialism proved so important. Eagleton feels that there is so little history in Joyce, that, he is unable to imagine revolutionary alternatives to the present order, that by taking language as the metaphor for the constitution of the social order, he was given over to an excessive emphasis on simultaneity.[90] Fairhill finds other limitations. Joyce, he argues, had no serious engagement with the Irish socialism of his day.[91] Because he ignored the slums, and distrusted all the 'big words [...] which make us so unhappy' (*Ulysses* 2: 264), Joyce is insufficiently aware of the necessity and practicability of socialism. There is some justice in these claims. Despite the clear awareness of social and economic questions he shows in the journalism he was writing before he started *Ulysses*, the proletariat are not the focus of the book. The book is set among the lower middle class and its locations skirt the worst of the tenement slums. It is, after all, written out of Joyce's own biography. However, I think Joyce does make a good case that the national, the religious and the colonial questions do shape and will shape Irish identities. Their effects cannot be dreamed away by hitching the Irish question to the engine of proletarian struggle. Indeed, the struggle for social justice, in many cases, has been based on mobilising people around elements of this unholy trinity. It is in this sense that I think that the agenda of Joyce's spatial poetics is not quite the same as, or at least is not predominantly defined by, the contemplation of time-space compression or its primary effects. I have argued here that the spatial themes of circulation, labyrinth and palimpsest raise quite other, if related, questions. Circulation embraces the flux of modern life but in order to emphasise freedom, or at least efficiency, through practical schemes, challenging the priorities of politicians. Labyrinth

90. Terry Eagleton, *Heathcliff and the Great Hunger: Studies in Irish Culture*, London, Verso, 1995, p318.

91. Fairhill, *Joyce and the Question of History*.

democratises the view of the city and its denizens, challenging elitism. Palimpsest provides a view of the urban scene as placing Irish identities in hock to historical grudges, grudges that divide those coincident persons who make up the citizenry. Each is related to stylistic innovations in *Ulysses*, a novel that draws attention to the constitution of the social order of the city through the circulation of texts, that makes of the novel a decentred maze to be explored in many equally adequate and exciting ways, and a book which takes seriously the injunction to historicise but equally to historicise a particular sense of history that sustains and may derail anti-colonial struggles. There is a hint, and more than a hint, in *Ulysses* of an alternative utopia, the 'New Bloomusalem', practical, egalitarian, and tolerant - difficult to imagine, but all the more vital for that.

I would like to thank the following for their advice: Millie Glennon, Stephen Heath, Mike Heffernan, Phil Howell, Paul Laxton, Steve Legg, Denis Linehan, Scott McCracken, John Morrissey, Katy Mullin, David Nally, Richard Philips, Simon Reid-Henry, Ray Ryan, Karen Till, Andy Tucker, and the anonymous referees for the journal.

Study, Marketplace and Labyrinth:
Geometry as Rhetoric

Jess Edwards

DIRTY OR CLEAN?

It is all too easy to think that we understand the power and the charm of the early modern map. In those often magnificent examples of global, regional and even local cartography, which have survived the centuries we imagine we perceive the spirit of European artists, rulers, merchants and landlords for the first time in possession of their material environment: bursting the bubble of Medieval parochialism and stretching out to govern a space as limitless as the geometry which framed it. And if we do not celebrate this breaking free from place to space then we mourn it, as the dawn of a new age of panoptic discipline and surveillance.

For many cultural historians the cartographic mathematisation of experience is a crucial marker of modernity, and of the revolution in ideas and values that fostered early modern capitalism and imperialism. If arts such as geography embraced mathematical technologies and aesthetics in the late sixteenth and seventeenth centuries they are held to have done so in an empiricist, pragmatic and mercantile spirit, treating the material world as so much dead matter to be cleanly abstracted, partitioned and exploited: subjected to a distinctly modern form of discipline. Graham Huggan sees in the 'reinscription, enclosure and hierarchization of space' executed by the post-Renaissance map, 'an analogue for the acquisition, management and reinforcement of colonial power'.[1] Samuel Edgerton finds in the orthogonal grid common to Ptolemaic cartographic projection and Albertian artificial perspective in painting, a 'symbol of cultural expansion'.[2] David Harvey observes that the geometric aesthetic of Ptolemaic cartography made the world in general seem 'conquerable and containable for purposes of human occupancy and action'.[3]

The problem with these judgements is encapsulated in Edgerton's 'symbol' as it is in Huggan's 'analogue'. How do we know what the geometry of early modern maps symbolised or seemed to their early modern makers and users? How can we judge the cultural currency of the early modern map?

Since the 1980s we have become used to regarding early modern cartographies as maps of cultural meaning, rather than simply of material space. But the critical history of early modern cartography that has developed over the past three decades is highly heterogeneous, and by no means agreed on the ways in which cartography is cultural. The most

1. Graham Huggan, 'Decolonizing the Map: Post-Colonialism, Post-Structuralism and the Cartographic Connection', *Ariel: A Review of International English Literature*, 20, 4 (1989): 115-131, p115.

2. Samuel Edgerton, 'From Mental Matrix to *Mappamundi* to Christian Empire: The Heritage of Ptolemaic Cartography in the Renaissance', in David Woodward (ed), *Art and Cartography: Six Historical Essays*, Chicago, University of Chicago Press, 1983, p22.

3. David Harvey, *The Condition of Postmodernity: An Enquiry into the Origins of Cultural Change*, Oxford, Basil Blackwell, 1989, p246.

materialist histories treat maps as what we might call 'dirty' entities, locating them in tightly specified local processes and transactions.[4] Other scholars have constructed relationships between maps and verbal texts, widely separated in historical time and material space, over the 'cleaner' common ground of symbolism and formal analogy. So is the map clean or dirty? Is it a text that we can read effectively in modern galleries, libraries and classrooms? Is it, on the other hand, a material commodity whose historical significance lies beyond it, in those local transactions and performances in which it was originally engaged?

This question has profound ramifications for the place we give to cartography in early modern culture, and for the way we read or decline to read the map. In this essay I will attempt an answer, reviewing past strategies and exploring the possibilities for reading cartography with writing. I will argue that early modern cartography was rhetorical: engendered and closely supplemented by processes of verbal argument and persuasion, and regarded in itself as a persuasive gesture. Early modern maps were used not just to represent space but also to negotiate the identity, the legitimacy and the agency of individuals, groups and ventures. As an element in these negotiations they were characteristically entangled in a web of words which all too frequently evaporates in idealist readings and materialist histories of cartography. Neither clean nor dirty, they were often intended as dusty metaphors for the liminal relationship between virtue and profit, knowledge and the world.

FROM TRANSPARENT WINDOW TO THICKENED TEXT

The traditional, positivist history of cartography is teleological and idealist.[5] Traditional cartographic history assumes consistent development towards a modern scientific practice founded on the discipline of geometric measurement and projection and treats individual maps as neutral contributions to a Platonic archive of geographic knowledge. It treats the geometric space delineated in early moden maps, if not as a Newtonian absolute category of the world, then as a Kantian absolute category of the mind. The first revolution in a critical history of cartography involved what might be called a thickening of the map, a shift from the essentially idealist habit of seeing through it, as a window on the world, to one of reading it, as cultural text. This revolution began in the history of art.

The iconological tradition in art history, inaugurated by Erwin Panofsky, treats the newly geometric spatiality of early modern maps and paintings not as 'a definitive victory over Medieval parochialism and superstition' but as a form of culturally specific, symbolic meaning which can be read.[6] This approach has informed a revisionist history of cartography which seeks to appreciate the geometric map as cultural text. Yet in the main this new history has acted only as a mournful counterpoint to traditional map history, reinforcing its idealism through a set of complementary assumptions about

4. See, for instance, Jerry Brotton, *Trading Territories: Mapping the Early Modern World*, London, Reaktion, 1997.

5. Matthew Edney, 'Cartography Without "Progress"', *Cartographica*, 30, 2/3 (1993): 57.

6. Samuel Y. Edgerton, *The Renaissance Rediscovery of Linear Perspective*, New York, Basic Books Inc., 1975, p9.

7. Michel Foucault, 'Space, Knowledge, and Power', in Paul Rabinow (ed), *The Foucault Reader*, Harmondsworth, Penguin, 1986, p254.

8. Michel Foucault, 'Panopticism', in Paul Rabinow (ed), *The Foucault Reader*, Harmondsworth, Penguin, 1986, pp208-9.

9. Denis Cosgrove and Stephen Daniels, 'Introduction: Iconography and landscape', in Denis Cosgrove and Stephen Daniels (eds), *The Iconography of Landscape: Essays on The Symbolic Representation, Design and Use of Past Environments*, Cambridge Studies in Historical Geography 9, Cambridge, Cambridge University Press, 1988, p1.

10. Harley, J.B., 'Maps, Knowledge, and Power', in Denis Cosgrove and Stephen Daniels (eds), op. cit., 277-312.

11. Ibid., p282.

12. See, for instance, Mark Koch, 'Ruling the World: The Cartographic Gaze in Elizabethan Accounts of the New World', *Early Modern Literary Studies* 4, 2, Special Issue 3 (September, 1998): 11, <http://purl.oclc.org/emls/04-2/kochruli.htm>; William Boelhower, 'Inventing America: a model of

the modernity of the early modern map, and shadowing the traditional view of cartographic 'discipline'.

MAPS, KNOWLEDGE AND POWER

If it learns from iconology in its preparedness to read the map, the new cartographic history also owes much to French structuralism, and specifically to Michel Foucault, in its account of what the map might say. Foucault's analysis of the uses and the politics of Enlightenment space is notoriously pessimistic, treating modern modes of spatial thought and planning as inextricable from the exercise of power. Linnaean botany and the sciences of madness and penalogy map out common ground for Foucault in a 'spatialisation of knowledge' working to define and subject nature and humanity and embodied in the pun of 'discipline'.[7] In both of its senses 'discipline', notes Foucault, 'fixes; it arrests or regulates movements; it clears up confusion ... it establishes calculated distributions'.[8] Foucault's descriptions of the 'spatialisation of knowledge' and of the disciplinary uses of spatial planning and representation have proved vastly fertile in revisionist studies of cartographic history, and most prominently in the work of Brian Harley.

One of the most widely read of Harley's essays is included in Denis Cosgrove and Stephen Daniels's 1988 collection *The Iconography of Landscape*. Harley's essay reads cartography as a Panofskian 'cultural image', and Harley's title 'Maps, Knowledge and Power' makes clear the Foucauldian parameters within which he intends to read the map.[9] Harley regrets that cartographic history has been dominated to date by a positivist teleology of evolving accuracy. What this history elides, he suggests, is the partiality of modern maps as simply a 'way of conceiving, articulating, and structuring the human world'.[10] In fact, Harley argues, the 'Euclidean syntax' privileged in post fifteenth-century cartography did not just reflect the world, but 'structured European territorial control'.[11] The particular rhetoric of 'authority' explicit in the Medieval map had not gone away, but was now hidden by this 'silent' geometric syntax.

FROM PRODUCT TO PROCESS

Harley's interventions laid out the ground for a critical history of cartography which examines the role of maps in the cultural making of knowledge. Much of what has followed has reproduced Harley's pessimistic reading of the 'Euclidean syntax' of cartography.[12] Yet several notes of warning have been sounded in recent years which have worked to undermine this simultaneously Foucauldian and iconological approach. These warnings have come primarily from two directions: one, that of traditional, positivist map scholarship; the other, an alternative fork to Harley's in the path of a newly cultural history of geography.

In his introduction to the posthumous collection of Harley's essays *The New Nature of Maps* (2001), map historian J.H. Andrews poses the following rhetorical question: 'positivist historians have plenty to do when confronted with a previously unknown map ... What can the non positivist scholar do except say, 'Just as I thought: more glorification of state power'.[13] The problem, as Andrews sees it, is that whilst it is easy for the positivist historian, and even the lay map reader to decode simple layers of cartographic meaning - inductively, or by using a key - 'there is nowhere they can go to verify the presence of the abstract ideas allegedly embodied in the map'.[14] In the absence of any specifically cartographic evidence for these 'abstract' meanings, Andrews finds Harley relying on 'an analogy with other art forms whose practitioners have been more communicative'.[15] And this strategy of analogising leads him to consider not only what Andrews considers inadmissible evidence from other disciplines - 'art history, literary criticism, architecture, and music' - but also 'non-cartographic' elements of maps themselves, including 'decorative embellishments'.[16]

Andrews's critique suggests that Harley's iconology over-reads the map: reifying and totalising its meaning; filling its apparent silences with misplaced rhetorics from elsewhere. Similar warnings have been sounded from a rather different direction. Since Foucauldian New Historicism became conspicuous as a movement in literary studies a host of materialist cultural critiques have focussed on the way in which this approach can seem to further the work of the representational practices it describes, perfecting their forms and re-incorporating that which escapes them as part of the 'system'. Responsibility for this theoretical totalising can be traced directly to Foucault: firstly for the closure which he attributes to the modern 'disciplinary society' and its 'indefinitely generalizable mechanism of panopticism', and secondly for the formalism by which he models it.[17] Foucault himself acknowledged - in dialogue with a group of geographers - his use of an analytic lexicon replete with unexamined spatial metaphors: of 'implantation, delimitation and demarcation ... the organisation of domains'.[18]

New cartographic historicists, to coin a rather awkward label for Foucauldian map-readers in the style of Brian Harley, can seem highly vulnerable to this materialist critique. Rather than relating representations to their specific local conditions of meaning and use they often map formal patterns discovered in their texts onto spatialities still more abstract and idealist than those of Enlightenment geometry. Moreover they can often seem to elide the gap between these aesthetic and conceptual spatialities and the space of practical activity, as if the map really were an ideal encapsulation of the world. In his analysis of American cartography, for example, William Boelhower projects a battle between an imperialist geometry which seems to have its own agency, and resistant cartographic toponyms whose inherent particularity opens 'a trap door ... in the written surface of the map'.[19] Julia Lupton writes similarly of rebel resistance to English cartography in Ireland 'cracking, piercing and mutating' the colonial

cartographic semiosis', *Word and Image* 4, 2 (1988): 475-497; Bernhard Klein, *Maps and the Writing of Space in Early Modern England and Ireland*, London, Palgrave, 2001.

13. J.H. Andrews, 'Introduction', in J.B. Harley and Paul Laxton, *The New Nature of Maps: Essays in the History of Cartography*, Baltimore, MD and London, Johns Hopkins University Press, 2001, pp31-2.

14. Ibid., p11.

15. Ibid.

16. Ibid.

17. Michel Foucault, 'Panopticism', op. cit., p206.

18. Michel Foucault, 'Questions on Geography: Interview with the Editors of *Hérodote*', in Colin Gordon (ed) *Power/Knowledge: Selected Interviews and Other Writings 1972-1977 by Michel Foucault*, Brighton, Harvester Press, 1980, p72.

19. William Boelhower, op. cit., p494.

20. Julia Lupton, 'Mapping Mutability; or, Spenser's Irish Plot', in Brendan Bradshaw, Andrew Hadfield and Willy Maley (eds), *Representing Ireland: Literature and the Origins of Conflict, 1534-1660*, Cambridge, Cambridge University Press, 1993, p93.

21. Henri Lefebvre, *The Production of Space*, Donald Nicholson-Smith (trans), Oxford, Blackwell, 1991, p4.

22. Ibid., p16.

23. Peter Jackson, *Maps of Meaning: An Introduction to Cultural Geography*, London, Unwin Hyman, 1989, pp7-8.

24. Denis Cosgrove, 'Introduction: Mapping Meaning', in Denis Cosgrove (ed), *Mappings*, London, Reaktion, p1.

25. Ibid., p2.

26. Peter Jackson, op. cit.

27. C.D. Pocock, 'Interface: Geography and Literature', *Progress in Human Geography*, 12 (1988): 87-102.

geometric plane.[20]

From the materialist point of view these idealist slippages between abstract and concrete space are the product of a characteristically Foucauldian over-estimation of representation itself. Attacking the dominant language model of cultural analysis and demanding a Marxian critical shift from products to processes, Henri Lefebvre has complained of Foucault that he 'never explains what space it is that he is referring to, nor how it bridges the gap between the theoretical (epistemological) realm and the practical one, between mental and social, between the space of the philosophers and the space of people who deal with material things'.[21]

Panofsky encouraged the student of art to read widely in order to historicise their intuitive interpretation of artistic symbolism. In his monumental history and critique of spatial production Lefebvre constantly urges caution in this critical turn to language. Real space for Lefebvre is social space, and it is produced through processes in which the abstractions of verbal media play no especially privileged role. Why, he asks, should language be granted the special status Foucault and his ilk implicitly accord it? 'Does language ... precede, accompany or follow social space? Is it a precondition of social space or merely a formulation of it?'[22]

Materialist cultural geographies have often accorded with these warnings about language and representation. Peter Jackson, like Denis Cosgrove a geographer highly instrumental in importing cultural studies methodology into his discipline, insists that his call for a 'more expansive view of culture' shouldn't lead to the over-privileging of linguistic cultural forms.[23] In writing published since *The Iconography of Landscape*, Denis Cosgrove has worried about the de-historicising universalism of criticism preoccupied with reading the aesthetics of the map itself.[24] When we shift our focus from product to process, he suggests, we soon see the 'aesthetics of closure and finality dissolve'.[25]

These materialist critiques suggest that we should tread very carefully indeed before reading maps as 'cultural images', rather than local interventions in material social processes. Yet notwithstanding the warning signs staked out along disciplinary boundaries a new cultural history of geography has placed considerable emphasis on the literary text, as an element within processes of cultural reproduction, and has also pushed the analogy of reading far beyond the bounds of written texts, exploring the iconology of spatial forms from homes to landscapes to cartographic maps themselves as cultural 'maps of meaning'.[26] The 'interface', as one scholar calls it, between literary and cartographic study is proving massively fertile ground, and yet what or where exactly is this interface?[27]

IDEALIST ANALOGIES AND THE POST-STRUCTURALIST CRITIQUE

Much of the most recent work on the relationship between geography and literature seeks to establish a broader context for spatial representation than that of local processes and transactions. At its most challenging, this kind of work relates literature and cartography in terms of overlapping modes of cultural production, subject to distinct but related social pressures, mediated by distinct but related generic codes. In its attention to the local limitations both of social process and of generic form it is able to ward off much of the cultural formalism of which New Historicism stands accused. But this formalism persists in the tendency of most literary readings of cartography to make their comparisons over the abstract and idealising common ground of formal analogy, 'reducing' the cultural specificity of their subjects.

Most literary scholars of cartography can be accused to some degree of that preoccupation with the aesthetic associated with Foucauldian New Historicism. Moreover rather than re-integrating the formal abstractions of cartography and literature with the local processes of production and consumption which generated them, these readings often reinforce them through idealising analyses of the 'space' engendered by cartography and literature.

In their seminal work on literature and cartography Richard Helgerson and John Gillies both give considerable weight to the formal correspondences between maps and literary texts.[28] In Helgerson's case these resemblances are mapped onto the more general common ground of cultural pressures. Helgerson is explicit in his focus on cultural 'forms' and is inclined to construe the politics of cartography in formal, generic terms. On the one hand, he regards Jacobean estate maps and country house poetry as broadly conservative in their centrifugal focus on manorial stewardship. On the other, he regards chorographies as proto-whiggish and politically centripetal; and projections of a nation composed of localised individuals.[29] In John Gillies's case, the general common ground underpinning particular, aesthetic resemblances between maps and literary works is shaped not just by contemporary political consciousness, but also by subconscious human impulses to stratify and thereby textualise space, marking the scene, the obscene, and so on. Gillies reads maps and texts for a 'poetic geography' which originates not in history but in human nature.

The most common relationship between maps and verbal texts discovered in recent scholarship is similarly formal and phenomenological. Most critics reach for a mobile, metaphorical definition of what maps and literary texts are and do which will accommodate and permit comparison. Both Tom Conley and Rhonda Lemke Sanford, for instance, identify early modern literary works which seek, like conventional cartography, 'to contain and appropriate the world they are producing in discourse and space through conscious labours of verbal navigation'.[30] Bernhard Klein, in turn, has argued that both literary and cartographic texts can be categorised as either static map or mobile itinerary, depending on the relationship they establish between reader and space.[31] Like Gillies, Klein reads a 'semiosis of desire' in the formal characteristics of the new geography: its views from above and its all-encompassing atlases and globes.[32] Like Helgerson he foregrounds the cultural politics apparently implicit in cartographic and literary form.

28. Richard Helgerson, *Forms of Nationhood: The Elizabethan Writing of England*, Chicago and London, University of Chicago Press, 1992; John Gillies, *Shakespeare and the Geography of Difference*, Cambridge, Cambridge University Press, 1984.

29. See especially Richard Helgerson, 'Nation or Estate: Ideological Conflict in the Early Modern Mapping of England', *Cartographica*, 30 (1993): 68-74.

30. Tom Conley, *The Self-made Map: Cartographic Writing in Early Modern France*, Minneapolis and London, University of Minnesota Press, 1996, p5, cited in Rhonda Lemke Sanford, *Maps and Memory in Early Modern England: A Sense of Place*, New York and Basingstoke, Palgrave, 2002, p13.

31. Bernhard Klein, *Maps and the Writing of Space in Early Modern England and Ireland*, London, Palgrave, 2001.

32. Ibid., p35.

Above all, Klein traces in the common formal strategies of maps and texts the symptoms and the mechanisms of a pervasive 'mathematization of experience' estranging early modern subjects from the social experience of space.

All of these literary studies have made highly valuable contributions to a new cultural history of cartography. Yet they perpetuate the presumption of the most traditional, positivist histories that the primary function of maps, and of the geographic text in general, is to represent space. The danger in their tendency to read maps and literary texts in terms of abstract spatial analogies is that it formalises in advance our view of particular social processes. It assumes that spaces 'framed' by geometry or 'navigated' in verse felt to early modern readers much as they feel to us, and thereby naturalises the advent of 'modern' forms of spatiality and representation however much it may appear to mourn them. It cleans up the dirtiness of the early modern map. But where positivist and materialist critiques have blamed an excessive post-structuralism for these abstractions, a final and most telling critique of the new cartographic history blames an insufficiency.

In his critical introduction to Brian Harley's essays, self-confessed positivist J.H. Andrews finds Harley asking his reader to question the 'assumed link between reality and representation' but notes with relief that Harley draws back from the post-structuralist brink of finding nothing 'outside the text'.[33] Barbara Belyea, on the other hand, finds this hesitancy problematic.[34] To bring ornament to the centre of the map is to accept that maps, like other texts, do indeed - in Andrews's incredulous phrase - 'create noncartographic reality as well as representing it'.[35] And yet, Belyea points out, Harley's work on cartography consistently supposes a normative physical reality, politics, ethics and human subjectivity which cartography distorts and represses.[36] Whilst this supposition is in perfect harmony with the idealist, Kantian basis of Panofsky's approach, it does not sit well with the post-structuralism with which Harley tries to mix his iconology.[37]

For Foucault and Derrida, Belyea observes, political power is not external to the text, and executed upon or through it, but is inextricable from, and a product of textuality and discourse.[38] Truth is not something which human subjects misrepresent and suppress through textuality and discourse, as Harley suggests in his readings of cartographic 'silence', but is a product of textuality and discourse themselves. As, for that matter, is the human subject. Maps do not simply 'hide' power in those margins which positivist scholars would have us believe are not part of cartography. Rather, they make it possible precisely in their marking of the boundary between centre and margins, truth and ornament, representation and reality.

Belyea's critique suggests that the characteristic slippage between practical and aesthetic we find in Harleyan readings of cartography is the product not of an over-estimation of representation and language, as materialists have suggested, but of a half-hearted post-structuralism which sees representation as the 'tool' of political agencies operating somehow

33. J.H. Andrews, op. cit., p21.

34. Barbara Belyea, 'Images of Power: Derrida/Foucault/ Harley', *Cartographica*, 29, 2 (1992): 1-9.

35. Andrews, op. cit., p11.

36. Ibid., p4.

37. Ibid., p2.

38. Ibid., p3.

beyond it. I would apply the same critique to recent readings of cartography and literature which have sought in phenomenology a refuge from Foucauldian pessimism and an idealised common ground beyond cartographic discipline.

For the phenomenological tradition in philosophy there is no possibility of Cartesian detachment and the 'cogito ergo sum'.[39] No possibility, that is, of a subject that might regard the world objectively and separately from the thinking self, and that might conceive of an objective space which is a condition of this world detached from the thinking self. Being, as Martin Heidegger put it, is always *'dwelling'*, or *'being-in-the-world'*, and the self, rather than being limited by physical boundaries separating it from the world, is constituted through such boundaries.[40] Phenomenology appeals for us to examine images, whether visual or literary, not as substitutes for an objective 'reality', but as the way in which we experience our world.

Whilst phenomenology is indebted to Kant for its sense of the mental mediation of space, it rejects the Kantian notion of space as an absolute category even of the mind. Space, to use Edmund Husserl's language, is 'intentional'; or, to use Heidegger's, imbued with 'care'. It is constituted and shot through with human negotiations, processes and desires.[41] The best the philosopher can do is search, as Husserl does for geometry, for the essence of the human experience of a phenomenon: the sense it must have had for its first discoverers, with all the intervening overlay of history bracketed or reduced.

Much of the most influential cartographic theory and history written in the last few decades has taken a broadly Panofskyan view of representational space as symbolic, and thereby cultural. But it also shares the phenomenological conviction that lies behind Panofsky's work, articulated seminally for Panofsky by Ernst Cassirer, that the arrival of an abstract spatial consciousness separating the self symbolically from the world is an essential milestone in the evolution of human cultures. In its human absoluteness, mapping is viewed by most historians as a form of cognition and communication somehow prior to, beyond, and thereby merely analogous with language. In 1976 Arthur Robinson and Barbara Petchenik made what they regarded as the first attempt at a general theory of cartography, defining the 'communications model' in a text which remains influential.[42] 'Mapping', they write, 'is basically an attempt at communication between the cartographer and the map percipient ... all maps have as their aim the transfer of images of the geographical milieu'.[43] Elsewhere, to the same effect, Robinson and Petchenik quote founder of cultural geography Carl Sauer: 'the map speaks across the boundaries of language'.[44] By the time Brian Harley came to write his introduction to the Chicago *History of Cartography*, another attempt at timely disciplinary synthesis, this Sauerian mantra needed no attribution. 'There has probably always been a mapping impulse in human consciousness', writes Harley in his opening paragraph, and he goes on to describe the power of maps to 'speak across the barriers

39. Mike Crang, *Cultural Geography*, London and New York, Routledge, 1998, p107.

40. Ibid., p107.

41. Ibid., pp108-10.

42. Arthur H. Robinson and Barbara Bartz Petchenik, *The Nature of Maps: Essays toward Understanding Maps and Mapping*, Chicago and London, University of Chicago Press, 1976.

43. Ibid., p42.

44. Quoted in ibid, p2.

45. J.B. Harley, '1. The Map and the Development of the History of Cartography', in J.B. Harley and David Woodward (eds), *The History of Cartography, Volume One: Cartography in Prehistoric, Ancient, and Medieval Europe and the Mediterranean*, Chicago, Chicago University Press, 1987, p1.

46. Jacques Derrida, *Edmund Husserl's 'Origin of Geometry': An Introduction*, John P. Leavey (trans), David B. Allison (ed), New York, N. Hays and Hassocks, Harvester, 1978, pp61-6.

of ordinary language'.[45]

For all its insistence on an essential subjectivity and humanity, the phenomenologist's quest for the heart of the phenomenon remains an idealist one: an attempt to re-ground knowledge on something absolute and eternal. In recent years it has been subjected to a persistent post-structuralist critique, most prominently in the work of Derrida. Derrida brought this critique to bear specifically on Husserl's attempt to re-ground geometry on realities beyond history and language. It applies with equal force to the attempts made by cartographic historians and more recently literary critics to read in textual and cartographic images the traces of archetypal human experiences of space, apparent to any reader.

Husserl insists - 'obstinately', in Derrida's view - that the objectivity typified in geometry lies behind, and is the condition of possibility for language and history itself.[46] This insistence begs an archetypal Derridean question: if geometry is prior to language and history, and yet not absolutely ideal, why and how was it invented, and by what means might the pure sense of this invention be experienced and transcribed? Since language and history are the only media for either moment of invention, no phenomenology can give this question a satisfactory answer.

Derrida's question about the relationship between geometry and language matches and answers the Lefebvrean one. Language is neither prior to the human experience and representation of space nor posterior to it. Writing, geometry and practice are not analogous but inextricable and the same. A thoroughly post-stucturalist critique of the new critical history of cartography suggests that its revolution has been incomplete. But it does not accept that we are wrong to 'read' when we do cartographic history, simply that we are wrong to read the map itself as an analogy or alternative to language and especially wrong to attempt intuitive readings of geometry and space.

Derrida's critique of phenomenology moves us beyond a post-Kantian divide between language and geometry, and towards a historicised conception of their relationship: a relationship fully acknowledged in the seventeenth century. Far from exploding history, it helps us do history properly. We cannot, as Husserl hoped, share the experiences of early modern subjects by imagining the geometries and other spatialities encoded in their texts. We cannot do this because these experiences are not extricable from history and language. And when we abandon this Husserlian quest and appreciate the written-ness of early modern geometries and geographies we find, in fact, that they were far from being what they seem intuitively to us. Far from being the symbolic form through which early modern subjects inevitably perceived their worlds, far from being the 'silent' ground, the naturalised basis for a 'disciplined' experience of space, the meaning of geometry and the map was contingent on a cacophony of rhetorics conditioning and negotiating their interpretation. As literary historians have suggested in analyses of those early modern meta-narratives that accompanied the birth of the novel, these rhetorics were often simultaneously rhetorics of 'truth' - of the right way to represent - and rhetorics of 'virtue' - of the legitimacy of those individuals and communities who represent and are represented.[47] Moreover maps themselves were conceived not formally, as frames of or routes through 'space', but as gestures in rhetorical contests and negotiations.

CARTOGRAPHY AND RHETORIC

I want to ground my argument for the rhetorical nature of early modern cartography on a historicised understanding of rhetoric itself: something often missing in post-structuralist appropriations of the term.[48] The importance of the classical rhetorical tradition in European culture from the Renaissance to Romanticism is widely underestimated, principally because of its strangeness to post-Romantic habits of mind.[49] Classical theories of rhetoric established the habit of systematising the art of speaking for which the tradition would later become notorious. Aristotle distinguished three species of rhetoric in terms of their social function. The function of judicial rhetoric was to influence a judge's decision over past events by accusation or defence; the function of deliberative rhetoric was to influence a politician's decision over future events by encouragement or discouragement; and the function of epideictic rhetoric was to influence the good conduct of any citizen by praising virtue and mocking vice.[50] Further, argued Aristotle, all of these species of rhetoric should pursue three species of persuasion: teaching, delighting and moving.[51] Finally, classical rhetoric divided the processes involved in rhetoric into the successive stages of invention (the identification of the correct commonplaces, figures of speech and tropes to use); disposition (planning and laying out the speech); and elocution (performing it).[52]

Renaissance humanists promoted rhetoric as the definitive civic art, and the orator as the culture hero of the *vita activa*. The Renaissance orator was celebrated as a guide uniquely capable of navigating the virtuous course defined by Aristotle as lying always at the mean of two extremes: between pure truth and pure utility; between retired scholarship and the venality of the world.[53] Humanists recognised the need for any form of speaking or writing, including the scientific, not just to teach its reader, but to delight and move them - to 'draw' and 'winde' them in, in the words of one sixteenth-century theorist.[54] In sixteenth-century England, rhetoric came to enjoy an extraordinary prominence not just in Universities, but at the root of education. By 1575 there were 360 grammar schools in England in which pupils learnt from ancient and modern sources how to identify and use the figures and tropes of classical rhetoric.[55] In an age of print their teachers came increasingly to treat rhetoric as a written, as much as a spoken art, and theorists of literature such as Sir Philip Sidney followed classical precedent in treating literature or 'poesy' as a close relative or derivative of

47. Michael McKeon, *Origins of the English Novel, 1600-1740*, Baltimore, Johns Hopkins University Press, 1987.

48. See 'Epilogue: The Future of Rhetoric', in Brian Vickers, *In Defence of Rhetoric*, Oxford, Clarendon, 1988, pp434-479.

49. This case is made by Brian Vickers, op. cit.; Quentin Skinner, *Reason and Rhetoric in the Philosophy of Hobbes*, Cambridge, Cambridge University Press, 1996. I am extremely grateful to one of the anonymous readers of this article for their encouragement to develop further the Renaissance rhetorical context.

50. Vickers, op. cit., p21; Skinner, op. cit., pp42-5.

51. Vickers, op. cit., p74.

52. Skinner, op. cit., pp45-6.

53. Ibid., pp154-5.

54. Quoted in ibid., p89.

55. Vickers, op. cit., pp257-8.

56. Skinner, op. cit.,
p109.

57. See 'Plato's
Attack on Rhetoric',
in Brian Vickers, op.
cit., pp83-147;
Quentin Skinner, op.
cit.

58. Vickers, op. cit.,
p266.

59. Ibid., p284.

60. Ibid., pp343-5;
Skinner, op. cit.,
pp188-97.

61. For examples of
'judicial' mapping
see Clarence
Winthrop Bowen,
*The Boundary Disputes
of Connecticut*,
Boston, James R.
Osgood, 1882.

62. For an excellent
account of this kind
of mapping see Sara
Stidstone Gronim,
'Geography and
Persuasion: Maps in
British Colonial New
York', *William and
Mary Quarterly*, 58,2
(2001): 373–402.

rhetoric.[56]

However much they might have been suspicious of the excesses of rhetoric and of Machiavellian perversions of its power, early moderns did not in general swallow Plato's argument that true knowledge must do without metaphors, or buy Hobbes's attempt to ground natural, civil and moral science on pseudo-mathematical deductive reasoning.[57] Instead they tended to regard truth, justice, public benefit and moral good as best revealed by processes of negotiation and persuasion, and to prize the Ciceronian skill of speaking *in utramque partem* (on both sides). Rather than regarding the rhetoric of early modern science as a guilty secret, as we are wont to do and as only the most anti-rhetorical early moderns saw it, it is more accurate to see rhetoric as the benchmark against which arts and sciences of more doubtful value - including mathematics and cartography - were obliged to prove themselves. It is worth remembering that rhetoric was not only given a superior place in the humanist curriculum to mathematics, judged a barbarously solitary and un-civic science, in some instances it actually displaced it.[58] But how might early modern cartography have been rhetorical?

It isn't necessary to reach for abstract notions of extra-linguistic cognition and communication to answer this question since the connection can be made concretely historical. Rhetorical theory placed considerable value on the visual as the perceptual register most intimately connected with the passions and therefore as a horizon to which verbal rhetoric must aspire. Moreover it treated visual images themselves as part of the arsenal of the grand style in rhetoric, ranged alongside the most potent figures.[59] Along with rhetorical theories of poesy, the Renaissance quickly generated rhetorical theories of painting. These matched rhetorical invention with the painter's selection of a novel, sometimes even 'far-fetched' subject, guaranteed to rouse the viewer's passions. Disposition was matched with the geometric process by which this subject was tempered, brought back within the familiar bounds of sound design, elocution with the painter's artful colouring and finishing of the work.[60]

Like Renaissance paintings, early modern maps resemble rhetoric in kind. In fact their functions correspond far more closely than those of painting to the functions according to which Aristotle defined rhetorical species. Early modern maps were made most frequently, if often most ephemerally, in the judicial mode, commissioned by court authorities or by opposing parties to influence the negotiation of a just decision.[61] They were also made in the deliberative mode, commissioned to persuade the powerful that a given action, or kind of action was both virtuous and profitable.[62] Finally, many early modern maps were made, like poems and paintings, in the epideictic mode, to celebrate the honourable achievements of proud landlords and imperial nations.

In style, early modern maps range, like rhetoric, from the plain style of everyday estate management and the lawcourts, through the middle style of armchair travellers' tales to the grand style of scholarly cosmography: of geographies inspiring heroic imperial endeavour, of the atlas and the globe. At their grandest, like the grandest style of rhetoric and painting, they arouse the reader's passions, bringing them specimens of novelty and strangeness, but tempering these passions through the familiar, domesticating logic of mathematical design. Understood as rhetorical, there is nothing strange in the 'bizarre congruence of the geometric and the mysterious' to be found in sixteenth-century atlases.[63] The exotic aspect of such geographies is not necessarily a form of distancing and 'aloofness': the expression of an innate human tendency to spatialise distinctions between the familiar and the foreign.[64] It is more a rhetorical appeal through wonder to the passions, marshalled through the rational logic of geometry.

Finally, if they are like it in kind, early modern maps are also like rhetoric in process. They take a piece of subject matter from the world and re-present it according to scholarly principles of good design and artful qualities of skill and discretion. The cartographer selects the places they represent as the orator or poet chooses their arguments or their stories. They make their mathematical measurements and cast them up as the orator lays their arguments out. They ornament, colour and fill in the details of their map as the orator embellishes their speech.[65]

These are not exact or necessary correspondences - I make no absolute claims as to whether the colouring on a map corresponds meaningfully to metaphor in poetry, or to the performance of a speech. Neither, however, are they speculative associations with no basis in early modern culture. J.H. Andrews may be right, at least for the eighteenth and nineteenth centuries, when he judges modern cartography an intrinsically silent art: 'before about 1930, cartographers made few general pronouncements of any kind about their subject'.[66] But for a substantial part of the sixteenth and seventeenth centuries, cartography was distinctly noisy. Sixteenth and seventeenth-century mathematicians and geographers worked hard to advertise the parameters within which they wanted their work to be understood, and these parameters were distinctively rhetorical.

BETWEEN THE STUDY AND THE MARKETPLACE

The best-known aspect of early modern writing on mathematics and cartography has fuelled the idealist conception of a clean mathematical panopticism: a mathematics beyond rhetoric. But it is only one side of the story. Geography, claims mathematician and physician William Cuningham in *The Cosmographical Glasse* (1559), 'delivereth us from greate and continuall travailes. For in a pleasaunte house, or warme study, she sheweth us the hole face of all th'Earthe, withal the corners of the same'.[67] Dedicated to Elizabeth I's favourite Robert Dudley, Cuningham's treatise promises to teach its reader how to draw a map for 'Spaine, Fraunce, Germany, Italye, Graece, or any perticuler region: yea, in a warme and pleasaunt house,

63. Bernhard Klein, op. cit., p35.

64. See John Gillies, op. cit., pp28-30, on Elizabethan exoticism.

65. See Leonard Digges and Thomas Digges, *Pantometria*, London, Henrie Bynneman, 1571. This manual gives an account of the whole procedure of taking a survey which, like the Renaissance painting treatises discussed by Brian Vickers, appears to mimic the three stages of the rhetorical process.

66. J.H. Andrews, op. cit., p5.

67. William Cuningham, *The Cosmographical Glasse*, London, John Daye, 1559, sig.A6r.

68. Ibid., p120.

69. Bernhard Klein,
op. cit.

70. Denis Cosgrove,
*The Palladian
Landscape:
Geographical Change
and its Cultural
Representation in
Sixteenth-Century
Italy*, Leicester,
Leicester University
Press.

71. William
Cuningham, op. cit.,
sig.A4r.

72. Ibid, sig.A2r.

73. Ibid., sig.A2r.

74. William
Leybourn, *Cursus
Mathematicus*,
London: Thomas
Basset, Benjamin
Tooke, Thomas
Sawbridge,
Awnsham and John
Churchill, 1690.

75. Ibid., p47, p48.

76. Thomas Hood, *A
Copie of the Speache
Made by The
Mathematicall Lecturer
... at the House of
Thomas Smith*,
Amsterdam,
Theatrum Orbis
Terrarum, 1974.

without any perill of the raging Seas: danger of enemies: losse of time: spending of substaunce: wearines of body, or anguishe of minde'.[68] Cuningham's offer to place his patron and his reader above the world beyond travail, outside even their bodies, represents by far the best known aspect of the early modern 'cartographic transaction'.[69] It is a manifestation of that 'Euclidean ecstasy' which infused early modern scientific culture from the sixteenth century onward, inspiring aspirations for a new dominion over nature and humanity.[70] It looks much like the Husserlian crisis which sees the European self finally gaining perspective on its world. Yet equally common in mathematical writing are figures and rhetorics of a more equivocal nature: figures which dirty somewhat the clean lines of geometric discipline.

Cosmographia also tells of maps which Alexander, 'the mighty Conqueroure,' would have made of the country 'with which he would warre,' and would have 'hanged in open markets for all men to behold, wherby the Capitaines did forsee, and seke out where was the easiest places to arrive, and the Souldiors allured with the commodities of the Countries, were made the willinger to the thinge'.[71] These maps take us far from the scholar's study and into a world of strategies, commodities, material pain and pleasure. Moreover, alongside alternate images of scholarly detachment and worldly engagement, Cuningham presents images which equivocate in typical rhetorical fashion between the two.

In an account derived from Ovid's *Metamorphoses* Cuningham tells of Daedalus 'that excellent Geometrician', who saw the 'Monster Ignorance' with 'the eyes of knowledge' and, with wings prepared '(throughe Science aide)', flew 'oute of hir mooste filthy Prison','her lothsome Labyrinthe', 'Ascending to the Sterrye Skie'.[72] Knowledge, concludes Cuningham, shuns ignorance, brings man closer to God and permits the invention of arts through which man has 'sought out' worldly 'Secretes'.[73] But we and every imaginable contemporary reader of Cuningham's treatise know two things that complicate this story: that Daedalus's son Icarus paid a terrible price for starry soaring in the flight from Crete, and that the labyrinth from which the pair escape was built by Daedalus himself. Science, it appears, is both escape route and trap, both of the world and out of it. All the more need, then, for a guide like Cuningham to lead us rhetorically along the Daedalean middle path.

Cuningham's invocation of the Daedalus myth compresses into almost emblematic form the claims of a wide array of mathematical popularisers and publicists that mathematics and its various derivations could do what rhetoric did. It could teach, delight and move. It could tread a middle path between virtue and profit. Exemplary here is the corpus of mathematical writer William Leybourn, which ranges from the plainest, most practical texts, to expensive subscription volumes designed for wealthy consumers. In *Cursus Mathematicus* (1690), which falls into the latter category, Leybourn fashions a mathematics neither scholarly nor pragmatic, but somewhere in between: a mathematics of the rhetorical middle style, designed to please as well as teach.[74] This book, whose reader must be 'Mathematically affected', looks not merely to 'agree with his *Stomach*', being profitable, but also to 'please his *Palate*'.[75] Exemplary too is a speech given in 1588 by Thomas Hood to a city audience composed in part of the militia got up to counter the Armada.[76] Hood's speech appeals to his audience both as greedy merchants and as lofty scholars, and fashions a mathematics equivocal between these apparently polar interests.

That mathematicians were obliged to advertise their discipline in this tentative manner should remind us of its doubtful status in the sixteenth and seventeenth centuries. In Francis Bacon's words, 'The *Labyrinth* is an excellent Allegory, whereby is shadowed the nature of Mechanicall sciences … for Mechanicall arts are of ambiguous vse, seruing as well for hurt as for remedy, and they haue in a manner power both to loose and bind themselues'.[77] This rather equivocal view of scientific artfulness sits uncomfortably with Bacon's place in early modern cultural history. Yet Bacon's equivocation and the 'excellent' labyrinth allegory itself are entirely characteristic of the ambivalence of Protestant humanism and of its accomodation in the rhythms of classical rhetoric.

DISCIPLINE AND RHETORIC

Francis Bacon is famous for his articulation of a radical humanism which shifted the origins and ends of science from idealist contemplation to the improvement of the human condition, and which subjected the material world to mathematical abstraction and manipulation: to 'discipline'. Bacon regarded mathematical reduction as first principle of a rigorous intellectual engagement with and improvement of the material world, recommending "that all natural bodies be, as far as is possible, reduced to number, weight, measure, and precise definition".[78] The Baconian philosophy of discipline and improvement was enthusiastically embraced by Puritans and revolutionaries envisioning a new dominion over nature, forming, in Charles Webster's words, almost 'the official philosophy' of the English revolution.[79] Neither was Baconianism exclusive to Puritan social networks, however much the soil of Puritanism may have nourished the spread of Baconian ideas.[80] It is widely viewed as the ethos informing both the mathematisation of seventeenth-century geography, and the economic reformism and imperial expansionism for which this new world view is held to have served as instrument and ideology.[81] Yet even the most pragmatic, worldly streams of Puritan and Baconian thought, equating truth and virtue with utility, contended over a long period with a residual discourse of Calvinist asceticism, associating practical art and economic individualism with moral and social corruption.

Treatises promoting improvement, economic reform and the colonisation of waste American soil were matched throughout the mid-seventeenth

77. Francis Bacon, Viscount St Albans, *The Wisedome of the Ancients*, Sir Arthur Gorges (trans), London, John Bill, 1619, pp93-94.

78. Quoted in Charles Webster, *The Great Instauration: Science, Medicine and Reform, 1626-1660*, London, Duckworth, 1975, p351.

79. Charles Webster, op. cit., p25.

80. See Nicholas Tyacke, 'Science and Religion at Oxford before the Civil War', in Donald Pennington and Keith Thomas (eds), *Puritans and Revolutionaries: Essays in Seventeenth-Century History presented to Christopher Hill*, Oxford, Clarendon, 1978, pp73-93. Where Charles Webster stands in a still flourishing tradition tracing the rise of experimental science to Puritan social origins, Tyacke contests this thesis, pointing to vigorous experimentalism amongst Royalist groups in the Universities and arguing that there is no positive correlation between Puritanism and science.

81. See, for instance, Bruce McLeod, *The Geography of Empire in English Literature, 1580-1745*, Cambridge and New York, Cambridge University Press, 1999.

82. See, for instance, Robert Powell, *Depopulation Arraigned, Convicted and Condemned, by the Lawes of God and Man*, London, R.B., 1636; John Moore, *The Crying Sin of England, of Not Caring for the Poor...*, London, Antony Williamson, 1653.

83. David Armitage, 'Literature and Empire' in Nicholas P. Canny (ed), *The Oxford History of the British Empire, I: The Origins of Empire*, Oxford, Oxford University Press, 1998, pp109-10.

84. See P.D.A. Harvey, 'English Estate Maps: Their Early History and their Use as Historical Evidence', in David Buisseret (ed) *Rural Images: Estate Maps in the Old and New Worlds*, The Kenneth Nebenzahl, Jr Lectures in the History of Cartography, Chicago and London, University of Chicago Press, 1996, pp27-61; Sarah Bendall, 'Estate Maps of an English County: Cambridgeshire, 1600-1830', in David Buisseret, op. cit., pp63-90.

85. Fulke Greville, Baron Brooke, 'A Treatise of Monarchy', in *The Remains*, G.A. Wilkes (ed), London, Oxford University Press, 1965, book IX.

century by sermons and print diatribes denouncing individualism and acquisitiveness.[82] Although the tide of legislation began to turn in favour of enclosure in the mid-seventeenth century, supported by Baconian discourses valuing utility and general benefit over custom, the customary rights of common users, whether English or Native American, were widely argued. The perception persisted throughout the seventeenth century that colonies, in particular, threatened the moral and material economies of the commonwealth, diverting the attention of the nation's guardians to the mirage of foreign gold when it should be focussed on the stewardship of their own immediate charges.[83] Early moderns felt as anxious about the binding, loosing forces of economic change as they did about the arts that might forward it. It is this anxiety that haunts the 'excellent allegory' of the labyrinth and that should oblige us to reconsider our view of mathematical 'discipline' in the seventeenth century.

In the light of a sustained ambivalence about economic individualism and reform, it should be unsurprising that much seventeenth-century geography conveys a mixed message about what is virtuous in the use of land, and what is true in representing it. Close-grained archival research has demonstrated that traditional discursive and court-based practices of land management and representation co-existed throughout the seventeenth century with the new arts of mathematical surveying and cartography.[84] Such research suggests that we may be misguided if we treat those expensive, ostentatiously mathematical maps conspicuous amongst seventeenth century survivals as symptomatic of a widespread 'mathematization of experience'. Moreover even where mathematics did flourish, it played a rhetorical role, connoting balance and constraint, the middle path between custom and reform; the study and the marketplace; liberal virtue and worldly profit. If seventeenth-century space was disciplined, then mathematical discipline was not the limit and the end of rhetoric, the advent of a silent dawn of capitalist and imperialist system; but was itself a species of rhetorical negotiation.

An implicitly or explicitly mathematical and geographic language of design, surveying and reduction was common currency amongst seventeenth century reformers - advocates of commerce, agrarian improvement and colonisation - for whom it served the rhetorical function of negotiating between virtue, grace and providence and the chaotic energies of history and commerce. We can see this mathematical language at work in a wide variety of texts negotiating the meaning and value of controversial capitalist and colonial enterprises, and of economic artfulness in general. Amongst these, maps take their place.

A rhetoric of mathematical balance and constraint is at the heart of an argument made by Jacobean courtier Fulke Greville for the benefits of trade.[85] 'A Treatise of Monarchy' (composed c.1610) was one of five long verse treatises, all of which negotiate the same rhetorical middle path between a Calvinist pessimism, which shrinks in horror from man's worldly and intellectual ambitions, and a humanist optimism which sees redemption in the artful ordering of government and society.[86] Greville cannot clean commerce of its traditional taint of wasteful luxury: of the toys on which prodigal sons waste their father's wealth, defaulting on their responsibilities of patriarchal stewardship. But he finds in 'art' itself the most certain guarantee that the products of artful commerce will not corrupt. The core of such artistic virtue he figures in explicitly mathematical terms:

> Yet must there be a kynde of faith preserv'd
> Even in the commerce of the vanitie,
> That with true arts their marketts may be serv'd,
> And creditt kept to keape them greate, and free;
> Weight, number, measure trulie joyn'd in one,
> By Trade with all states, to inrich our owne.[87]

Mathematics serves here to constrain the threat of luxurious individualism by generalising its benefits. '[I]n States well tempered to be rich', writes Greville, 'Arts be the men's, and men the Prince's are; / Forme, matter, trade so worckinge everie where, / As governement may finde her riches there'.[88] So long as their individual artfulness is tempered, Greville urges, kings should not see competition in the self-advancement of the skilful artisan and tradesman:

> Wherefore with curious prospect theis prowde Kings
> Ought to survey the commerce of their lande;
> New trades and staples still establishinge,
> So to improve the worcke of everie hand.[89]

Greville's rhetoric of mathematical tempering, of confident prospects which 'survey' and master a landscape of burgeoning individualism and improvement, typifies the public discourses of enclosure and of American colonisation, both of which were highly controversial enterprises in the seventeenth century. Whilst mathematical surveying for pragmatic purposes was remarkably slow to evolve in America, a public discourse of balance and proportion frequently drew upon mathematics, and in some instances generated actual maps. The best known examples of a conspicuously mathematised and thereby 'disciplined' American 'space' were not, as Brian Harley and others have consistently suggested, expressions of a proto-Enlightenment culture of systematic domination, but were more characteristically gestures in an anxious rhetoric of self-constraint: attempts to negotiate contemporary scepticism and anxiety about the virtue and the benefit of colonial expansion.

An anonymous New England tract titled 'Essay on the Ordering of Towns' (c.1635) seeks to establish 'comfortable Communion' in the embryonic Puritan community through a plan 'square 6 miles euery waye. The howses

86. Matthew Woodcock, "'The World is Made For Use": Theme and Form in Fulke Greville's Verse Treatises, *Sidney Journal*, 19, 1/2 (2001): 143-59.

87. Fulke Greville, op. cit., p132.

88. Ibid., p132.

89. Ibid., p129.

90. Anon., 'Essay on the Ordering of Towns', *Winthrop Papers*, 5 vols, Boston, Massachusetts Historical Society, III (1943): 182, p181.

91. Ibid., p182.

orderly placed about the midst, especially the Meetinghouse, the which we will suppose to be the Centor of the wholl Circomference'.[90] Geometry here is neither simply a pragmatic mode of laying out the standard town, nor does it simply clear the land for private property. Rather it moralises the expansive work of settlement through limitation. Like Fulke Greville, the anonymous author of the essay is certainly preoccupied with 'Improvement', regarding it as a 'principall Condicion of that Grand Couenant assigned' to man by God.[91] Yet at the same time the author assures his reader that all 'within Compas of the wholl towne' will be 'bownd with the suerest Ligaments'; each man limited to 'his due proportion' (184, 183).

This mathematised morality of compassing and proportion was re-invoked where New England towns began to test their bounds. In 1667 the residents of the southern, Chebaco district of Ipswich town petitioned Massachusetts General court successfully for parish status, supporting their application with a plan (Fig 1). The plan showed the proposed site for a

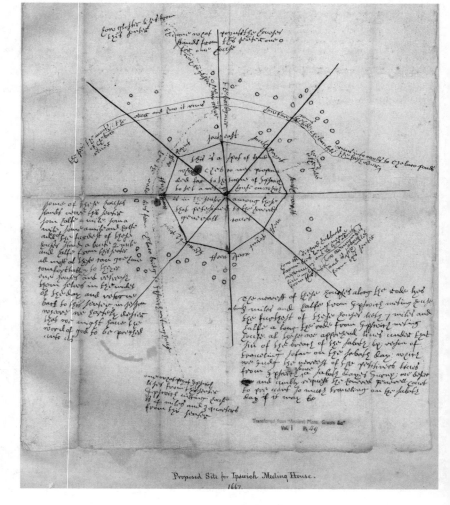

Fig 1, Unknown draftsman: Map of Chebaco, Massachusetts Archives Collection Third Series (v.1 p35), 1667. Reproduction courtesy of Massachusetts Archives

Proposed Site for Ipswich Meeting House.
1667.

new meeting house at the center of an octagonal shape. This geometry conveyed a distinctly spatial, and at the same time a distinctly moral rhetoric. It was designed to demonstrate that none of the houses of the new parish would be more than two and a half miles distant from 'comfortable Communion', whereas some of them were currently seven and a half miles distant from the Ipswich meeting house. In the first histories, travelogues and cartographies of New England the rhetorical oscillation between expansion and limitation made graphic in the Chebaco plan is played out on a larger scale. This oscillation, rather than the confidently expansionist trajectory across a blank Cartesian plane, is the true rhythm of American improvement.

MIDDLE MEN

Cartographic rhetoric served the Protestant-humanist and Puritan cultures of sixteenth and seventeenth-century England as a means of negotiating the problematic status of artfulness, profit and the world. It also allowed mathematicians and geographers themselves room for manoeuvre: for self-fashioning.

Early modern mathematicians and geographers who published to promote their knowledge and their arts typically hedged their bets, like William Cuningham, between liberal scholarship and profit and between the study and the marketplace. They wanted their readers to believe that they and their arts could do what rhetoric did: could steer a middle course between individual pleasure/profit and public benefit; could teach and yet also delight; could weigh the pros and cons; the wrongs and rights of a subject and a course of action; and could draw or persuade a reader and an audience to see things in the just-est, true-est and most virtuous light. The Harleyan, New Historicist account of early modern cartography sees it as clean and disciplinary, intolerant of the slightest departure from impersonal, mathematical authority. Yet seventeenth-century geographers make these departures remarkably conspicuous. Exemplary here is the Virginia colonist John Smith, who made clear both in the margins of his *Map of Virginia* (1612), and in the narrative account that accompanied it, that he had relied upon the help of Indian informants.[92] Like other colonial cartographers, who variously boasted of surveying with a 'Rod cut out of the Hedge', and of leaving their 'compasses at home', Smith advertises his capacity to cope without a cleanly disciplined perspective, commenting on another map: 'Thus have I walkt a wayless way, with uncouth pace, / Which yet no Christian man did ever trace'.[93]

Pragmatic, dirty geographies such as these were intended to thicken out the cartographic text, reminding the commissioners of colonial maps that their view from the panoptic mathematical 'study' of cartographic consumption was impotent without the mediating agency of the tough, experienced surveyor. In the language of classroom mathematics they present

92. Captain John Smith, 'A Map of Virginia', in *The Complete Works of Captain John Smith (1580-1631)*, Philip L. Barbour (ed), 3 vols, Chapel Hill, University of North Carolina Press, 1986, I, p151.

93. John Love, *Geodaesia; or, The Art of Surveying and Measuring of Land Made Easie*, London, W.Taylor, 1715, 2nd edn; first published 1688, *Appendix*, p7; William Wood, *New England's Prospect*, London, Iohn Bellamie, 1634, p70; Captain John Smith, *The Generall Historie of Virginia, New England, and the Summer Isles*, in *The Complete Works of Captain John Smith (1580-1631)*, Philip L. Barbour (ed), 3 vols, Chapel Hill, University of North Carolina Press 1986, II, p107.

not just solutions, but also the 'work' it cost to produce them. They construct geographers as mediators in the rhetorical tradition between their readers, patrons or clients and a dangerous, doubtful, sinful world. And they remind us that a mathematics which truly conformed to the Husserlian ideal, with all its historical and cultural residues reduced, would be as empty and as meaningless as the disciplined spaces of Brian Harley's maps. To have agency and meaning, as both Bacon and Derrida have recognised, mathematics must be wrapped in the binding, loosing labyrinth of language.

MAPPING WORDS

Miles Ogborn

It is, it seems, time for a re-evaluation of the relationships between Geography and Literary Studies, or, to be more inclusive of the broad interdisciplinary field which is involved, of the relationships between words and spaces. The essays collected here, and the range of works that they cite and use, signal a shift that now has more than ten years' work behind it away from interpretations based on the notion of 'representation', toward a range of other ways in which spaces and texts are imbricated one with the other. By briefly mapping out these involvements (a cartographic metaphor that will not be appreciated in some quarters), I want to indicate the choices and questions that now face those who seek to explore the possibilities for understanding words and their geographies.

There are two approaches that now seem to have had their day. First, a series of crises of representation both produced and then cut the ground from under literary and geographical studies which set out the ways in which spaces are represented in texts. Accounts of images of the city, descriptions of the countryside, and discourses of the Orient all took their impulse from the notion that there was a space to be represented, and that it could be represented in different ways in different contexts. As Clive Barnett argues, the very language of text and context on which this approach depended enacted the spatialisation of a series of 'insides' and 'outsides' which is of little help in understanding how words make their way in the world. Second, a process of metaphorical appropriation seems to have first illuminated the nature of texts and spaces through difference (as metaphors do) and then obscured them via familiarity. The 'mapping' of this and the 'cartographies' of that, and the landscape or city as 'text', promised to reveal new dimensions of spaces and texts but ultimately failed to do any more than indicate that each was 'a bit like' the other, denying in the end, as Richard Cavell notes, the specificity of both material spaces and of things that might be read.

Both of these approaches, via representation and via metaphor, relied for their effect upon the *differences* between spaces and texts. In the first, spaces were what was represented, texts were where they were represented. In the second, as has been noted, the difference in seeing texts as spaces, or spaces as texts, initially promised new forms of interpretation. What has replaced this are arguments and approaches which rely upon treating spaces and texts in parallel – which is not to say that they are treated as the same thing – and drawing out interpretations and connections from that. As many of the essays here point out, a genealogy for this can be traced back to the convergence of Marxist interpretations of postmodernism in both Geography and Literary Studies in the late 1980s. Frederic Jameson, David Harvey and Ed Soja all seemed to be saying the same thing. They were all attempting to counter the challenge of Lyotard and Baudrillard by regrounding postmodernism in a newly refurbished historical and geographical materialism. They were all arguing that there was a contemporary transformation in the nature of space and time which was not so much represented in literature (or cinema) but manifest there just as it might be manifest in the shape of the city or the experience of post-Fordist production regimes. This converged around the paradigmatic geographies of Los Angeles's Bonaventure Hotel and the unlikely figure of Kevin Lynch whose notion of 'cognitive mapping' was used by Jameson to signal a process, or more appropriately a confusion, that might be provoked just as well by a text or a space.

Allegiances to Jameson, Harvey and Soja clearly differ, but I would suggest that this parallel theorising and treatment of spaces and texts has worked in four ways. First, following Henri Lefebvre, both spaces and texts are treated as 'cultural productions' that work along the same sorts of lines. They are both something made. They could have turned out differently under different circumstances. This is, it must be said, a more radical proposition for spaces than it is for texts. However, treating them in parallel means that considerations of dead, decentred or multiple authorship raises serious questions about how the mode of literary cultural production actually works. In many ways this is a response to the crises of representational understandings of literary geographies. It recognises that neither spaces nor texts can be the *a priori* basis for the other. Instead, texts are part of the cultural production of spaces and spaces are part of the cultural production of texts. For example, Andrew Thacker's interpretation of the production of meaning in Jean Rhys's novel *After Leaving Mr Mackenzie* (1930) works by filling out the significance of the spaces her characters inhabit, pass through or pass by to indicate a gendered geography of fragmentation and marginality. These meaningful spaces animate the novel. In turn, Gerry Kearns demonstrates how James Joyce in *Ulysses* makes meaning with Dublin towards particular political ends. Neither the city nor the text are the sole locus of the meanings Joyce produces between them. Finally, Ian Buchanan reads Vladimir Nabakov's *Lolita* and Hitchcock's *Vertigo* alongside the spaces – shopping malls and chain motels – produced by the deterritorializing and reterritorializing economics of land rent. Neither, he suggests, simply represents postmodern space. Instead, they are each surfaces upon which its condition is revealed. In all of these cases the concern is as much with form as with content and in this we can trace another manoeuvre.

Second, then, spaces and texts are understood as sharing a formal aesthetic. In an early example of this John Bender argued in *Imagining the Penitentiary* (1987) that the eighteenth-century novel and the modern penitential prison had the same narrative structure. This sort of argument is clearly evident in Jameson, Harvey and Soja's interpretations of postmodernism (and in Buchanan's use of Deleuze to the same end here).

It is also evident in interpretations of early twentieth-century modernist texts and the spaces of the modern city. Traffic, jazz and modernist experimentation in poetry and prose have a shared aesthetic. Thus, for Kearns, the figures of circulation, the labyrinth and the palimpsest give form to both Joyce's text and to the city. This dissolves any distinctions between the real and the imaginary. Thus, for Peter Brooker, interpreting writing on New York after 9/11 where such distinctions are particularly unhelpful, the relationship between writing and the city is reconceived as one of 'indirect resonance' or as a shared 'urban imaginery' which are manifest as evidently in movements of the pen, of the reading eye, or of bodies in the streets. Interpretations and disagreements are then generated in debates over which aesthetic characteristics are the significant ones. In Jess Edwards' interpretation of early modern cartography the visual aesthetic of a rigid geometry shared between colonial maps and colonized territories, both making manifest the mathematization of experience, is replaced with a shared rhetorical structure which makes evident the negotiation of the meaning of both texts and spaces. In all these cases interpretation does not rely upon a model of causation from space to text or vice versa, but on one in which texts and spaces are treated in parallel.

Third, in various ways there is an emphasis on the materiality of both spaces and texts. This is, in part, a response to the seeming separation of a concern with representations, metaphors and discursive constructs from the determinations, violence and messiness of the material world. It is also a recognition that words become material too. Roger Chartier's distinction between texts and the material forms in which they are instantiated in the world, or Donald McKenzie's notion of a sociology of texts, lead us towards a history of the book which is pursued through material histories of production and dissemination that pay attention to such things as paper, type, binding, and the mechanics of distribution. That texts cannot exist outside some form of materialisation (however immaterial that may seem), and that this matters to writers, publishers and readers is signalled in various ways here. There are indications that the page of any book is a material space on which typography imprints its own geography. Clive Barnett, drawing on Gerard Genette, offers an account of the active role of publishing practices – of cover colours, author photographs, cheap paperbacks, and educational politics – in the making of the Heineman *African Writers Series*, and with it the construction of a particular canon of African writing with a specific geography. In their essays Jody Berland and Richard Cavell each reworks an earlier Canadian theorist of the material geographies of words. Berland uses Harold Innis's enigmatic *Empire and Communication* (1950) to set out how an east-west communication system based on train tracks and radio stations gave shape to the uncertain geographies of Canadian citizenship. Cavell adapts Marshall McLuhan's 1960s meditations to revisit the ways in which electronic texts and technological spaces are shaping lifeworlds at the level of affect, performance and embodiment rather than simply through representation. His quotation of Michael Denning's suggestion that the internet be taken as one of the most significant 'cultural texts' of the last ten years raises significant questions about the materiality of texts and also questions any separation between literary and other texts. Indeed, it is already evident that Bruno Latour's notion of 'inscriptions' – anything from a restaurant table number, to the graph drawn by a laboratory instrument, to an encyclopedia – is being used as a way to take seriously the variety of forms of writing and to, as he puts it, go beyond extending literary criticism to the technical literature, by examining the material forms of inscriptions and detailing the ways that they are used to act in and on the world. In all of these ways, therefore, texts are necessarily geographical in that they exist in particular material forms – literally taking up space – and are made mobile within particular distributive technologies which have their own geographies.

Finally, both spaces and texts, and the relationships between them, are coming to be seen as matters of performance and enactment. This turn to embodied practice is partly a reaction to the overdetermined readings of spaces and texts produced through notions of representation. The idea of non-representational theory, as developed within Geography, wishes to rethink spaces and their making beyond the notion of representation in text or image, but that need not necessarily send a shiver down the spine of those concerned with words on the page. As Richard Cavell points out there are parallel theoretical moves in literary studies which seek to expand the range of spatial practices through which texts are approached. Both developments share a common concern with performativity, affect and the body, and some shared theoretical foundations. In a more empirical and historical vein, the history of reading has begun to knit together concerns for texts, spaces and embodied practices in pursuit of the making of meaning. Indeed, as steps towards a geography of reading, works such as Jim Secord's *Victorian Sensation* (2000) are beginning to show how reading is undertaken in fundamentally different ways in different places. The same text takes on quite different meanings, and is put to very different uses, as readers interpret and appropriate texts through distinct reading practices. In this way both texts and spaces are connected (in the place of reading) and opened (in their enactment in practice) to a range of appropriations. In these accounts of practice, the range of readings of a novel and the range of uses of a shopping mall are not exhausted by the singular interpretations of literary or geographical critics.

In each of these four ways of going beyond the notions of representation or metaphorical appropriation spaces and texts are treated in parallel: as culturally produced, as sharing a formal aesthetics, as material, and as differentially enacted through embodied practice. The productiveness of these ways of exploring what the editors term the spatial imaginary is evidenced by the essays presented here and by many of the works that they cite. However, in mapping out these approaches and directions it is also evident that there is a significant division in modes of analysis and interpretation. On the one hand are those who use notions of cultural production and formal aesthetics to produce ever more complex readings of the meanings of texts, spaces and their conjunctions. On the other hand are those whose concern with the geographies of production and dissemination, and with the embodied practices of reading and writing, serves to generate a material historical geography of texts which often eschews literary theory, and may even refuse to comment on the content of the texts themselves. Therefore, it is not yet clear whether these different versions of what it means to investigate textual geographies or the geographies of texts can actually speak productively to each other. The question that must now be faced is how to work across these different possibilities if we are to find appropriate ways of mapping words.

WALTER, LENI, WALT AND MICKEY

Laura Marcus

Esther Leslie, *Hollywood Flatlands: Animation, Critical Theory and the Avant-Garde*, London, Verso, 2002, 344pp; £20 hardback.

Flatland was the title of a novel of the 1880s written by English headmaster Edwin Abbott Abbott to explore and explain geometry, by means of a fantastical adventure story in which the worlds of different dimensions (from zero to three) meet and clash. In *Hollywood Flatlands*, Esther Leslie charts the ways in which the two-dimensional world of the animated cartoons produced in the early decades of the twentieth century became subordinated to an illusionistic realism and depth. Walt Disney's 'fight against flatness' in films from the late 1930s onwards, she suggests, was part and parcel of the cartoon's increasing self-distancing from the art of the avant-garde, 'which takes fragmentation and disintegration into its law of form, making clear how constructed not only it is but also the social world - ripe for transformation'.

Such an account of modernist self-reflexivity may be a familiar one, but there is nothing obvious or derivative about the ways in which the arguments of *Hollywood Flatlands* proceed. The book starts and ends with the expressed desire to challenge facile assumptions about an irreconcilable divide between high and mass culture in modernist contexts. The animated cartoon - emblematic of 'popular culture' – fascinated modernist theorists and artists, shaping their theories and art in its own shifting and subversive forms. A similar point is made by Paul Wells in his interesting study *Animation and America* (Edinburgh University Press, 2002), in which he asserts that animation 'is a child of the modernist principle ... the bastard child of [America's] own avant garde' (9). The model of filiation is not particularly useful here, but the broader point stands: cartoons are exemplary instances of, in Esther Leslie's phrase, a 'demotic modernism'. As she argues, the relations between intellectuals and popular culture in the early twentieth century was *productive*, 'in the sense that both intellectuals and mass culture producers recognised, in some way, that all was to play for, that transformation was a virtue, a motive and a motif, that dissolution of form, including the form of the mass itself, was on the agenda, indeed that there was a chance to return to the drawing board of social formation'. The question of the utopianism implied here is fully addressed in a subsequent chapter on 'Mickey Mouse, Utopia and Walter Benjamin'. In its first appearance, however, the set of claims is part of a polemical argument that the productivity of modernist/mass cultural relationships was replaced by a postmodern cultural theory which merely affirms an existing mass culture, rather than finding in that culture, as did modernism, its own critique.

This argument might be held to merit question, or at least, discussion. In fact, given that Leslie's book pursues neither animation nor cultural theory much beyond the 1930s, it receives little of either. Fortunately, *Hollywood Flatlands* is exceptionally productive, to borrow its own term, in its exploration of film and critical/cultural theory leading up to the mid-twentieth century. There are absorbing discussions of pre-cinematic animated cartoons; of the relationship between animated films and the 'absolute film' of the European avant-garde; of film and the rise of Fascism; of colour theory and film. Conceptually, the study pushes far beyond most of the existing literature on animation. Leslie draws on Goethe, Marx and Freud in her analyses, but turns most often to the writings of Adorno, Kracauer, and, above all, Benjamin. She explores the part played by optics in Benjamin's work, his fascination with children's books and toys, and his interest in the nineteenth-century caricaturist Grandville, in whose animating fantasies Benjamin found a relationship to Marx's theory of fetishism and whose graphic transmutation skills were his legacy to later animators.

There is also a tracing-through of the many, though dispersed, references to Disney, and to Mickey Mouse in particular, in Benjamin's writings. Leslie reads the different versions of his most cited essay, 'The Work of Art in the Age of its Mechanical Reproducibility' - revised predominantly at the urging of Adorno - in relation to the issue of animation. In the first version of the essay, Benjamin suggested that animation was the most legitimate film form, in its abstraction from a recorded reality and its foregrounding of the graphic dimension of film. The second version includes the caveat, in a footnote, that the counter side of animation's comicality is horror, and a violence which had become part of the everyday brutality of the Nazi regime. Benjamin's thesis moves closer to Adorno's pessimism about mass culture, anticipating the criticism of Disney cartoons expressed by Adorno and Horkheimer in *Dialectic of Enlightenment*. In the third version of the essay, references to Brecht come to replace those to Mickey Mouse and Disney. Yet in abandoning Disney, Leslie argues, 'Benjamin was rejecting something that had changed anyway', as the cartoons of the late 1930s 'became naturalistic, moralistic and tamed'.

In this account, animation is at the heart of debates and struggles over culture and politics. *Hollywood Flatlands* traces these not only through the central premise that animation's art of mutation and metamorphosis is intertwined with a politics of transformation, but, in more directly historical terms, in relation to the rise of Fascism. The chapter on 'Leni and Walt' opens with the encounter in 1938 between the Nazi propagandist film-maker Leni Riefenstahl and Walt Disney, the only Hollywood celebrity who would receive her. Disney's films had generated a good deal of debate in Germany, due in substantial part to his use of German fairy-tales. While the 'how German is it?' question was raised by critics and commentators in relation to Disney's versions, 'it could not be denied that Disney had tapped into something dear to the Teutonic "soul" .... In this era, for Riefenstahl and for Disney, the "German feeling" was a code word for restitution. It acted to wipe out the futuristically propelled avant garde', replacing it with Kitsch. The connections multiply: Disney's Fordist methods find their parallels in the monopolistic culture industry in which Riefenstahl worked; both Riefenstahl's film *Olympia* and Disney's *Snow White* stage a battle over beauty in which Nordic classicism and 'spick and span Gothic' respectively become a denial of technological modernity. It was not until the close of 1941, when Germany declared war on America, that it also said goodbye to Disney.

Ten years before Riefenstahl's meeting with Disney in Hollywood, Sergei Eisenstein had travelled to meet him. The encounter received a brief paragraph in Ivor Montagu's *With Eisenstein in Hollywood*; Leslie weaves an entire chapter around it, which she titles 'Eisenstein Shakes Mickey's Hand in Hollywood'. During the period in which debates over the proper use of sound in film were at their height, Eisenstein found in Disney an exemplum of experimental sound, 'associating the action in Mickey Mouse', as Montagu wrote, 'with sound chosen for its arbitrary effect'. To this account, Leslie adds a discussion of Eisenstein's long-standing interest in drawing - from his childhood sketches, in which he transposed animal and human forms and characteristics, onwards. Like Benjamin, he was absorbed by, and a collector of, the images of Grandville. Eisenstein found in caricatures and cartoons a primal energy which he called 'protoplasmic', an evolutionary understanding of life forms. Animation is also animism. The correlation ties in, on the one hand, to modernist 'primitivism' and, on the other, to socialist dialectics and, in Leslie's account, to Trotsky's commitment both to 'an organic, dynamic, energy-laden vision of the development of the human race' and to an affiliation between men and animals. At the heart of animation lie fundamental questions of the identity, relationship and difference between man, animal and machine.

We can find a similar testing of boundaries in the films of Charlie Chaplin, whose 'gags' so often revolve around the drama of objects or things, and transformations of the human body, often as a form of camouflage or self-erasure. The film theorist André Bazin described this well: 'Driven into a corner by a terrible and unavoidable danger, Charlie hides behind appearances like a crab burying itself in the sand. And this is no mere metaphor. At the opening of *The Adventurer* we see the convict emerging from the sand in which he was hiding, and burying himself again when danger returns'. Victor Shklovsky wrote that 'Chaplin's movement is dotted'. The connections with the techniques of animated film are striking. Leslie notes the ways in which the cartoon character Felix the Cat, who first appeared in 1919, borrowed the gestures of Chaplin, and the imaginative play with props, though she also emphasises the differences between the cartoon world and that of Chaplin the actor, who is bound to the physical universe, ultimately unable to dissolve himself fully into the film.

Nonetheless, Disney and Chaplin are part of the same modernist world, and of the same European avant-gardist embrace of American popular culture and technology.

There are shades of opinion that the schema of *Hollywood Flatlands* tends to exclude. When Aldous Huxley, for example, celebrated the world of Felix the Cat in 1926, it was perhaps less a reaching out to avant-gardism or to popular culture than a defensive manoeuvre, a demand that film abandon adaptation, leave narrative to the writer, and stay within its own ludic sphere. Leslie for the most part leaves aside the question of literature's relationship to the cinema, including the ways in which novelists and avant-garde artists found common cause in their resistance to narrative film. It would, however, be churlish to ask for any more than this study provides, when it is already so richly researched, so alive to complexity, so imaginative in its connections, so powerfully argued, so vividly written and so beautifully produced.

TEDDIE AND THE PHILOSOPHERS

David Cunningham

Brian O'Connor, *Adorno's Negative Dialectic: Philosophy and the Possibility of Critical Rationality*, Cambridge, MA and London, MIT Press, 2004, 204pp; £22.95 cloth.

In one of his famous letters to Walter Benjamin, Adorno complains of the undialectical approach that he finds apparent in the unfolding method of the *Arcades Project*. 'Only theory', he advises Benjamin, 'can break the spell: your own merciless, good, speculative theory'.[1] A lack of 'theory' is not, of course, something of which Adorno often found himself accused. Rather the reverse. Few twentieth-century writers have such a 'merciless' reputation. Yet, while Adorno's standing within both contemporary social and aesthetic theory is probably higher than it has been at any point since the 1960s, the specifically *philosophical* import of his work remains largely ignored, or at least under-represented, within the available secondary literature.

1. Theodor Adorno, 'Letters to Walter Benjamin', in Ernst Bloch et al, *Aesthetics and Politics*, London, New Left Books, 1977, p129.

At first sight, then, Brian O'Connor's new book seems perfectly placed to remedy this neglect, insisting, as it does, upon the significance of the 'purely philosophical parts' of Adorno's oeuvre. Indeed, for O'Connor, viewed from this perspective, Adorno's thought is revealed as sticking 'remarkably close to what might be considered a traditional concern of "'pure" philosophy' (ix). *Adorno's Negative Dialectic* thus develops a reading of Adorno which - deliberately marginalising both the sociological studies and the writings on music, art and literature - stresses the 'positive contribution' to be found in his pursuit of a classically 'epistemological task': the critical elaboration of a rationally articulable account of experience, which, O'Connor argues (with some qualifications), continues to be of relevance to the concerns of contemporary philosophy, as much within the 'analytical' tradition as within the so-called 'continental' one.

Like all Critical Theory, Adorno's thought was marked by its broadly Hegelian-Marxist devotion to the possibility of an alternate 'critical rationality', other to those forms of rationality sanctioned within the 'distorted reality' of social life under capitalist modernity. The principal philosophical argument to be explicated here concerns Adorno's critical treatment of modern western thought's dominant account of the subject-object relation, and thus his rejection of its 'cardinal error': the belief that 'the power of thought is sufficient to grasp the totality of the real' (4). Through this *negative* articulation of 'the way things ought to be', Adorno elaborates his central philosophical claim that the only possible coherent account of the structure of experience entails a recognition of the *reciprocal* and *transformative* relations of subject and object; a recognition which, he argued, remained ultimately lacking in each of Critical Theory's main theoretical competitors, from Husserlian and Heideggerian phenomenology to Neo-Kantianism and Logical Positivism. O'Connor does a fine job of reconstructing Adorno's criticisms here, while returning, each time, to their central underlying point: the *essential* role of mediation in all experience. This is a radically dialectical argument, insofar as mediation is understood not as a process of 'connecting two separate independently meaningful moments', but as 'constitutive of subject and object' as such (48). While Adorno, therefore, refers polemically to 'the priority of the object' - marking a recognition of the necessary non-identical moment in experience by virtue of the irreducibility of objects to concepts - in truth, object and subject each reciprocally 'requires the other in order to be thought at all' (48).

In its exposition of Adorno's 'epistemological task', this book covers, then, some fairly familiar ground, but it does so in an unusually detailed and analytical fashion. What gives weight to O'Connor's exegesis is its painstaking - and, one would have to say, at times rather laborious and repetitive - attempts to give more rigorous philosophical definitions to the key concepts deployed in Adorno's writings, in particular 'mediation' and 'nonidentity'. And while *Adorno's Negative Dialectic* is a pretty dry read - deliberately so, one suspects - it is certainly both lucid and persuasive. This is most apparent in the complex relations that O'Connor establishes, in the main part of the book, between Adorno's work and that of Kant and Hegel, lending his analyses an obvious philosophical grounding. Focusing on such relations is evidently justifiable to the extent that Adorno consistently situated his own project through his engagement with these canonical figures. Moreover, aspects of O'Connor's analyses are genuinely novel. For example, the argument that Kant's theoretical treatment of antinomies is actually more influential on Adorno's thinking than Hegel's speculative dialectic is one which I, at least, find both original and compelling.

This is O'Connor's strong point. Yet, even given the justifications for this rather conventionally restricted focus, it also indicates the book's limitations. For there is surely something dubious about a study of Adorno's philosophy that never even *mentions* the likes of Freud, Weber or Simmel. At times such exclusions are deeply problematic: some of the confusion O'Connor seems to display regarding the link Adorno makes between conceptualisation and identification might, for example, have been dispelled had he traced its roots in Nietzsche (as much as in Hegel) (17-18). Similarly, given the key debt that Adorno acknowledges, in a range of works, to psychoanalysis - admittedly not always the happiest of influences on his thought - there is something bizarre about a section which claims to read him in the context of questions in the 'philosophy of mind' without once referring to Freud (92). The same kind of peculiar omissions are also apparent in relation to Adorno's closest contemporary associates: Marcuse gets one mention in the index; extraordinarily, neither Horkheimer nor Bloch nor Benjamin get *any*. (This despite the - I would have thought obvious - fact that so much of Adorno's work, from the early essay 'The Idea of Natural History' onwards, can be read as an effective commentary on aspects of Benjamin's fragmentary philosophy).

The reasons for such omissions, and for what stands in their stead (rather than Freud we get six pages on Nagel and Searle, while Strawson gets a more extended treatment than Marx) are, I think, complicated, and have much to do with the very conception of philosophy with which O'Connor works. It should be said, too, that there is, no doubt, something refreshing about a book which is less interested in Adorno's convergences with Derrida or Foucault than in how certain of his arguments might be related to Frege's delineation of the elements of the proposition (181). Yet, such novelty notwithstanding, there is also, shall we say, a certain whiff of desperation for a particular kind of philosophical *respectability* apparent in all this - one which demands that all those weird arty types that Adorno was so fond of get edited out of the story. (The reader dependent upon this book would, for instance, have no idea of the profound impact of Schoenberg upon Adorno's thought, not only on the aesthetic theory but also on its 'purely philosophical parts'). At the same time, the nature of O'Connor's insistence upon Adorno's significance as a *philosopher* - despite its undoubted exegetical merits - suggests grounds for some fairly serious misgivings as regards this book's overall project and its general claims.

Perhaps most important among these would be the book's key assertion that Adorno is best read as doing what O'Connor unhesitatingly describes as *transcendental* philosophy. The rationale for this, perhaps, is fairly uncontentious: Adorno is concerned with the conditions of possibility of experience *per se*; *ipso facto* he makes an implicitly transcendental claim for 'a notion of experience that *exclusively* is consistent with the rational expression of philosophy' (3). Yet there are good reasons why Adorno himself never defined his own thought in these terms. In one of his responses to criticisms of *Specters of Marx*, Derrida notes, *a propos* of Negri, that the word 'ontological' never appears in Marx, and that 'one should perhaps not be too quick to reinsert it in his text'.[2] Much the same could be said as regards the 'transcendental' in Adorno. At the very least one needs to consider, as O'Connor does not, *why* Adorno resisted such a characterisation.

Such resistance also tells us something about the status of 'philosophy', more generally, in Adorno's writings, to the extent that 'philosophy's historical fate' is itself frequently thematised there. Echoing Marx's famous eleventh thesis on Feuerbach, and its unfulfilled promise of the *actualisation* of the alienated universality of philosophical rationality, *Negative Dialectics* famously begins: 'Philosophy, which once seemed obsolete, lives on because the moment to realise it was missed'.[3] All of Adorno's contributions to the 'traditional concern[s] of "pure" philosophy' must be read with this in mind. O'Connor recognises this (sort of), but its significance for the relationship between philosophy and Critical Theory - a central concern of two famous essays from 1937 by Horkheimer and Marcuse - is consistently marginalised. For Adorno, as for Horkheimer and Marcuse, a critique that wills emancipation has also

2. Jacques Derrida, 'Marx & Sons', in Michael Sprinker (ed.), *Ghostly Demarcations: A Symposium on Jacques Derrida's* Specters of Marx, London and New York, Verso, 1999, pp257-8.

3. Theodor Adorno, *Negative Dialectics*, E.B. Ashton (trans), London, Routledge, 1973, p3.

to involve a reflection upon the conditions of knowledge entailed by the contradictions present within existing *social* reality - contradictions which require, therefore, more than merely *philosophical* resolution, or, indeed, analysis, insofar as philosophy itself is rooted in a division of labour which derives from these contradictions. The extent to which this conception of theory colours *all* of Adorno's work must bring seriously into question, even given the caveats that O'Connor dutifully inserts, his intention to 'consider Adorno's negative dialectic in isolation from the sociological specifics of his critical theory', as a way of identifying its 'purely philosophical justifications' (x-xi). The philosophy cannot simply be severed from the social theory without misrepresenting the arguments that are, precisely, the most philosophical in Adorno's works. No account of his philosophy should forget its attention to what Marcuse described as the 'untruth' always inherent in 'transcendental philosophy' as such. True, O'Connor notes that the 'largely abstract' concerns of the philosophical texts upon which he focuses are, nonetheless, always written in view of an 'authentic concretion', serving as a 'theoretical foundation of the sort of reflexivity - the critical stance - required by critical theory' (ix). Yet, if this is something different from a classical transcendentalism (and it is), then the broader *interdisciplinary* and *collaborative* nature of Critical Theory's project - and the *re-inscription* of the transcendental-empirical opposition itself that it entails - needs to be much more forcefully recognised than it is in O'Connor's account. That it is not may well have something to do with what is happening, institutionally, to philosophy within the academy right now. With the (endlessly re-iterated) waning of 'Theory', and *its* (at least speculative) transdisciplinary promise, the reassertion of a classical, if slightly expanded, disciplinary identity is on the agenda again. If, as Adorno once wrote, 'no theory today escapes the marketplace', the marketplace here has less to do with the pure commercial logic of sales than with the internal marketplace of academia in a situation governed by the imperatives of the Research Assessment Exercise and the like. This has been accompanied by a certain amount of to-and-fro across established continental and analytical divides - the former referencing Bernard Williams or Donald Davidson; the latter finally acknowledging there might be something of interest in that Hegel chap after all. Clearly this is not an entirely unwelcome development, yet, too often, it is underpinned by fundamentally conservative and depoliticising tendencies. Adorno and the likes of Wilfred Sellars cannot simply be put alongside each other as if they operated within some straightforward continuum of shared problems and conceptions of the 'philosophical' itself.

In this regard, too, it is more than a petty gripe to observe the extent to which O'Connor lacks any feeling for Adorno's *style*, and its inseparability from his philosophical content (something which, for example, Gillian Rose captured so well in *The Melancholy Science*). For, lacking an account of the dialectical fabric of Adorno's texts, O'Connor finds logical 'inconsistency' when it isn't really there. Adorno seems at one point to assert the primacy of the social, at another to launch a devastating assault on all 'sociologism' (136); at one point to defend Kant's notion of the thing-in-itself as a recognition of the 'nonidentical', and at another to criticise it (61-2). Yet, surely what O'Connor worries about as inconsistency just is the textual movement of negative dialectics.

That *Adorno's Negative Dialectic* is dominated by a strange apologetic tone would seem, in part, to be a function of this perplexity and of a concomitant strategy of justification. Adorno's readings of Kant are legitimised as anticipating 'the famous criticisms of Strawson' (121), while, for example - summarising Adorno's attack on logical philosophy - O'Connor appends a typically conciliatory parenthesis: 'This is, no doubt, a rather quaint view of the business of logic' (58). Why, exactly, we are not told. Elsewhere, Adorno's 'mining' of the works of German Idealism is, O'Connor assures us, also 'fashioned in ways that would have been the cause of grievous consternation to Kant and Hegel' (172). No doubt. But, then, one would hope so! (After all, in part, Adorno's claims for the 'potentially revolutionary resources' to be found in what O'Connor calls 'idealistic looking concepts' has to do with what he takes to be their historically-conditioned homology with the actual idealism of capitalist form). This odd litany of apologies leads up to an extraordinary (if, by this point, not entirely unexpected) concession - so extraordinary I quote it at some length - in the concluding pages of the book:

> Undoubtedly the history of philosophy will find in Habermas's writings a significantly more comprehensive and sophisticated version of critical theory ... The line of thought I emphasise in Adorno - his epistemological strategy - certainly provides only a limited contribution to the complex and detailed questions raised by the second generation of critical theory - it is, after all quite abstract in its procedure (169-70).

Leaving aside the question of what this says about O'Connor's reasons for writing this book in the first place, and how exactly the 'abstract' is to be *philosophically* understood here, I think that there is considerable doubt that the history of philosophy will come to anything like this conclusion. Indeed, it is a mark of much *third* generation Critical Theory of the last decade or so - not least in the English-speaking world - that it precisely starts from a move back to Adorno and away from Habermas's neo-Kantian, and fundamentally undialectical, project. Intended as a 'contemporary' defence of the coherency of Adorno's philosophical position, against Habermas's charge that it is limited by an obsolescent theory of consciousness, the failure to acknowledge the degree to which such a charge has been countered by a range of other commentators - some of whom even describe themselves as philosophers - risks making O'Connor's book itself look somewhat obsolescent.

Despite my misgivings, that would be something of a shame, because, in its restricted way, there is much that is genuinely innovative here, and, at the very least, it raises some compelling questions. Whether it redeems Adorno for the contemporary discipline of philosophy is however more doubtful. More to the point, would it be such a good thing if it did?

Disruption and Flickering in the Weimar Republic

Janelle Blankenship

Frances Guerin, *A Culture of Light: Cinema and Technology in 1920s Germany*, Minneapolis, University of Minnesota Press, 2005, 360pp; US$74.95 hardback, US$24.95 paperback.

Daguerre in the 1820s referred to the invention of photographic art as 'sun painting'. From his photography to the dawn-to-dusk daylight effect of Daguerre's diorama and beyond, sun-inspired light has served a double purpose: to both expose and manipulate reality, ultimately, our vision of time and space. Frances Guerin's study focuses on 1920s Germany, certainly a period of heightened experimentation in the arena of lighting and 'living pictures'. Although the earliest cinematographers were forced to film outdoors in the atelier of the sun, technically manipulated light sources opened up new possibilities for indoor studios in the early 1910s. Guerin explains that German directors had a somewhat belated introduction to the 'culture of light' that revolutionised filmmaking. Even after 1908, when the first 'quicksilver lamps' were used by Oskar Messter, German directors often used daylight or petroleum and gas as the only available artificial means of lighting in the cinema. Yet, according to Guerin, several years after the First World War the disquieting effect of technological modernity punctured the modern spectacle of German film, in the form of the brilliance and intensity of electric light, a cinematic commodity imported from American and European studios. Although German filmmakers did not develop the lighting strategies and setups, Guerin makes the compelling claim that they interiorised the theme of electric energy, using it as compositional material, an agent and bearer of 'discursive meaning'.

As exemplified also in the 1920s art of light as avant-garde medium, the interaction of glass and light forged new conceptions of the public and the private in Weimar Germany; in residential buildings and in aesthetic theory alike the formations 'inside' and 'outside' became integrated. Interwar German artists, architects and media theorists contemplated how light transformed human perception and vision: Bruno Taut, Paul Scheerbarth, László Moholy-Nagy had a utopic vision of light as a new space of mobility and sheer transparency, one that dissolved the tension in our fractured and alienating social landscape. Yet the reformulation of space through light in interwar German cinema does not first and foremost speak of a cohabitation or togetherness of technology and the human. Rather, it often highlights an invasion or intrusion of the public onto the private sphere. As Guerin importantly explains in her treatise, the heterosexual 'happy end' to many of the German films born of a 'culture of light' is an artificial escape from the 'harshness of modernity through a retreat to a morally conservative' nostalgia, feigning at best a resolution of an ideal social harmony. Light is a melodramatic force in films such as *Varieté* (1925) and *Sylvester* (1923), but in a narrative built on disruption and flickering, it is precisely the force and weight of this 'melodrama' that is put in question. As Guerin asks with *Varieté*, does the light spectacle mirror or hinder the moral resolution of the artificial 'happy end'?

In the most extreme version of this melodrama of a new medium, *Jenseits der Straße* (1929), 'light' only highlights oppressive, unrelenting gloom: here there is no alternative to the vice, immorality and 'illogic' of the city. As an alien power, the sources of the street lighting are invisible. Even the elaborate sign of the 'Electric Bar', the neon night-time semiotic, according to Guerin, is an enigma that appears entirely separate from the building to which it should be attached. Here we are reminded of a moment in Siegfried Kracauer's famous study, *From Caligari to Hitler*, when he lingers briefly on the glowing eyes of an optician's shop, an illuminated pair of spectacles that follow the protagonist of Karl Grune's *Die Straße* (1923), writing that 'for the first time, on the German screen window dressings participate in the action'. Guerin is also interested in capturing such magical moments of a haunted *mise-en-scène* of modernity, and it is not insignificant that this image of the optician eyes that Kracauer describes is used as a cover illustration for Guerin's text. After all, lighting can be used to 'lie', as a 1920s article in *Filmtechnik* explains - to shift our understanding of time and space, of public and private spheres. In *Die Straße*, the euphoric notion of the street as home, a popular theme of *flânerie* literature (Walter Benjamin and Asja Lacis praise this inversion of the public-private in their essay on Naples) is overturned. The street we now encounter is a horror of haunting and alienation. During the 1920s, when the number of electrically lit streetlights nearly doubled in Germany, electrical light was used as a primary vehicle in German cinema to represent the abrasions and interruptions of technological modernity. It bespoke the alienation of the metropolis, and the fear that the public and private spheres were corroded. Guerin's study, which highlights this exterior-interior drama, thus intersects nicely with Miriam Hansen's work on moral reform and the 'light play' [*Lichtspiel*] as a presumed threat to patriarchal division of public and private.

Another fascinating subject of Guerin's gaze is a little-known film of the 1920s avant-garde, Arthur Robison's *Warning Shadows* or *Schatten* (1923). Its German version also bore the subtitle 'A Nocturnal Hallucination', 'Eine nächtliche Halluczination'. In this film, it is not the nocturnal street scene that is presented as spectacle, but an interior night-time labyrinth that unfolds as primary attraction. An itinerant magic lantern showman 'projects' hidden desires of guests at an aristocratic dinner party (the company of a count). The plot is love and intrigue, a play within a play; guests are hypnotised and their shadows set free. The subconscious of the characters act out their passions, an affair and murder, a horrifying public spectacle. In keeping with the magic lantern pre-cinematic reference, we are only presented with shadows: even the light of the lantern is implied, more or less imaginary. The light and darkness of this shadow art indicate not a metropolis-fed mania or neurosis, and the hypnotism is strikingly different from the omnipresent observation of the illuminated eyes of the optician shop. Rather, the shadow play here points to a cure, light therapy or psychoanalysis, as Kracauer states, and as the Marxist author Peter Weiss also asserts in his 1956 book *Avantgarde Film*.

Schatten is the one film of Guerin's text that takes us far beyond the reified capitalist spectacle and deep into an interior drama of the psyche; it too has a clichéd, moralistic ending. Yet Guerin's analysis of *Schatten* skirts this issue of psychoanalysis and desire, focusing instead on the uncertainty of the framing event of this 'film within a film'. As a result, she does not discuss the end of the film, when a new day with sober, natural lighting, symbolising the light of reason, spills into the scene. Instead she focuses on the 'shadow play' as an 'openness', a cause of confusion and uncertainty for the spectator. She even writes that 'contemporary audiences were nevertheless arrested by the confusion of this new medium and its proximity to reality, because, despite its confusion, it was preferable to the tedium and insubstantiality of daily life'. Overlooking the psychoanalytic aspect and the German subtitle of this film (which is nowhere quoted in her study), Guerin concludes that spectators of *Shadows* read the story as a straightforward narrative, and as a result find it difficult to differentiate between the main plot and the framing story embedded as a magic lantern 'film within the film'. Certainly there are multiple versions of these early films now available in archives, and it is highly possible that Guerin based her analysis on a different print. Yet it is still worth noting that, precisely at the moment when light and shadow could point to a cinematic language of affect and desire, Guerin initially hesitates, although elsewhere her analysis cogently highlights what such a terrain might look like. This is most provocative and promising when she speaks of lighting as an emotional 'excess', above all as it is articulated in a First World War documentary *Das Stahlwerk der Poldihütte* (1917), where utopian aspirations are perfectly situated in the brilliance of steel. The soft light that would typically showcase a film star here showcases mechanised, manufactured creation. Bathed in soft light, steel is given the space and face of a human protagonist, whereas human figures are banished to a visual and conceptual background.

This celebratory mode of light reminds us that light and lighting in these twenties films are not only replications of the alienation of modernity. They can also serve as an 'attraction', displaying a new technological vision and a stunning focus on exhibition that was dominant during the earliest years of 'living pictures'. When discussing the harmony and joy of the rustic sepia colour in Richard Eichberg's little-known *Das Bacchanal des Todes* (1917), Guerin celebrates the ceremonial use of colour, demonstrating how it was used along with lighting in early cinema to create a new cinematic code for affect, enhancing intense emotions. In her discussion of early German detective film, such as Franz Hofer's *Der Steckbrief* (1913), Guerin also celebrates an electricity (here an electrically operated cable car) that is used to playfully frame emotional tension. The dramatic social drama of 1914 that Guerin also analyses, *Und das Licht erlosch* (1914), again is a powerful tale of light as pulsating passion, a lighthouse beam that creates a sense of urgency and anxiety, but also underlines the 'intense emotions' and romantic passions of the characters.

As these dates illustrate, Guerin does not limit herself to Weimar film. She provocatively uses her theme to move backwards and forwards in film history. From tinting and the image of magic lantern technology, to electricity as a corrupt, Faustian pact or design of the devil (*Algol*, 1920), to the spotlights and searchlights of Nazi Germany, she weaves a fine web for a powerful narrative of *mise-en-scène* and modernity. Simultaneously, she examines films that celebrate and criticise technological change. Paradigmatic of this is another early twenties film that is caught between two worlds: the power of early modern myths and the power of the machine. In Guerin's reading, *Der Golem* (1920) marries the spectacular technologies of cinema to the centuries-old rituals of the Cabala in an ambiguous take on the image and modernisation. Light is a brilliant spectacle and sign, an openness that bespeaks the future - but it could also be interpreted as a crippling force in the narrative. She concludes that *Der Golem* encourages a critical audience reception, as it perpetually oscillates between myth and modernity. Light is here a compositional element, but also a means for cultural transformation. When analysing *Faust* (1926), Guerin notes that lighting technology is part of a larger discourse on the transformation of time and space, in particular human-centred time and history. *Faust* highlights a technologically modern world that is marked both by instantaneity and its other, the slow dissolve. A star metamorphoses into the word 'love' in a prolonged moment of filmic desire; elsewhere in *Faust*, the *mise-en-scène* is interrupted by frenzied flashes of broken light. Guerin's study gives us a valuable technical language to examine the pioneering work behind such editing techniques of superimposition and dissolve (here the trick is Carl Hofmann's 'Two-Sun-Phenomenon').

Perhaps as a result of her intense focus on lighting as a primary phenomenon of the 1920s, at times Guerin tends to dismiss the earliest years of cinema and the pre-cinema period that was so important for film's development. Without any sources or information to back up such a claim, she actually states in her text that 'the development of the pre-First World War German film aesthetic was retarded by relatively unsophisticated technologies' (49). The idea that a German film aesthetic in its early years was 'retarded', when German directors and technicians did pioneering work in slow motion, time lapse, and so on, goes completely against the grain of current film scholarship, which undoes the narrative of the early years as 'primitive'. The danger is that one extrapolates from Guerin's study to conclude that Germany always had a belated introduction to new 'cinematic' technologies. Nothing could be further from the truth. *Schatten* tells us, for example, that it was not cinema alone that inaugurated fantastic journeys through time and space, the interior of the mind as well as the exotic of the exterior. Microscopes, magic lanterns, and dioramas/panoramas were used for centuries in the grand German tradition of optics for the purpose of life science pedagogy and playful 'projected' entertainment/edutainment. In fact, as early as the 1890s there were German magic lantern shows that thematised the introduction of electric light to the hectic metropolis, a spectacle that was presented as both dangerous and edifying. Certainly it is worth mentioning that Weimar film was not the first or final flirtation with a new culture of electricity, as Carolyn Marvin elucidates in her study, *When Old Technologies Were New: Thinking About Electric Communication in the Late Nineteenth Century* (1988).

That said, Guerin's book is an absolute first in the field. Even if Guerin fails to trace her 'culture of light' back to other 'light' moments of modernity that are now popular in early cinema scholarship - such as Loïe Fuller's light-display serpentine dances, turn-of-the-century 'ladies of electricity', the electrical scenes of the colonial expositions, or Röntgen's wondrous 'new light' (X ray) - her amazing use of archival sources and technical sources tells us that there is much, much more to the German cinema of the teens and twenties than we had previously imagined. *A Culture of Light* is a dazzling study that puts old films on the map in an entirely original and innovative way.

Resistance Incarnate: on Rancière

Peter Sjølyst-Jackson

Jacques Rancière, *The Politics of Aesthetics: The Distribution of the Sensible*, Gabriel Rockhill (trans), London and New York, Continuum, 2004, 116pp; £14.99 hardback. Jacques Rancière, *The Flesh of Words: The Politics of Writing*, Charlotte Mandell (trans), Stanford, CA, Stanford University Press, 2004; 169pp; US$19.95 paperback, US$50.00 hardback.

The Politics of Aesthetics situates Jacques Rancière's oeuvre in relation to his break with 'structuralist Marxism'. The translator, Gabriel Rockhill, records in a brief overview of his career that Rancière was closely affiliated to Althusser's circle as a contributor to the collective volume *Reading 'Capital'* in 1965, but that he distanced himself from this 'philosophy of order' in the wake of 1968, because it 'anaesthetized the revolt against the bourgeoisie' (*PA* 1). In an afterword to the volume, Slavoj Zizek replays the moment with comical gusto, evoking how it didn't take long for 'Rancière's unique voice to explode in a thunder which rocked the Althusserian scene' (*PA* 69). Such, perhaps, is the narrow frame through which Rancière has come to be recognised, or ignored, in the world of Anglo-American criticism. So why read him now? In 'our time of the disorientation of the Left', Zizek contends, Rancière 'offers one of the few consistent conceptualisations of *how we are to continue to resist*' (*PA* 79).

What these two new books resist most stridently are the habits of compartmentalisation in literary and cultural studies, which, according to Rancière, endlessly trace ruptures between the old and the new, from realist representation to modernist anti-representation, from progressive modernity to postmodern disenchantment. Demonstrating a formidable knowledge of European intellectual and cultural history, *The Politics of Aesthetics* ranges across philosophy, literature, painting, photography, film and music. Originally published as a series of responses to questions from Muriel Combes and Bernard Aspe, the translator supplies this English edition with an interview with the author, an illuminating glossary of conceptual terms, and a bibliography of primary and secondary sources in French and English. The style is dense and programmatic, but this gives way, in *The Flesh of Words*, to lucid analyses of the 'work of incarnation' in literature and philosophy. Rancière traces here 'the power by which words are set in motion and become deeds' in poems by Wordsworth, Byron, Mandelstam and Rimbaud; the figure of 'the word made flesh' in different interpretations of the Gospels by Erich Auerbach, Frank Kermode and St Augustine; the 'theologies of the novel' in Cervantes, Balzac and Proust; and finally, the problematic of writing and incarnation in Althusser and Deleuze. Throughout the readings, commentaries and programmatic statements in both books, Rancière attempts to elucidate the manifold conditions under which art and literature circumscribe the possibilities for change, through their diversion and alteration of sensible perceptions, inscribing themselves on the landscape, the flesh, and into the very rhythms and movements of bodies. In *The Flesh of Words* this is shown to involve a democratic malady that is peculiar to literature. As textual matter, literature cannot embody its incarnation, and remains 'separate' from its inscriptions on the social body. But this provokes a paradoxical response in literary and philosophical texts, which attempt to 'escape the fate of the letter released into the world' by inscribing the body of their incarnation within themselves - as though their 'deeds' could be programmed in advance. It is a self-defeating struggle, says Rancière, because literature 'lives only by evading the incarnation that it incessantly puts into play'. And yet, he affirms that this struggle 'must always be begun anew' (*FW* 4-6).

The Politics of Aesthetics attacks notions of 'artistic modernity' that separate the 'aesthetic' sphere of art from the industrial world of labour. Rancière rejects this 'lazy and absurd schema' with contempt, and lampoons the 'vain debates' that worry about whether the arts are politically submissive or artistically autonomous. Although there are specific interventions on Benjamin's notion of mechanical reproduction and Lyotard's elaboration of the sublime, Rancière's targets of criticism seem to be many and diffuse. This lack of specific reference doesn't serve his argument well, especially when transplanted into the Anglophone context, whereupon the number of potential targets is vastly increased. Nonetheless, it is a restrictive conception of 'aesthetics' he rejects, one that would 'consign art to its effects on sensibility' or, alternatively, link 'the conquests of artistic innovation to the victories of emancipation' (*PA* 10). Both of these prevent a clear understanding of the relationships between art and collective experience, obscuring 'the struggles of the proletariat to bring labour out of the night surrounding it, out of its exclusion from shared visibility and speech' (*PA* 45).

Rancière's starting point for a different elaboration of aesthetics relates, precisely, to this field of 'shared visibility and speech'. 'Aesthetics' is a historically mediated 'distribution of the sensible' which, in its 'primary' definition, refers to 'the system of *a priori* forms determining what presents itself to experience' (*PA* 13). In opposition to any theory of sensible affects, Rancière's project is to 're-establish' the conditions of intelligibility proper to aesthetics as 'a specific regime for identifying and reflecting on the arts' (*PA* 10). In order to explore the implications of this 'aesthetic regime of art', he contrasts it to the 'ethical regime of images' established in the formulations of Plato, and the 'representative regime of art' founded by Aristotle. In the ethical regime, there is no distinction between art and politics, since, for Plato, there are only 'ways of doing and making', divided between knowledge based 'arts' with 'precise ends', and their devious counterparts: the 'simulacra that imitate simple appearances' (*PA* 21). While this confines reflection upon all 'arts' to questions of truth, purpose and end results, the representative regime of art, ushered in by Aristotle, will isolate 'imitation' as a separate branch of the arts, to be judged on different criteria. Here, the simulacra of painting, poems and the stage are legitimised according to a twofold *division of labour*. The 'ways of doing and making' are categorised into restricted occupations, while the artistic products themselves are judged according to fixed norms of evaluation. Included in these norms are 'the privilege accorded to tragic action' and 'the hierarchy of genres according to the dignity of their subject matter'. The practices and products of art would thus enter into 'a relationship of global analogy with an overall hierarchy of political and social occupations' (*PA* 22). The obligation to produce a 'distribution of the sensible' in line with social hierarchy - 'tragedy for heroes and nobles, comedy for the people of meagre means' - comes to an end as art bestows honour on the commonplace and confers visibility on 'anonymous individuals' by turning them into acceptable subjects of art. The 'aesthetic revolution', says Rancière, was first carried forth in nineteenth-century literature, as 'an epoch and a society were deciphered through the features, clothes, or gestures of an ordinary individual (Balzac); the sewer revealed a civilization (Hugo); the daughter of a farmer and the daughter of a banker were caught in the equal force of style as an 'absolute manner of seeing things (Flaubert)', (*PA* 32).

A brief sketch like this invites hasty dismissal: Isn't this simply a re-compartmentalisation of 'beginnings' and 'ends', substituting a relatively even chronology for a bizarrely lopsided one, jumping from Ancient Greece to nineteenth century Europe? This dismissal, however, would ignore Rancière's frequent reminders that the three regimes are not mutually exclusive, that the new does not abolish the old, and that, at 'any given point in time, several regimes coexist and intermingle' (*PA* 50). Art is still identifiable by reference to ethics, truth and intention - often as a means to oppose dominant systems of representation. As evidenced in Terry Eagleton's celebration of Erich Auerbach's *Mimesis*, for instance, it is still possible to make a virtue of singling out novelistic realism 'as the morally and artistically serious representation of unvarnished everyday life, as the common people enter the literary arena long before they make their collective appearance on the political stage'.[1] When Rancière recasts this frequently observed shift in terms of the 'aesthetic revolution', however, it is not simply to affirm what Eagleton evokes as the irresistible rise of the proletariat, from literary representation to political materialisation. Of more crucial importance, for Rancière, are the *uncertain* possibilities of political subjectivity in the wake of this 'silent revolution', which entails new preconditions for recognising art - that is to say, in relation to politics. No longer grasped along the Platonic or Aristotelian lines of 'division within ways of doing and making', artistic products are now ascribed a 'sensible mode of being' (*PA* 26). Severed from its previous contexts of identification, the 'autonomous' art work is now liable to be interpreted against the stated intentions of artists. It is 'inhabited by a heterogeneous power, the power of a form of thought that has become foreign to itself' (*PA* 22). This has complex implications for political subjectivity, some of which can be discerned in Rancière's distinction between the 'two major variants' of modernist discourse. The first, 'purist formalism',

1. Terry Eagleton, 'Pork Chops and Pineapples', *London Review of Books*, Vol. 25, No. 20, October 2003, p23.

rejects the cultural uses of representation (in painting), communication (in literature) and emotive expression (in music), and sees in modern art the recovery of its proper autonomy, internal to its distinctive forms. If hybrid postmodernism has marked a decisive break from this, Rancière holds, it has done so by disavowing the second major form of the modernist paradigm: 'modernatism'. This strange term is presumably intended to evoke a point of convergence between social projects of 'modernity' and artistic endeavours of 'modernism'. Its trajectory, according to Rancière, passes from Schiller's 'aesthetic state', through the 'aesthetic programme' of Hegel, Hölderlin, Schelling and German Romanticism, to the Marxist revolution of producers and artisans. In contrast to purist formalism, which seems to *exclude* the social in its pursuit of artistic autonomy, the paradigm of 'modernatism' identifies new and radical possibilities of the social *within* the autonomy of art. Calling for a 'total revolution' of the sensible, it seeks in art 'the material realization of a humanity still only existing as an idea' (*PA* 26-7). To recall a formulation from *The Flesh of Words*, such art 'gives itself the body of its incarnation', as though it could programme its deeds within itself, prior to its circulation in the social world (*FW* 4).

To combat any hasty claims that the revolutionary arts must always adhere to a totalitarian logic, Rancière draws a distinction between different ideas of the 'avant-garde' which, he says, proceed from two different political subjectivities: 'archi-politics' and 'meta-politics'. In the archi-political version, the avant-garde operates as an advanced detachment, issuing the rules for historical interpretation and social action. It imposes, in Rancière's terms, a 'police order', a homogenous social space premised on the rigid exclusion of the fractured process of 'politics' as such. The meta-political avant-garde, by contrast, radicalises political disruption, using art as a model for 'a total life programme'. Deploying, after Schiller, an aesthetic of anticipation, it invents new sensible forms and material structures for a life to come (*PA* 29-30). As a utopian form of socialism, however, it runs up against a paradox; the utopia it anticipates is identical to the homogenous social space of archi-politics. And yet, it is the same utopian impulse that generates artistic resistance to 'the obvious sensible facts in which the normality of domination is rooted' (*PA* 40). As such, its politics are ambivalent, anticipating a utopia that is both a place of closure, and a radical opening.

Rancière's fascination is with the openings made possible in art and literature. Their 'fictions', he says, are '*material* rearrangements of signs and images' that can spread 'lines of fracture and disincorporation'. As such, they do not produce 'an organism or a communal body', but rather, contribute to the formation of 'uncertain communities', 'unspecified groups of people', 'enunciative collectives that call into question the distribution of roles, territories, and languages' (*PA* 39-40). The democratic disorder of literature which Rancière calls 'literarity' resonates strongly with Derrida's elaboration of 'dissemination' as the unending possibilities of digression, divergence, accident and fragmentation. Rancière does not acknowledge this resonance, but it is particularly evident in his frequent recourse to Plato's *Phaedrus*, which, he says, 'for more than two millennia has regulated thought about writing in the West' (*FW* 102). If, for Derrida, Plato's denunciation of writing involves a risk of dissemination that remains unthinkable for philosophy, in *The Flesh of Words* Rancière restricts the focus to writing as 'an imbalance of the legitimate order of discourse, of the way it is distributed and at the same time distributes bodies in an ordered community' (*FW* 103). Rancière traces this notion of writing through Balzac's novel *The Village Priest*, which he considers an 'exemplary fable of democracy', despite the fact that it was written for conservative moral edification in an age of post-revolutionary emancipation. More surely than the modern perfection of plotting in Sterne, James, Poe or Borges, this 'badly designed' novel highlights the paradox of writing, strung between literarity and incarnation. The story of Véronique, torn from her proper destination in manual labour or housekeeping - thanks to her reading a book full of dreams of the tropics and chaste loves - reflects the obsession of the age: the 'misfortune' of *déclassement*, of 'working-class bodies torn from their natural goals by the course of the letter and thrown by it into ways of wandering and misery, suicide and crime' (*FW* 98-105). Véronique's fateful encounter with the book, says Rancière, recalls the testimonies of autodidacts in the nineteenth century, where the encounter with a book makes a new world possible, by unmaking an older one. Balzac's novel is thus obliged to remedy this 'disorder of writing' through the figure of the Catholic priest, 'an engineer of souls in the Saint-Simonian manner', who guides Véronique in her renunciation of books. As Rancière shows, this entails the substitution of one form of writing for another, a renunciation of literature and the adoption of a form of writing incarnate in the landscape and in the social body. This writing 'inscribed in the texture of things' would be the healthy, ordered and yielding work of irrigating the soil. As Balzac's Véronique testifies: 'I have marked … my repentance in indelible lines on this earth. It is written in the fertilized fields, in the enlarged mountain town, in the streams directed from the mountain to this plain, which had previously been uncultivated and wild, but is now green and productive' (*FW* 107). Balzac attempts, in other words, to give his novel the body of its incarnation, in a paradoxical attempt to write his way out of the democratic disorder of literature. The great difficulties he had in finishing the novel, Rancière makes clear, occurred only after its initial serialisation in *La Presse* in 1839. Despite his reactionary conservatism, the irony is that Balzac was always writing 'for those men and women who *should not* read' (*FW* 108-9).

It is at such moments that Rancière's work undermines the standard criticism that his work offers nothing much beyond a backward looking fervour, and a romantic attachment to nineteenth century rebellion.[2] In Rancière's defence, Zizek points to the proliferation of creative protest, and the subversive potential of body-piercing, cross-dressing, absurdist 'flash mobs' and cyberspace. In relation to the internet, however, we should also observe the more obvious fact that it is *writing* that survives, indeed disseminates, more unpredictably than ever. The tensions, contradictions and aporias of democratic disorder, and of the utopias that try to order them - traced by Rancière through the histories of philosophy, art and literature - have not gone away. They remain in the uncertain communities, where people read things they shouldn't.

2. See for instance the reviews of Rancière's *The Politics of Aesthetics* and *The Philosopher and His Poor* by Stewart Martin and Mark Neocleous respectively, in *Radical Philosophy* 131, May/June 2005, pp39-46.